THE PSYCHOLOGY OF C. G. JUNG

THE PSYCHOLOGY
OF C. G. JUNG

An Introduction with Illustrations

by
JOLANDE JACOBI

YALE UNIVERSITY PRESS

NEW HAVEN AND LONDON

First published in England 1942
by Routledge & Kegan Paul Ltd.
Broadway House, 68–74 *Carter Lane*
*London, E.C.*4 *and in the United States of America in* 1943
by Yale University Press

English Edition 1973

Library of Congress catalog card number: 72–96174
ISBN 0–300–01673–5 *(cloth);* 0–300–01674–3 *(paper)*
Translated by Ralph Manheim From the German
DIE PSYCHOLOGIE VON C. G. JUNG

Text printed in the United States of America by
BookCrafters, Inc., Chelsea, Michigan.

16   18   20   22   24   23   21   19   17

CONTENTS

PLATES

(Between pages 96 and 97)

FOREWORD

by C. G. Jung

THE present work, I believe, meets a generally felt want which I myself up to now have not been in a position to satisfy—the wish, namely, for a concise presentation of the elements of my psychological theory. My endeavours in psychology have been essentially pioneer work, leaving me neither time nor opportunity to present them systematically. Dr. Jacobi has taken this difficult task upon herself with a happy result, having succeeded in giving an account free from the ballast of technical particulars. This constitutes a synopsis that includes or at least touches upon all essential points, so that it is possible for the reader—with the aid of the references and the bibliography of my writings—to orient himself readily wherever needful. It may be regarded as a merit of this work that the text has been supplemented with a number of diagrams, which aid in understanding certain functional relations.

It is a particular satisfaction to me that the author has been able to avoid furnishing any support to the opinion that my researches constitute a doctrinal system. Such expositions slip all too easily into a dogmatic style which is wholly inappropriate to my views. Since it is my firm conviction that the time for an all-inclusive theory, taking in and describing all the contents, processes, and phenomena of the psyche from one central viewpoint, has not yet arrived, I regard my concepts as suggestions and attempts at the formulation of a new scientific psychology based in the first place upon immediate experience with human beings. This is not a kind of psychopathology, but a general psychology which also takes cognizance of the empirical material of pathology.

I hope that it may be the lot of this book not only to give the general reader an insight into my researches, but that it will also save him much laborious searching in his study of them.

August, 1939   C. G. JUNG

ix

PREFACE[1]

THE REASON for my writing this book—the first Swiss edition appeared in 1940—was the ever-growing public demand for a comprehensive but concise account of the elements of the teachings of C. G. Jung, with a view to easing the approach to his extraordinarily fertile and multidimensional work. The wide interest the book evoked has allowed me to go on expanding it, to adapt it to Jung's most recent findings, and to present it in steadily clearer form. To condense a man's whole lifework, the fruit of sixty years of research, into so narrow a compass is an almost insoluble task, and the result must necessarily remain a mere sketch. Such a book may nevertheless encourage the interested reader to take the plunge into Jung's voluminous writings and to experience for himself the plenitude of psychological and human insights that touch upon nearly every area of life and domain of knowledge.

The text of the eighth English edition remains unchanged. For a better understanding of concepts that often had to be presented in tightly compressed form, I have again illustrated it with six diagrams as visual aids to clarification and a series of nineteen "pictures from the unconscious," to direct attention to a new field of psychic expression and symbolism opened up by Jung for the therapy of adults. (Jung was the first to use painting as a therapeutic aid in the treatment of non-schizophrenics; previously, psychotherapists had reserved it for children and psychotics.) The short biographical sketch has been included once more, and a number of corrections have been made in the footnotes, as well as in the bibliography of Jung's publications in English.[2]

[1] Replacing the prefaces to the previous English editions (New Haven and London, 1942–1968). Translated by R. F. C. Hull.

[2] References are now fully in accord with the Collected Works of C. G. Jung, and quotations have been revised when a significant revision had been made in the Collected Works translation. When a quotation is from the older translation, the citation includes "Cf." Paragraph citations are given for the more recent editions. The Collected Works are published by Princeton University Press (as Bollingen Series XX) and Routledge & Kegan Paul, London. For contents, see list at the end of this book.

One of my main concerns in each successive edition has been to demonstrate with all possible clarity that Jung never abandoned the empirical method and always remained within its boundaries even at those points where one or another of the specialist sciences accused him of having encroached upon its territory. Because of the generic nature of its material, Jungian psychology has always been compelled to draw upon other specialist fields. But the objective observer will soon discover that these alleged encroachments are more apparent than real. Psychic phenomena, no matter whether they derive from the sound or the sick, can only be grasped through a total vision that considers every single detail from all sides at once, so that a widely ramified knowledge far beyond the ordinary is needed for their elucidation.

In this book I have carefully avoided any kind of polemic, firstly because of a certainty that in the end it never convinces anybody but merely puts the reader's back up, and secondly out of respect for any and every serious scientific line of research or school of thought however controversial it may be. The world of the psyche is beyond all human differences and beyond all happenings in time. The beginning and end of all human activities are contained within it. Its problems are perennial and are always of the same burning actuality. Those who immerse themselves in these problems will find in them not only the key to all the terrible things perpetrated by man, but also the creative seeds of everything high and holy that mankind has ever produced, and upon which is founded our never-failing hope of a better future.

In the epilogue to a seminar delivered in Basel in 1934 Jung wrote: "It is my conviction that the investigation of the psyche is the science of the future. Psychology is the youngest of the sciences and is only at the beginning of its development. It is, however, the science we need most. Indeed, it is becoming ever more obvious that it is not famine, not earthquakes, not microbes, not cancer but man himself who is man's greatest danger to man, for the simple reason that there is no adequate protection against psychic epidemics, which are infinitely more devastating than the worst of natural catastrophes. . . . It is therefore in the highest degree desirable that a knowledge of psychology should spread so that men can understand the source of the supreme dangers that threaten them."[3]

If at least this insight were to be bestowed upon man, if he were but granted a drawing realization of the dark powers that dwell in his psyche—so that he could draw the necessary conclusions and tame those powers by making them an organic part of his psychic structure instead of letting them make him their plaything—then he would never be reduced to a ravening beast through dissolution in the masses, and then a truly momentous step would have been taken towards the creation of a real and lasting culture. Unless man begins at last to create order within himself, he will never be anything but a spineless, supine victim, the obedient servant of a mass organization, and can never become the free member of a community.

Every collective, every nation, reflects in magnified form the psychic state of its individual components, the average man, and its actions in the molding of history reveal the depths and heights inherent in the psyche of each of them. But the man who, undaunted, sets foot on the "inward way" and, overcoming its perils, courageously follows it to the end, will be able to take the "outward way" equally fearlessly, the way into the world of external reality. He will master the challenges of life in the collective with the bewildering profusion of tools given into his hand for the conquest of nature, neither losing himself in the labyrinth of the inward way nor vanishing in the anonymity of the mass, but preserving in both adventures the unique value of the individual personality.

And now I would like to pay homage to the memory of C. G. Jung, in gratitude for the understanding and encouragement he gave me ever since the first appearance of this book, as attested by his appreciative foreword to the first edition, the beneficent influence of which is still palpable today. I am also indebted to the late Toni Wolff for her checking of the original manuscript, as well as to Prof. K. W. Bash for the first translation into English. Nor should those many readers be forgotten whose encouragement helped to launch the book on its worldwide journey.

Zurich, January 1972   JOLANDE JACOBI

[3] Roland Cahen (ed. and trans.), *L'Homme à la découverte de son âme* (6th edn., Paris, 1962), pp. 339f. The epilogue, written in 1944, is included in Jung's Collected Works, vol. 18.

INTRODUCTION:

THE PSYCHOLOGY OF C. G. JUNG

THE psychology of C. G. Jung may be divided into two parts, one theoretical and the other practical. The theoretical part, in turn, breaks down into two main subdivisions that may roughly be designated as (1) the structure of the psyche and (2) the laws of the psychic processes and forces. The practical part, based on the theory, is concerned with therapy in the strict sense.

In order to gain a sound understanding of Jungian theory, we must first adopt Jung's point of view and recognize the *full reality of all psychic phenomena*. Strange as it may seem, this attitude is relatively new. For up to a few decades ago psychology was not regarded as autonomous, subject to laws of its own, but was looked upon and explained as a derivative of religion, philosophy, or natural science. This made it impossible to discern the true nature of the psyche.

For Jung the psyche is no less real than the body. Though it cannot be touched, it can be directly and fully experienced and observed. It is a world of its own, governed by laws, structured, and endowed with its own means of expression.

Whatever we know of the world or of our own being comes to us through the mediation of the psyche. For 'the psyche is no exception to the general rule that the universe can be established only so far as our psychic organism permits'.[1] From this it follows that 'in respect of its natural subject matter and its method of procedure, modern empirical psychology belongs to the natural sciences, but in respect of its method of explanation it belongs to the humane sciences.' 'Our psychology,' says Jung, 'takes account of the cultural as well as the natural man, and accordingly its explanations must keep both points of view in mind, the spiritual and the biological. As a medical psychology, it cannot do otherwise than pay attention to the whole man.' It 'inquires into the reasons for the pathogenic failure to adapt, following the slippery trail of neurotic thinking and feeling until

[1] Jung, C. G. 'Religion', p. 41.

I

it finds the way back to life. Our psychology is therefore an eminently practical science. It does not investigate for investigation's sake, but for the immediate purpose of giving help. We could even say that learning is its by-product, but not its principal aim, which is again a great difference from what one understands by "academic" science.'[1]

Jung built his system on this premise and it is with this premise that we must approach it. But he does not—after the manner of pure psychologism—disparage other ways to knowledge, nor does he, with psychism or panpsychism, suppose all reality or all existence to be of a psychic nature. His purpose is to investigate the psyche as the organ with which we apprehend the world and being, to observe and describe its phenomena, and to arrange them in a meaningful order.

Theology, psychology, history, physics, biology, and numerous other disciplines can all in equal degree serve as starting point for the investigation of being; they are interchangeable and to a certain degree they may even be transposed, each having its relevance according to the problem under discussion or the investigator's personal viewpoint. Jung, as it happens, adopts the psychological approach. He builds on his profound knowledge of psychic reality, so that his edifice is no abstract theory born of the speculative intellect, but a structure resting entirely upon the solid foundation of experience. Its two main pillars are:

1. the principle of psychic totality
2. the principle of psychic energism.

In examining these two principles and the practical application of Jung's doctrine, we shall, as far as possible, work with Jung's own definitions and explanations and identify them as such. It should be particularly noted that in so doing the expression 'the unconscious', which has been used throughout to designate the sphere of those contents of the psyche which are not joined to consciousness, is in fact an illicit hypostatization. It has, however, proved useful as a working hypothesis. Jung designates his teachings in regard to the practice of psychological analysis as 'analytical psychology'. He adopted this

[1] Jung, C. G. 'Education', pp. 86, 90, 93. N.B.: In the following pages all works cited in the footnotes by title only are those of C. G. Jung.

term after his break with Freud in 1913 to avert confusion with the 'psychoanalysis' of the Freudian school. Later he coined the term 'complex psychology', which he always uses when the emphasis is on basic principles and theory. By it he wished to stress that his teachings, in contrast to other psychological doctrines (e.g. the mere psychology of consciousness or Freud's psychoanalysis that reduces everything to instinctual elements), are concerned with extremely complicated psychic contexts. The term 'complex psychology' has steadily lost ground in the last few years, because when translated into foreign languages the word 'complex' has given rise to misunderstandings. Today the term 'analytical psychology' is employed for Jung's doctrine as a whole, both in its theoretical and practical aspects.

THE NATURE AND STRUCTURE OF THE PSYCHE

CONSCIOUSNESS AND THE UNCONSCIOUS

BY 'psyche' Jung means not only what we generally call 'soul' but the totality of all psychic processes, conscious as well as unconscious, hence something broader and more comprehensive than the soul, which for Jung is only a certain 'limited functional complex'.[1] The psyche consists of two complementary but antithetical spheres: CONSCIOUSNESS and the UNCONSCIOUS.[2]

[1] The word 'soul' has a specific meaning in Jungian terminology; here we use it in the sense of a definite, circumscribed functional complex which might be characterized as a kind of 'inner personality', as the 'subject' to which the ego-consciousness of the individual is related in the same way as to an outward object. Jung's definition runs: 'The subject, conceived as the "inner" object, is the unconscious. . . . The "inner personality" is the way in which one behaves in regard to one's inner psychic processes; it is the inner attitude, the character, that one displays toward the unconscious. . . . [This] inner attitude I term the *anima*, or *soul*. . . . The same autonomy that very often characterizes the outer attitude is claimed also by the inner attitude. . . . As experience proves, it usually contains all those general human qualities the conscious attitude lacks' (*Types*, pars. 801, 803 f., slightly modified). By 'intellect' we mean the power of conscious thought and understanding, the purely rational side of the individual. 'Spirit' is to be taken as a faculty which pertains to the realm of consciousness but also has a natural bond with the unconscious; it leads primarily to meaningful artistic, ethico-religious accomplishments, in the form of insights and utterances, but it can also lend a definite coloration to thoughts and judgements as well as emotional attitudes. 'Spirit' in this sense comprises both the intellect and the soul; it forms a bond between them and is a meaningful 'sublimation' of both; it is a formative principle constituting the contrary pole to the unformed, instinctual, biological nature of man, thereby sustaining the continuous tension of opposites on which our psychic life is based. These three terms are taken to denote 'partial systems' of the psychic totality; where I speak of all aspects of this totality, of a whole that takes in the conscious as well as the unconscious side, I have always employed the term 'psyche', or 'psychic'.

[2] The first scientific investigation of the manifestations of the unconscious is the lasting achievement of Sigmund Freud, who may be regarded as the founder of modern depth psychology.

Our ego has a share in both. Diagram 1 represents the ego standing between the two spheres, which not only complement one another but also stand in a compensatory relation to each other.[1] In other words the dividing line that separates the two of them in our ego can be displaced in both directions, as is indicated by the arrows and dotted lines in the drawing. Of course the situation of the ego in the exact centre is only an abstraction. If the dividing line is shifted upward, consciousness

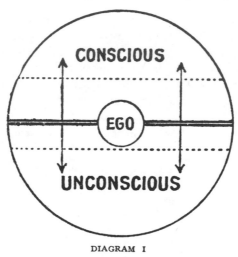

DIAGRAM 1

will be more restricted; if it is shifted downward, consciousness will be broader.

But if we consider the relations of these two spheres to one another, we see that our consciousness constitutes only a very small part of the total psyche. We know from the findings of anthropology that it is a product of late differentiation. It floats like a little island on the vast, boundless ocean of the unconscious which in fact embraces the whole world. In Diagram 2

[1] This diagram, like all that follow, is merely an aid to understanding. The reader should be warned against regarding them as anything more than an admittedly inadequate and oversimplified attempt to illustrate highly complicated and abstract functional relations. The circle expresses the relatively self-contained wholeness of the individual psyche; totality has been symbolized by the circle or sphere from time immemorial. 'In neo-Platonic philosophy the soul has definite affinities with the sphere. . . . Cf. also the spherical form of Plato's Original Man' (*Alchemy*, par. 109 and note).

the black point in the centre marks our ego; surrounded and sustained by consciousness, it represents the side of the psyche which, especially in our Western culture, is primarily oriented towards adaptation to outward reality. 'By the ego,' says Jung,

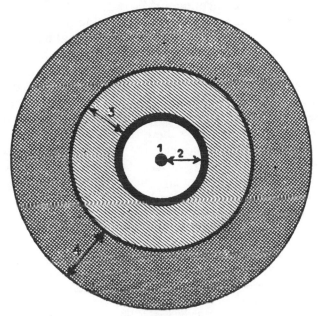

DIAGRAM 2

1. Ego.
2. The sphere of consciousness.
3. The sphere of the personal unconscious.
4. The sphere of the collective unconscious.

'I understand a complex of representations which constitutes the centre of my field of consciousness and appears to possess a very high degree of continuity and identity.'[1] He also calls the ego 'the subject of consciousness'.[2] He defines consciousness

[1] Cf. *Types* par. 706.

[2] In recent years various hypotheses on the development of the ego have been put forward by certain of Jung's disciples, particularly Fordham in London and Neumann in Israel. So far, however, none of them seems entirely satisfactory. One of the theories best grounded in experimental science, though it does not take the specific views of depth psychology into account, is that of J. Piaget, which he has set forth in numerous works. In any event the Freudian view—and this is also Jung's opinion—remains fundamental.

as 'the function or activity which maintains the relation of psychic contents with the ego'. All our experience of the outer and inner world must pass through our ego in order to be perceived. For 'relations to the ego, insofar as they are not sensed as such by the ego, are unconscious'.[1]

The next circle shows the sphere of consciousness, surrounded by contents lying in the unconscious, contents that have been set aside—for our consciousness can hold only a very few contents at once—but which at any time can be restored to the level of consciousness, and also contents that we repress because they are disagreeable to us for various reasons—in other words, 'forgotten, repressed, subliminally perceived, thought, and felt matter of every kind'.[2] Jung calls this sphere the PERSONAL UNCONSCIOUS[3] to distinguish it from the COLLECTIVE UNCONSCIOUS, as is shown in Diagram 3.[4] The collective part of the unconscious does not include personal acquisitions specific to our individual ego, but only contents resulting 'from the inherited possibility of psychical functioning in general, namely from the inherited brain structure'.[5] This heritage is common to all human beings,

---

[1] *Types*, par. 700. In everyday speech 'consciousness' is often confused with 'thinking'. This is inadmissible, for there is a consciousness of feeling, of will, of fear, and of all other manifestations of life. Nor should 'life' be equated with 'consciousness', as occurs only too often, since a man who has fallen asleep or fainted, for example, has life but no consciousness. There are different degrees of consciousness: on the one hand consciousness may represent an act of perception which is not elaborated; on the other hand it may perform an act of understanding, evaluating elaboration.

[2] Ibid., par. 842.

[3] Freud called those contents that can be raised to consciousness at any time 'preconscious'. He applied the term 'unconscious' only to those which cannot be made conscious without recourse to a special technique. Jung includes both kinds of contents in the 'personal unconscious'.

[4] In the diagrams either the ego or the collective unconscious may occupy the centre, according to the orientation of our discussion. When we speak of the 'spheres' or 'strata' of the unconscious, or attempt to illustrate them graphically, we are, as it were, translating a genetic approach into spatial terms.

[5] *Types*, par. 842. The term 'brain structure', which Jung employs here where one might expect 'psychic structure', must be correctly understood. It points to the connection between the psyche and biology. For the psyche, as it presents itself—as it is experienced by us—is inseparable from our physical being. But this by no means implies a biological 'dependency'. 'The psyche deserves to be taken as a phenomenon in its own right; there are

perhaps even to all animals, and constitutes the foundation of every individual psyche.

'The unconscious is older than the consciousness. It is the

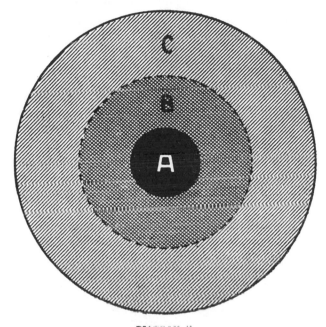

DIAGRAM 3

A. The part of the collective unconscious that can never be raised to consciousness.
B. The sphere of the collective unconscious.
C. The sphere of the personal unconscious.

"primal datum" out of which consciousness ever arises afresh.' Thus consciousness 'is only a secondary phenomenon built upon

---

no grounds at all for regarding it as a mere epiphenomenon, dependent though it may be on the functioning of the brain. One would be as little justified in regarding life as an epiphenomenon of the chemistry of carbon compounds' ('Energy', p. 8). And Jung further declares: 'We may establish with reasonable certainty that an individual consciousness as it relates to ourselves has come to an end [in death]. But whether this means that the continuity of the psychic process is also interrupted remains doubtful, since the psyche's attachment to the brain can be affirmed with far less certitude today than it could fifty years ago' ('The Soul and Death', p. 412). On the contrary, the psyche does not seem to be limited by space and time. Everything unconscious manifests itself as though it were outside space and time.

the fundamental psychic activity, which is a functioning of the unconscious'. The belief that man's essential attitude is that of consciousness is a fallacy, for 'we spend the greater part of our life in the unconscious: we sleep or daydream. . . . It is undeniable that in every important situation in life our consciousness is *dependent* on the unconscious.'[1] Children begin their lives in a state of unconsciousness and grow into consciousness. Whereas the so-called personal unconscious comprises 'forgotten, suppressed, repressed, subliminally perceived' contents originating in the life of the individual, the collective unconscious is made up of contents which, regardless of historic era or social or ethnic group, are the deposit of mankind's typical reactions since primordial times to universal human situations, such as fear, danger, the struggle against superior power, relations between the sexes, between children and parents, hate and love, birth and death, the power of the bright or the dark principle, etc.

The unconscious—and this is one of its essential properties—exerts a power of compensation. Whereas under normal conditions consciousness responds to a situation by an individual reaction adapted to outward reality, the unconscious supplies a typical reaction, arising from the experience of mankind and consonant with the necessities and laws of man's inner life. Thus it enables the individual to take an attitude in conformity with the totality of the psyche.

THE FUNCTIONS OF CONSCIOUSNESS

But before we proceed to a further discussion of the unconscious, let us take a closer look at the psychology and structure of CONSCIOUSNESS. Diagram 4[2] may serve as an example. The circle again symbolizes psychic totality;[3] at the four cardinal

---

[1] *Kindertraumseminar*, 1938–39.

[2] It should be noted that for the sake of simplicity the *thinking type*—the type which apprehends the contents of the inner and outer world predominantly through thinking, or cognition—has been taken as a model in all the diagrams. But of course with a corresponding shift of the functions any of the other types might serve as a model.

[3] By 'totality' Jung means more than unity or wholeness. The term implies a kind of integration, a unification of the parts, a creative synthesis, comprising an active force. It is a concept that should be identified with the 'self-regulating system' (see p. 53).

points stand the four basic functions which are constitutionally present in every individual: thinking, intuition, feeling, and sensation.[1]

By a psychic function Jung means 'a certain form of psychic activity that remains theoretically the same under varying circumstances' and is completely independent of its momentary

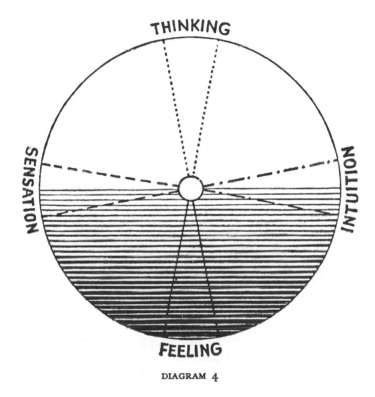

DIAGRAM 4

contents.[2] From this point of view the essential is not, for example, *what* one thinks, but the fact that one employs one's intellectual function, rather than that of intuition, for instance, in apprehending and elaborating the contents that present themselves from without or within. Here we are concerned

[1] 'Feeling' and 'sensation' should not be confused, as often occurs in English. In French the distinction here intended is clearly indicated by the two entirely different concepts of 'sentiment' and 'sensation'.

[2] Cf. *Types*, par. 731.

primarily with a mode of apprehending and assimilating psychic data regardless of their content. Thus thinking is the function which seeks to apprehend the world and adjust to it by way of thought or cognition, i.e. logical inferences. The function of feeling, on the other hand, apprehends the world through an evaluation based on the feelings of 'pleasant or unpleasant, acceptance or rejection'. Both these functions are termed *rational*, because both work with evaluations and judgements: thinking evaluates through cognition from the standpoint of 'true–false', feeling through the emotions from the standpoint of 'pleasant–unpleasant'. As determinants of behaviour, these two basic attitudes are mutually exclusive at any given time; either the one or the other predominates. It is obvious, for example, that certain political figures make decisions on the basis of their feelings and not their reason.

Jung calls the other two functions, sensation and intuition, the *irrational* functions, because they circumvent the *ratio* and operate not with judgements but with mere perceptions which are not evaluated or interpreted. Sensation perceives things as they are and not otherwise. It is the sense of reality, par excellence—what the French call the '*fonction du réel*'. Intuition also 'perceives', but less through the conscious apparatus of the senses than through its capacity for an unconscious 'inner perception' of the inherent potentialities of things. The sensation type, for example, will note all the details of a historical event but disregard the general context in which it is set; the intuitive type, on the other hand, will pay little attention to the details but will have no difficulty in discerning the inner meaning of the event, its possible implications and effects. Or another example: in viewing a lovely spring landscape the sensation type will note every detail; the flowers, the trees, the colour of the sky, etc., while the intuitive type will simply register the general atmosphere and colour. It is evident that these two functions are just as antithetical and mutually exclusive as our first pair, thinking and feeling; they cannot operate simultaneously.

This mutual exclusiveness is in keeping with the facts, i.e., observation (it cannot be overemphasized that Jung is above all an empiricist), but it also follows from Jung's theory, which is in turn derived from experience. This becomes clear when we consider that since, for example, the two basic functions of thinking and feeling are both 'evaluative', they cannot be employed at the same time. For one cannot simultaneously apply two systems of measurement to the same thing.

Although all men constitutionally possess all four functions, enabling us to 'orient ourselves with respect to the immediate world as completely as when we locate a place geographically by latitude and longitude',[1] experience shows that in each of us one function predominates. This function—probably the individual constitution determines which it is to be— usually undergoes the most pronounced development and differentiation; 'it becomes the dominant function of adaptation and gives the conscious attitude its direction and quality'.[2] It is always available to the individual's conscious will. Thus the psychological type amounts to a *general habitus*, which can take on all manner of variations according to the social, intellectual, and cultural level of the individual.

Diagram 4 shows the relations between the four functions. The upper half is light, while the lower half is dark; this is intended to show that the SUPERIOR FUNCTION pertains entirely to the light, conscious side, while its opposite, which we call the INFERIOR FUNCTION, is wholly confined to the unconscious. The two others lie partly in consciousness, partly in the unconscious zones,[3] indicating that in addition to his main function an individual usually makes use of a second, AUXILIARY FUNCTION, which is relatively differentiated and directed. The third function is seldom available to the average man; the fourth, the inferior one, is as a rule entirely beyond the control of his will. All this, of course, applies only to the individual who has developed naturally and possesses a relatively 'healthy' psyche; where the psyche is 'disturbed', in a neurotic, for example, the situation is different. Here the development of the main function may have been impeded, or a function which should constitutionally have occupied only second or third place has been pushed to the fore by compulsion or training, so that it takes the place of the main function. Another important factor in the relative development of the functions is the individual's age. In general

---

[1] 'A Psychological Theory of Types', par. 958.

[2] Toni Wolff, *Studien zu C. G. Jungs Psychologie*, p. 92.

[3] This diagram is only a theoretical model; in actual practice, we never encounter so radically one-sided a development of the functions.

one may say that all the functions should fall into their proper order and be appropriately differentiated by the middle of life (a moment which, to be sure, comes at different times for each individual).

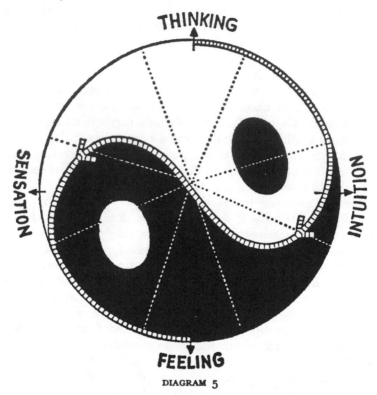

DIAGRAM 5

The Chinese sign *t'ai chi t'u*, reproduced in Diagram 5, offers a striking and perhaps not wholly accidental analogy to the value and direction of the functions. The course of the process of differentiation is indicated by the broken line; the 'way' follows not the periphery but an inner line corresponding to the relation between the functions as described above. *T'ai chi t'u* is a product of inner vision and one of the primal symbols of mankind. It represents the duality of light and dark, of masculine and feminine, as a unit, a totality.[1] 'The line at the same time

[1] In the iconography of symbols, the light ordinarily stands for the masculine, the dark for the feminine.

posits an above and a below, a right and left, front and back—in a word, the world of opposites.'[1] The path of the arrow, the way, does not take the form of a cross, as might have been expected, but moves from top to right (the two segments of the bright part of the circle might be called symbolic representations of father and son), then leftward where more dark enters (symbol of the daughter); in the end it descends to the fourth function, situated wholly in the darkness of the womb, the unconscious—all of which is in agreement with the findings of the psychology of functions. The differentiated and the auxiliary functions are conscious and directed; they are often represented, in dreams for example, by father and son or other figures representing the dominant principle of consciousness and that closest to it; the two other functions are relatively or wholly unconscious and are often represented, according to the same rule, by mother and daughter. But since the opposition between the auxiliary functions is by no means as great as that between differentiated and inferior functions, the third function can be raised to consciousness and thus become 'masculine'. But it carries along some of its contamination with the inferior function and so provides a kind of mediator with the unconscious. The fourth function is wholly interwoven with the unconscious; whenever circumstances raise it to consciousness, it draws with it the contents of the unconscious, it 'invades' the field of consciousness with its undifferentiated contents. The resulting confrontation creates the possibility of a synthesis between conscious and unconscious contents.[2]

Why does Jung select just these four as 'basic functions'? He himself writes: 'I can give no *a priori* reason; . . . I can only say that this conception has shaped itself out of many years' experience.' He distinguishes these four functions, 'because they are neither mutually relatable nor mutually reducible',[3] and

---

[1] *I Ching*, trans. Baynes, 3rd edn., p. lv.

[2] This example refers primarily to the psyche of the man, the unconscious parts of which have feminine traits. In a parallel symbolization of the unconscious female psyche, the third and fourth functions would have masculine traits, but nevertheless, since they belong to the unconscious realm, they would be 'dark', and thus no longer correspond to the usual symbol-iconography.

[3] Cf. *Types*, par. 731.

because in his observation they exhaust all the possibilities.[1] And indeed, the number four has been regarded from time immemorial as an expression of wholeness, completeness, totality: we need only consider the four fields of the customary system of co-ordinates, the four arms of the Cross, the four cardinal points, etc.

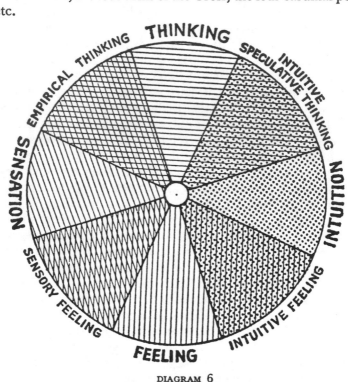

DIAGRAM 6

If all four functions could be raised to consciousness, the whole circle would be in the light and we should be able to speak of a 'round', that is to say a complete, man. Theoretically this is conceivable; but in practice only an approximation is possible. For no man can clarify all the darkness within him; to do so would be to cast off the last 'earthly vestige'. But although the

[1] Many psychologists regard the will as a basic function; in Jung's view, however, the will is a freely available psychic energy, present in each of the four basic functions. It can be 'directed' by an intervention of consciousness. Thus the scope and intensity of the so-called willpower are closely connected with the breadth of the field of consciousness and its degree of development.

mind cannot be dominated by more than one function at a time, an individual can, in the course of his progress toward fuller consciousness, differentiate the functions successively in a certain measure, so arriving at an approximation of 'roundness'. Once he has made the main function fully available and the accessory functions reasonably so, and has gained at least an idea of the nature of the fourth, inferior function and of when and how it is likely to spring into the foreground—and this is one of the ideal aims of analysis—he can, for example, first apprehend an object cognitively, then intuitively 'track down' its hidden potentialities, then palpate it with sensation, and finally —if feeling is the inferior function—evaluate it to a certain degree in regard to pleasantness or unpleasantness.[1]

Few people are clear about the function type to which they belong, although it is generally an easy matter 'to recognize from its strength, stability, consistency, and adaptedness whether a function is differentiated and to what extent'.[2]

The inferior function, on the other hand, is essentially characterized by its practical unreliability, the ease with which it can be influenced, its vagueness and unmannerliness. Or as Jung put it, 'You do not have it under your thumb; it has you'. It acts autonomously, emerging from the unconscious when it pleases. Because it is undifferentiated and wholly embedded in the unconscious, it has an infantile, primitive, instinctive, archaic character. This explains why we so often meet with moody, primitive, impulsive actions in individuals to whose nature as we know it they seem utterly foreign.

It goes without saying that the picture thus far presented is largely theoretical. In actual life the function types almost never appear in pure form, but in a variety of mixed types, as indicated in Diagram 6. Kant, for example, was a pure thinking type, while Schopenhauer must be regarded as an intuitive thinking type. We often find mixtures, but only of 'adjacent' functions, and when either component is pronounced, it is difficult to classify the individual according to his function type.

---

[1] Here as in the other examples thinking is used as the most differentiated function.

[2] Cf. 'A Psychological Theory of Types', par. 956. Sometimes the individual's inferior function can be inferred from the nature of the persons who appear in his dreams.

On the other hand, as their positions indicate, mixture is impossible between the opposites on the two axes: thinking–feeling and sensation–intuition. But there is always a compensatory relation between them. Where one function is overemphasized, in a one-sidedly intellectual individual for example, the opposite function, here feeling, will set up a compensatory drive. In the present case, of course, feeling will takes its inferior form. Quite unexpectedly the intellectual will be overcome by outbursts of infantile feeling; he is beset by fantasies and purely instinctual dreams against which he feels quite defenceless. And similarly, the neglected sensation function of the one-sided intuitive type will compel him, often by seemingly incomprehensible onslaughts, to take account of hard reality.

The complementary or compensatory relation between opposite functions is a structural law of the psyche. The overdifferentiation of the superior function, which is almost inevitable with the passage of the years, results nearly always in tensions that are among the main problems of the second half of life. Overdifferentiation leads to a disturbance of balance, which in itself can do serious harm.

THE ATTITUDE TYPES

The function type to which an individual belongs is an indication of his psychological character, but by itself it does not suffice. In addition we must determine his general attitude, i.e., his way of reacting to outer and inner experience. Jung distinguishes two such attitudes, EXTRAVERSION and INTROVERSION, which influence the entire psychic process. One or the other of these orientations is the reaction habitus that determines the way we respond to the objects of the outer and inner world, the nature of our subjective experience, and even the compensatory action of our unconscious. Jung calls this habitus 'the central switchboard from which on the one hand external behaviour is regulated and, on the other, specific experiences are formed'.[1]

Extraversion is characterized by a positive relation to the object, introversion by a negative one. In his adjustment and reaction pattern, the extravert orients himself predominantly by the outward, collective norms, the spirit of his times, etc. The

[1] Cf. 'A Psychological Theory of Types', par. 941.

attitudes of the introvert, on the other hand, are determined mainly by subjective factors. Often he is poorly adjusted to his environment. The extravert 'thinks, feels, and acts in relation to the object'; he displaces his interest from subject to object and orients himself primarily by the world outside himself.[1] For the introvert the subject is the basis of orientation, while the object plays at most a secondary, indirect role. His first move in every situation that confronts him is to recoil, 'as if with an unvoiced no',[2] and only then does his real reaction set in.

Thus while the functional types indicate the way the material of experience is apprehended and formed, the attitude type—extraversion or introversion—marks the general psychological attitude, that is, the direction of the 'libido', which to Jung means the general psychic energy. The attitude type is rooted in our biological make-up and is much more clearly determined from birth than is our function type. For although the dominant function is in general determined by a certain constitutional predisposition, the constitutional tendency can be considerably modified or even repressed by conscious effort. But a change in the attitude type can be brought about only by an 'inner reconstruction', a modification of the structure of the psyche, either through spontaneous transformation (which again would stem from biological factors) or by an arduous process of psychic development such as an 'analysis'.[3]

Consequently, the second and third function, i.e., the two auxiliary functions, are somewhat more easily differentiated than the fourth, inferior function, which is not only far removed from, and sharply opposed to, the principal function, but also coincides with the still unlived, hidden, and hence undifferentiated attitude type. Consequently the introversion of the extraverted thinking type, for example, has an overtone not of intuition or of sensation, but primarily of feeling.

Between extraversion and introversion there is also a compensatory relation. Where consciousness is extraverted, the un-

---

[1] Often, therefore, referred to by Jung as an 'orientation type'.

[2] 'A Psychological Theory of Types', par. 937.

[3] Concerning the relation between biologically and psychologically determined disorders and the effect of hormones on the psyche, there are numerous informative works (cf. Steinach, Freud, Meng, von Wyss, etc.).

conscious is introverted, and conversely. This is of crucial importance for psychological understanding. In her 'Einführung in die Grundlagen der komplexen Psychologie',[1] Toni Wolff writes: 'The extravert has an introverted unconscious, though precisely because this side of him remains unconscious, its introversion takes an undifferentiated, and compulsive or instinctual form. Thus when the unconscious counterpart breaks through, subjective factors make themselves violently felt. A positive-minded man, living at peace with the world, becomes temporarily or permanently a critical, carping, distrustful egocentric who suspects everyone of the most personal motives. He feels isolated and misunderstood and senses hostility on all sides. A frequent indication of this automatic transition from a conscious attitude to its unconscious opposite is that the individual finds his own negative aspects in an object—as a rule a person of the opposite, that is, the introverted type—or projects them upon it. Then, as one might expect, the object comes in for a shower of bitter and unjust reproaches.

'If the opposite unconscious attitude breaks through in the introverted type, he becomes as it were an inferior, maladjusted extravert. The outward object is covered with projections of subjective material and thus takes on a kind of magic significance.' Here we have a sort of 'participation mystique'. This condition, as one would expect, is particularly frequent in relations of love or hate, because an intense affect stimulates the projection mechanism.[2]

The attitudinal habitus of consciousness is maintained until the individual gets into a situation where his one-sidedness prevents him from adapting to reality. In a relationship with an object of the opposite type, the individual puts all the blame on the other when the opposites clash and misunderstandings arise, because the other possesses the qualities which he does not find in himself, which he has not developed, and which are therefore present in him only in inferior form. Thus difference in types is often the real psychological basis of marital problems, of difficulties between parents and children, of friction among friends and business associates, and even of social and political differ-

---

[1] *Studien zu G. G. Jungs Psychologie*, p. 87.

[2] 'Affects always occur where there is a failure of adaptation,' says Jung (*Types*, par. 808).

ences. In such cases everything of which the individual is un-aware in his own psyche is projected onto the object, and as long as he fails to recognize the projected content in himself, he makes a scapegoat of the object. The ethical task confronting him is to discern in himself the opposed attitudinal habitus, which is structurally present in everyone. By *consciously* accept-ing and developing it, the individual would not only achieve balance for himself but improve his understanding of his fellow men.[1]

As a rule, it is only in the second half of life that this opposi-tion of functions and of conscious and unconscious attitudes is exacerbated to the point of conflict; this, indeed, is the problem which announces the changed psychological situation of middle age. Often in his forties a capable man, well adjusted to his environment, will suddenly discover that despite his 'brilliant mind' his domestic difficulties are too much for him, that he is unsuited to his position, etc. This phenomenon should be taken as a warning that the inferior function has begun to claim its rights and that a confrontation with it has become a necessity. And indeed such a confrontation is all important as a first step in an analysis undertaken at this age.

At this point we must mention another disturbance of the psychic balance which is encountered almost as frequently today, namely the disorder that arises when none of the four possible functions has been developed, when all four have remained undifferentiated. This is the state of the child's psyche as long as his ego is not firmly consolidated. For the development of ego-consciousness is a slow and arduous process of centring and growth and runs parallel to the growth and consolidation of the principal function. It should be completed by the end of adole-scence, but many individuals arrive at a much more advanced age without having carried the development beyond its initial stages. Despite their years such individuals remain childish, characterized by a strange uncertainty, a constant vacillation in all their utterances, judgements, and actions. In every situa-tion such an individual seems to hesitate as though wondering which of his two possible attitudes or four possible functions he should exercise. He is highly impressionable, his personality

[1] Cf. also Jung's excellent description of these two antithetical types in 'Unconscious', pp. 81 ff.

changes from one minute to the next; or else—as a safeguard against this susceptibility—he puts on a rigid, conventional mask which is meant to hide his psychic underdevelopment. But experience shows that the immature psyche will make itself felt in the crucial moments and situations of life, leading to innumerable complications. Thus an insufficient development of the functions is as harmful as one-sided overdifferentiation. A frequent example is the perpetual adolescent, even when he takes the bright, lovable form of the *puer aeternus*. The 'eternal youth', however, may symbolize not merely a fixation at an early stage, i.e., a retardedness, but also, according to the individual case, a possibility of further growth, the potential unfolding that is present in whatever is still undeveloped.

The most essential psychic task of the young is to differentiate and isolate the function which, because it is most solidly rooted in the individual's constitution, will best enable him to gain a foothold in the world and meet the demands of his environment. Only after this has been done can the other functions be differentiated. For until an individual has firmly anchored his consciousness in the world around him—and this occurs only with the onset of adulthood or even later, after a certain amount of experience has been acquired—he should not confront his unconscious unless it is absolutely necessary.

The same applies to the attitudinal habitus. In the first half of life the habitus determined by his constitution should govern, because as a rule it is the attitude provided by nature that will best enable him to find his way in the world. It is only with the second half of life that it becomes important for him to let the opposite attitude come into its own. Obviously a born extravert will have an easier time than a born introvert in making the adjustment to the environment which is the main business of the first half of life. It seems safe to say that the extravert gets along more easily in the first half of life and the introvert in the second—the scales are more or less balanced and a relative justice prevails.

The danger threatening both sides is one-sidedness. An able man may be driven so far into the world that he can no longer find 'the way home'. His own innermost being has become alien to him. He keeps running away from it, until one day he cannot go on. Or else he has leaned too heavily on his reason, constantly exercising and strengthening his thinking function and it alone, until one day he becomes aware that he has alienated himself from his own living core; his feeling has become inadequate for communication even with those closest to him. But a one-sided orientation also creates difficulties for the introvert as he grows older. The neglected functions and attitudinal habitus revolt; they demand their place in the sun, and if all else fails, call attention to themselves by way of a neurosis. For the goal is always psychic totality, the ideal solution in which at least three of the four functions and both reaction types are made as conscious and available as possible. The individual must attempt at least once to achieve an approximation to this ideal, and he must get to know at least something of the fourth function and the danger it can represent for him. If he has not met the challenge at an earlier date, the noon of life represents the last summons. It is now or never that the psyche must be rounded out; otherwise it will be left unfinished and incomplete, to face life's evening.

THE TYPE PROBLEM IN CREATIVE PEOPLE

We have seen that a man is seldom aware of the function type to which he belongs. The same is true of his attitude type. Often it is very hard to distinguish, and a considerable psychological investigation is needed to disentangle it from the kaleidoscopic image that the psyche presents to the observer. The stronger the individual's natural relation to the unconscious, the more difficult this task becomes. This applies most of all to artistic natures. Creative men and artists possess an extraordinary natural relation, 'a direct line' as it were to the unconscious, and are hard to assign to a type, all the more so because an artist cannot automatically be equated with his work. Often one and the same artist is an extravert in his life and an introvert in his work, or the other way round. In this they follow the law of psychic complementarity, which seems particularly applicable to those artists who represent in their work what they themselves are not, in other words, their complement. In those artists, on the other hand, whose work does not represent their other, unlived aspect but a 'sublimation' of their conscious personality, an intensified, idealized self-portrait, work and individual should normally be of the same type. To this category belong the introverts who write subtle psychological novels about themselves, and the extraverts who make themselves the heroes of adventure stories. Jung believes that extraverted art springs from the artist's remoulding of outward experience, while introverted art is created when the artist is overwhelmed by inner contents.

As far as we can follow the creative process, it consists in activating the eternal symbols of mankind which lie dormant in the unconscious and in shaping and elaborating them to produce a finished work of art. 'But,' says Jung, 'he who speaks in primordial images speaks with a thousand voices; he enthralls and overpowers, while at the same time he lifts the idea he is trying to express out of the occasional and the transitory into the realm of the ever-enduring. He transmutes our personal destiny into the destiny of mankind, thereby evoking in us all those beneficent forces that have always enabled mankind to find a refuge from every peril and to outlive the longest night. That is the secret of great art.'[1]

Jung attaches great importance to the creative activity of fantasy, which he even puts in a category of its own, because in his opinion it cannot be subordinated to any of the four basic functions, but partakes of them all. He rejects the usual notion that artistic inspiration is limited to the intuitive type, that intuition is the dominant function in all artists. Fantasy is indeed the source of all creative inspiration, but it is a gift that can come to any of the four types. It may be equated neither with the 'active imagination' which raises the images of the collective unconscious to consciousness, activates and fixates them, nor with intuition, which is a way of apprehending psychic data—hence a function of consciousness. The functional type is revealed by the way in which intuitions as well as products of creative fantasy are apprehended and elaborated. Thus, by its whole tenor, a creative work may belong to a different type from the artist who creates it, and it is not only by the content that we may infer the artist's type but also by the way it is treated. Fundamentally, of course, the fantasy of the artist does not differ from that of the ordinary man; apart from the rich-

[1] 'On the Relation of Analytical Psychology to Poetry', pars. 129 f.

ness, originality, and vitality of the products of his fantasy, what makes the artist is primarily the formative power that enables him to give them shape, to weave them into an organic, aesthetic whole.

We often hear that it is dangerous for an artist to concern himself with the unconscious. A good many artists shun psychology, says Jung, 'because they are terrified that this monster will gobble up their so-called artistic ability. As if a whole army of psychologists could do anything against the power of a god! True productivity is a spring that can never be stopped up. Is there any trickery on earth which could have prevented Mozart or Beethoven from creating? Creative power is mightier than its possessor. If it is not so, then it is a feeble thing . . . and given favourable conditions will nourish an endearing talent, but no more. If, on the other hand, it is a neurosis, it often takes only a word or a look for the illusion to go up in smoke. Then the supposed poet can no longer write, and the painter's ideas become fewer and drearier than ever, and for all this psychology is to blame. I should be delighted if a knowledge of psychology did have this sanative effect and if it put an end to the neuroticism which makes contemporary art such an unpleasant problem. Disease has never yet fostered creative work; on the contrary, it is the most formidable obstacle to creation. No breaking down of repressions can ever destroy true creativeness, just as no analysis can ever exhaust the unconscious.'[1]

Another widespread error is the supposition that in producing a complete, well-rounded work an artist is necessarily perfecting himself. For in order to derive actual benefit for the process of psychic differentiation from one's 'dealings with the unconscious', in order to accomplish a desired development of the personality, one must humanly experience and understand the images, symbols, and visions that rise up from the depths; one must assimilate and integrate them *actively* or, as Jung says, 'face the figures of the vision actively and reactively, with full consciousness'.[2] But the artist often takes a passive attitude toward them, observing, reproducing, and at best allowing himself to be *acted upon*. Such experience has artistic value, but it is incomplete from a psychic point of view. Only a few of the very greatest artists are able to broaden and develop their personality

[1] 'Education', p. 115.   [2] 'Relations', par. 342.

and their work in equal degree. Only a very few have the strength to carry the work within and the work without to like perfection. For 'great gifts are the fairest, and often the most dangerous, fruits on the tree of humanity. They hang on the weakest branches, which easily break.'[1]

An attitude of extraversion or introversion is usually constant in the life of an individual. But at certain times the two attitudes can alternate. Certain phases in the life of the individual, or even in the lives of nations, are characterized more by extraversion, and others by introversion. In general, puberty is a more extraverted, the climacteric a more introverted, phase; the Middle Ages were a predominantly introverted period, the Renaissance was more extraverted. On the whole, the English are more introverted, the Americans more extraverted, etc. This in itself indicates that it is a mistake—though a very common one—to regard one or another of the two attitudes as more desirable. Both have their justification and both have their place in life. Each makes its contribution to the completeness of the world. Anyone who fails to recognize this only proves that he is a blind prey to one of the two attitudes and unable to see beyond it.

Combining the general attitudinal habitus with the four basic functions, we arrive at eight different psychological types: the extraverted thinking type, the introverted thinking type, the extraverted feeling type, the introverted feeling type, etc., which form a kind of compass by means of which we can orient ourselves in regard to the structure of the psyche. If we wish to give a complete schematic picture of the personality in accordance with Jung's theory of types, we may consider introversion—extraversion as a third axis running perpendicular to the two crossed axes of the four function types; by connecting each of the four functions of the two attitude types, we obtain a figure with eight determinants. And actually the idea of the quaternity is often expressed by the double four, the eight (ogdoad).

THE PERSONA

The degree of differentiation (or overdifferentiation) of one's consciousness also has a considerable bearing on what Jung calls the PERSONA, the form of an individual's general psychic

---

[1] 'The Gifted Child', p. 141.

attitude towards the outside world. Diagram 7 shows how the system of psychic relations, by which the individual comes into contact with his environment, casts a kind of cloak between the ego and the objective world. Here as in the other diagrams thinking is taken as the principal function; it dominates the

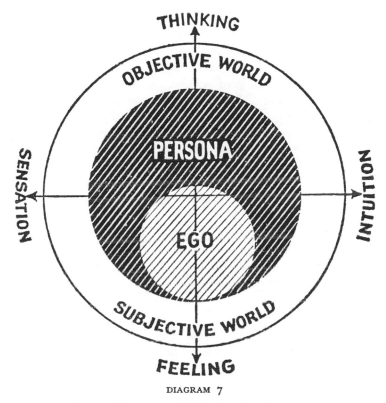

DIAGRAM 7

Ego and Persona, with the four function types.

persona, the cloak around the ego, almost entirely. The auxiliary functions have much less part in it, and the inferior function, feeling, has virtually none. The persona is actually a part of the ego, the part that is turned toward the outside world; Jung defines it as follows: 'The PERSONA is a functional complex which has come into existence for reasons of adaptation or necessary convenience, but by no means is it identical with the individuality. The function-complex of the persona is exclusively concerned with the relation to the object'[1]—that is, the outside world. 'The persona . . . is a compromise between individual and society as to what a man should appear to be.'[2] In other words it is a compromise between the demands of the environment and the inner structural necessity of the individual.

This means that a properly functioning persona must take account of three factors: first, the ego-ideal or wish image which every human being bears within him and on which he would like his nature and behaviour to be modelled; second, his particular environment's view of an individual 'after its own heart'; and third, the physical and psychic contingencies which limit the realization of these ideals. If one or even two of these factors is left out of account, as sometimes happens, the persona cannot do justice to its task; it becomes more of a hindrance than a help to the development of the personality. An individual whose persona is built up exclusively of traits approved by the external collectivity will have the persona of a mass man; while an individual who takes only his own wish image into account and neglects the other two factors will show the persona of an eccentric or even of a rebel. Thus the persona involves not only psychic qualities but also forms of social behaviour and our habits of personal appearance, posture, gait, dress, facial expression, the quality of our smile and our frown, even our way of wearing our hair.

In an individual well adjusted to his environment and his own inner life, the persona is merely a supple protective coating that makes for easy, natural relations with the outside world. But under certain circumstances it becomes too convenient to hide one's real nature behind the covering; the persona becomes mechanical. This has its dangers; the mask freezes and behind it the individual wastes away.[3] 'Identification with one's office or one's title is very attractive indeed, which is precisely why so many men are nothing more than the decorum accorded to them by society. In vain would one look for a personality behind this husk. Underneath all the padding one would find a very pitiable little creature. That is why the office—or whatever

[1] Cf. *Types*, par. 801.

[2] 'Relations', par. 246.

[3] Cf. Schopenhauer's fine essay, 'Von dem, was Einer ist und dem, was Einer vorstellt', in *Aphorismen zur Lebensweisheit*, II and IV.

this outer husk may be—is so attractive,'[1] providing, as it does, cheap compensation for personal inadequacies. We all of us know the professor whose whole individuality is exhausted by his professorial role; behind the mask, we find nothing but peevishness and infantilism. Thus despite its habitual and hence largely automatic mode of functioning, the persona must never become so impenetrable that an outsider cannot even suspect the traits of individual character that it covers over. Nor must it 'grow on' so rigidly that it can no longer be laid aside. Normally consciousness can dispose freely of a properly functioning persona, adapting it to the requirements of the moment or even exchanging it for another when necessary. An individual well adjusted to his environment will not attend a wedding, talk things over with the tax collector, and preside at a meeting with the same identical persona. To vary his persona in this way he must be relatively conscious of it, and this of course will be possible only if it is related to the superior function of his consciousness.

Unhappily—as it is easy to observe—this is not always the case. For the adaptation to the environment is sometimes attempted not with the superior function—as is and should be the rule—but with the inferior function. Or it may be forced upon the individual by his parents or the pressure of education. In the long run this can only have serious consequences. Such violence to the natural psychic disposition leads to a kind of 'compulsive character', if not to an actual neurosis. In such cases the persona inevitably takes on all the inadequacies of the inferior, undifferentiated function. Individuals of this sort make an unpleasant impression and often give those untrained in psychology a completely mistaken picture of their nature. All their lives, there is something false and mechanical about their conduct towards others. One such type 'never seems to have any luck'; another is the 'bull in the china shop', the eternal blunderer, who has no natural feeling for appropriate behaviour.

It is not only the representatives of the collective consciousness,[2] the socially prominent bearers of titles, honours, etc., that

[1] 'Relations', par. 230.

[2] By 'collective consciousness' we mean the aggregate of the traditions, conventions, customs, prejudices, rules, and norms of human collectivity which give the consciousness of the group as a whole its direction, and by

exert an attraction which tends to inflate the personality. Beyond our ego lies not only the collective social consciousness but also the collective unconscious, our own depths, which harbour equally attractive figures. In the first case a man can be thrown into the world by his official dignity; in the second, he can be carried away from it, i.e., engulfed by the collective consciousness. Identifying himself with an inner image, he suffers delusions of grandeur or insignificance. He takes himself for a hero, a saviour of humanity, an avenger, a martyr, an outcast, etc. The danger of succumbing to these 'inner figures' mounts when the persona becomes indurated and the ego's identification with it increases. For when this happens all the inner elements of the personality remain repressed, suppressed, undifferentiated, and charged with a menacing dynamic.

Thus a properly fitting and well-functioning persona is essential to psychic health and indispensable if the demands of the environment are to be met successfully. Just as a healthy, supple skin favours the metabolism of the tissues beneath it, while a withering, hardened skin cuts off the line of the body within, so a 'full-blooded' persona serves as an effective regulator of the exchange between the inner and outer worlds, but becomes an encumbrance or barrier when it loses its elasticity and permeability. Lasting identification with the persona—especially in an attitude that does not correspond to our true ego—leads invariably, around middle life, to disturbances that may assume the proportions of grave psychic crises and disorders.

THE CONTENTS OF THE UNCONSCIOUS

As we have already seen, the unconscious consists of two zones, one personal, the other collective[1] (Diagram 8). The personal unconscious is made up of 'forgotten, repressed, sub-

which the individuals of this group consciously but quite unreflectingly live. This concept coincides in part with the Freudian concept of the 'superego', but differs from it in so far as for Jung it includes not only the 'introjected' dos and don'ts of the environment, operating from within the psyche, but also those which pour in uninterruptedly from outside to influence the individual in his commissions and omissions, his feeling and his thinking.

[1] This attempt to divide the unconscious part of the psyche into 'zones' must of course be taken only as a working hypothesis which helps us to get our bearings amid the highly complex material of the unconscious and to group it conveniently.

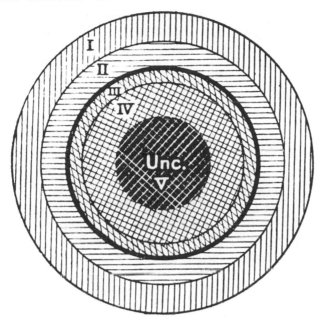

DIAGRAM 8 Sphere of the Unconscious.

I. Memories. ⎫
II. Repressed material. ⎬ Personal Unconscious.
III. Emotions.
IV. Irruptions.
V. That part of the collective unconscious that
    can never be made conscious.

liminally perceived and felt material of all kinds'.[1] The collec-

---

[1] The notions of 'preconscious' and 'subconscious', which are still widely equated with the personal or collective unconscious (a source of numerous misunderstandings), account for only a part of it. The preconscious (*Vorbewusstsein*), a term introduced by Freud, represents a kind of frontier of the personal unconscious. Bordering on consciousness, it is a realm of subliminal contents which are 'ready for action' so to speak, merely awaiting a summons before entering into consciousness. The subconscious (*Unterbewusstsein*; the term originated with Dessoir), on the other hand, refers to psychic processes situated between consciousness and the unconscious (such as certain states of trance and unremembered, unintentional, or unnoticed actions). The subconscious may be identified more or less with the personal but not with the collective unconscious, the contents of which go beyond personal experience. To venture a topographical description, one might say that the preconscious occupies the upper zone of the personal unconscious, bordering on consciousness, while the subconscious occupies the lower zone bordering on the collective unconscious. Thus Jung's 'personal unconscious' comprises both.

tive unconscious may also be broken down into zones which, figuratively speaking, may be considered as one above the other, though actually consciousness is surrounded on all sides by the unconscious. Jung goes so far as to say: 'In my experience the

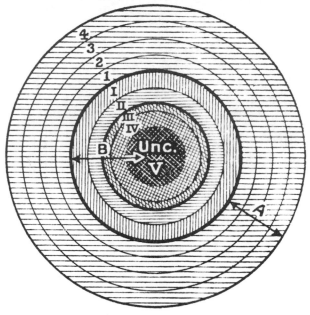

DIAGRAM 9

A. Consciousness.
B. Unconscious.

I. Forgotten material.
II. Repressed material.
III. Emotions.
IV. Irruptions.
V. That part of the collective unconscious that can never be made conscious.

1. Sensation.
2. Feeling.
3. Intuition.
4. Thinking.

conscious mind can claim only a relatively central position and must put up with the fact that the unconscious psyche tran-scends and as it were surrounds it on all sides. Unconscious contents connect it *backward* with physiological states on the one hand and archetypal data on the other. But it is extended *forward* by intuitions.'[1] But if we stick to our conception of layers, which are easier to visualize, we must take as our first zone that

[1] *Alchemy*, par. 175.

of the affects, and primitive instincts over which we can sometimes exert a certain control, upon which we can impose a
certain rational order. The zone below it comprises the contents
that erupt directly from the deep, dark centre of our unconscious,
which can never be made wholly conscious, which burst forth
with elemental force like foreign bodies, eternally incomprehensible and never wholly assimilable by the ego. They are quite

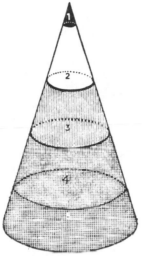

DIAGRAM 10

1. The ego.
2. Consciousness.
3. The personal unconscious.
4. The collective unconscious.
5. The part of the collective unconscious
   that can never be made conscious.

autonomous in character and provide the substance not only of
neuroses and psychoses but also of many of the visions and hallu-
cinations of creative men.

It is often extremely difficult to differentiate the various zones
and their contents. They usually appear in a kind of mixture.[1]
For one is not justified in conceiving of consciousness as Here and
of the unconscious as There. 'It is rather the case that the
psyche is a conscious–unconscious whole with continually
shifting borderlines of contact.'[2]

[1] It is only for the sake of clarity that the zones are divided by lines in the
diagrams.   [2] 'Nature', p. 200.

Diagrams 9 and 10 are intended to show the structure of the individual's total psychic system. The bottommost circle (in Diagram 9, the inner circle) is the largest. Each successive circle is smaller. The tip and culmination is the ego. Diagram 11 shows a kind of psychic family tree, the phylogenetic counterpart of the foregoing ontogenetic representation. At the very bottom

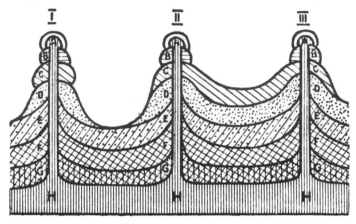

DIAGRAM 11
I. Isolated Nations.
II and III. Groups of Nations (e.g., Europe).

A. Individual.   E. Ethnic Group.
B. Family.   F. Primitive Human Ancestors.
C. Tribe.   G. Animal Ancestors.
D. Nation.   H. Central Energy.

lies the unfathomable, the 'central energy',[1] out of which the individual psyche has been differentiated. The central energy runs through all subsequent differentiations; it lives in them all and cuts across them to the individual psyche; it is the only factor that remains unchanged in every stratum. Above the 'unfathomable ground' lies the deposit of the experience of all our animal ancestors, and next that of our oldest human ancestors. Each segment stands for a further differentiation of the collective psyche, until, in the development from ethnic groups to national groups, from tribe to family, the summit, the individual human psyche, is attained. As Jung says, 'The col-

[1] This energy should not be taken as a metaphysical concept but as a heuristic term relating to an empirical finding.

lective unconscious contains the whole spiritual heritage of mankind's evolution born anew in the brain structure of every individual'.[1]

In contrast to the personal unconscious, which is an accumulation of contents that have been repressed during the life of the individual and is continuously being refilled with new materials, the collective unconscious consists entirely of elements characteristic of the human species. On the basis of a helpful working hypothesis Jung was able to distinguish between the various contents that are intermingled in the unconscious. He 'unscrambled' them, as it were, in order to point out their fundamentally divergent characters. The contents assigned to the collective unconscious represent the suprapersonal foundation both of the personal unconscious and of consciousness; it is 'neutral' in every respect; the value and position of its contents are defined only when they come into contact with consciousness. The collective unconscious is impervious to the critical and ordering activity of consciousness; in it we hear the voice of uninfluenced primal nature, and Jung accordingly calls it the *objective psyche*. The conscious mind is always directed toward the adjustment of the ego to the environment. The unconscious, on the other hand, 'is indifferent to the *egocentric* purposiveness and partakes of the impersonal objectivity of nature',[2] whose sole purpose is to maintain the undisturbed continuity of the psychic process, hence to oppose all one-sidedness that might lead to isolation, inhibition, or other pathogenic phenomena. At the same time it operates—for the most part in ways that are beyond our understanding—with a purposiveness of its own, directed toward the completeness and wholeness of the psyche.

So far we have spoken about the structure and functioning of consciousness and the manifestations and reactions by which we know them. We have also discussed the 'layers' of the unconscious. The question now arises: May one speak of a structure or morphology of the unconscious, and if so, how much do we know about it? Is it possible to obtain definite information about what is 'unknown' to consciousness? The answer is yes. Not directly, however, but *only* through such effects and indirect

[1] 'The Structure of the Psyche', p. 158.
[2] T. Wolff, *Studien zu C. G. Jungs Psychologie*, p. 109.

manifestations as the symptoms and complexes, images and symbols that we encounter in dreams, fantasies, and visions.[1]

THE COMPLEX

The phenomena most readily visible on the plane of consciousness are SYMPTOMS and COMPLEXES. A symptom may be defined as a physical or psychic indication of an obstruction of the normal flow of energy. It is a 'danger signal indicating that there is something drastically wrong or inadequate in the conscious attitude and that a broadening of consciousness is desirable'.[2] In other words, the obstruction should be removed, although there is no way of knowing a priori where it is or how to get at it.

Jung defines complexes as 'psychic entities that have escaped from the control of consciousness and split off from it, to lead a separate existence in the dark sphere of the psyche, whence they may at any time hinder or help the conscious performance'.[3] The complex consists first of a 'nuclear element', a vehicle of meaning, which is usually unconscious and autonomous, hence beyond the subject's control, and second of the manifold associations linked with it and marked by the same emotional tone; these in turn draw their content partly from original personal disposition and partly from outside experience.[4]

'The nuclear element has a constellating power corresponding to its energic value.'[5] Both in an individual and a phylogenetic sense, it is a kind of 'neuralgic point', a centre of functional disturbance, which becomes virulent in certain external or internal situations, when it may totally upset the psychic balance and dominate the whole personality.

Diagram 12[6] shows the rising complex. Under its weight the threshold of consciousness sags, permitting the unconscious to

[1] The parallel with the hypothesis of physics is obvious. We have no direct perception of waves and atoms but infer their existence from observed effects. They form the basis of hypotheses by which we try to explain the observed facts as coherently as possible.

[2] T. Wolff, *Studien zu C. G. Jungs Psychologie*, p. 101.

[3] Cf. 'A Psychological Theory of Types', par. 923.

[4] A detailed definition and description of the complex and of the two most important related concepts, the archetype and the symbol, may be found in my *Complex, Archetype, Symbol*.

[5] 'Energy', p. 12.

[6] This diagram is taken from the English report on Jung's lectures at the Zurich Eidgenössische Technische Hochschule, in 1934–35.

invade the conscious sphere. With this lowering of the threshold, '*l'abaissement du niveau mental*', as P. Janet called it, energy is withdrawn from consciousness. From an active, conscious state the individual falls into a passive 'seizure'.[1] An ascending complex of this kind acts as a foreign body in the field of consciousness. It is a self-contained whole with a high degree of

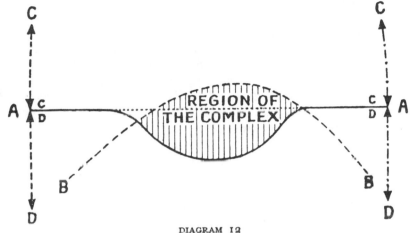

DIAGRAM 12

AA. Threshold of consciousness which is broken through at the dotted line, i.e., which has sunk into the unconscious.

BB. The path of the ascending complex.

CC. Sphere of consciousness.

DD. Sphere of the unconscious.

autonomy. It generally presents the picture of a disturbed psychic situation which has an intense emotional tone and proves incompatible with the usual conscious situation or attitude. One of its most frequent causes is moral conflict, which need by no means be sexual. 'The complex must . . . be a psychic factor which, in terms of energy, possesses a value that sometimes exceeds that of our conscious intentions.'[2]

Everybody has complexes. All sorts of slips, as Freud showed in his *Psychopathology of Everyday Life*[3], prove this unmistakably. Complexes do not necessarily imply any inferiority in the

[1] H. G. Baynes described the manifestations of this process in the Germany of the National Socialist period in his interesting book, *Germany Possessed*.

[2] 'A Review of the Complex Theory', p. 96.

[3] *Zur Psychopathologie des Alltagslebens* (1901, first published in book form in 1904).

individual who has them, but merely indicate 'that something incompatible, unassimilated, and conflicting exists—perhaps as an obstacle, but also, perhaps, as a stimulus to greater effort and even to new possibilities of achievement. Complexes are therefore, in this sense, focal or nodal points of psychic life which we would not wish to do without. Indeed they must not be lacking, for otherwise psychic activity would come to a fatal standstill.' According to their 'extent' and charge, or to the part they play in the psychic economy, we may thus speak of 'healthy' or 'sick' complexes, and here it depends solely on the state of consciousness, that is, on the relative stability of the ego-personality, to what extent they can be worked up, or whether they will ultimately have a beneficial or a harmful effect. But they always mark something 'unfinished' in the individual, or as Jung says, 'his weak spots in every sense of the word'.[1]

The origin of the complex is often a so-called trauma, an emotional shock, or something of the sort, by which a fragment of the psyche is 'incapsulated' or split off. In Jung's opinion it may spring from a recent event or current conflict just as well as from something that happened in childhood. But as a rule the complex has its ultimate cause in the impossibility of affirming the whole of one's individual nature.

It is only by practical psychotherapy that the actual significance of a complex can be shown or, when its influence proves to be harmful, that the individual can be freed from it. But its presence, its effective depth and emotional tone, can be determined by the association method elaborated by Jung some sixty years ago. In this method, a hundred 'stimulus words', selected on the basis of definite criteria, are called out to the subject, who must reply to each one with a 'reaction word', i.e. the very first word that occurs to him after hearing the stimulus word. Then, as a control, he must, after a certain lapse of time, reproduce all these word reactions from memory. It has been found that length of reaction time, absence of reproduction, false reproduction, and other forms of symptomatic reaction are determined by the relation of the stimulus word to the complex. The psychic mechanism points with clockwork accuracy to the complex-laden spots in the psyche.

---

[1] 'A Psychological Theory of Types', par. 925.

Jung has worked out the association method with extreme precision, taking the most divergent perspectives and possibilities into account. As a didactic and diagnostic method it has become an essential aid to psychotherapy, and it is still in standard use in psychiatric institutions, in courses of training in clinical psychology, in vocational guidance, and even in law courts. The term 'complex' originated with Jung. In *Studies in Word Association* (*Diagnostiche Assoziationsstudien*), his great work on the subject, published in 1904–6, he introduced the term 'feeling-toned complex' to designate 'groups of feeling-toned ideas in the unconscious'. Later the term was shortened to 'complex'.[1]

THE ARCHETYPES

It is not difficult to tell from the material provided by dreams, fantasies, and visions to what degree they transcend the personal sphere and involve the contents of the collective unconscious. Mythological themes, symbols rooted in the universal history of mankind, or reactions of extreme intensity always indicate the participation of the deepest strata. These motifs and symbols exert a determining influence on psychic life as a whole; they have a dominant functional character and an extremely high energy charge, which is why Jung at first spoke of them as 'primordial images' or 'dominants of the collective unconscious'. It was only later that he called them ARCHETYPES. Jung took the term 'archetype' from the *Corpus Hermeticum* (Scott, *Hermetica*, Vol. I, 140, 12b) and from Chap. 2, Par. 6, of the *De Divinis nominibus* of Dionysius the pseudo-Areopagite, which reads: 'But someone may say that the seal is not the same and entire in all its impressions. The seal, however, is not the cause of this, for it imparts itself wholly and alike in each case, but the differences in the participants make the impressions unlike, although the archetype is one, whole, and the same (τῆς αὐτῆς καὶ μιᾶς ἀρχετυπίας).'[2]

But he was drawn to the term above all by St. Augustine's definition of the *ideae principales*, the Latin equivalent of the

---

[1] The term 'complex' had already been used by Bleuler in reference to certain psychic findings, and it is still employed loosely for all manner of things.

[2] *Dionysius the Areopagite on the Divine Names . . .*, trans. Editors of The Shrine of Wisdom, Fintry (Surrey), 1957, p. 21.

Greek ἀρχετυπίαι. St Augustine writes: 'For the *principal ideas* are certain forms, or stable and unchangeable reasons of things, themselves not formed, and so continuing eternal and always after the same manner, which are contained in the divine understanding. And though they themselves do not perish, yet after their pattern everything is said to be formed that is able to come into being and to perish, and everything that does come into being and perish. But it is affirmed that the soul is not able to behold them, save it be the rational soul.'[1] Since 1946[2] Jung has distinguished (though not always explicitly) between the 'archetype per se' that is, the nonperceptible archetype which is present only potentially in every psychic structure, and the actualized archetype which has become perceptible and already entered into the field of consciousness. This actualized archetype appears as an archetypal image, representation, or process, and its form may change continuously according to the constellation in which it occurs. Of course there are also archetypal modes of action and reaction and archetypal processes, such as the development of the ego or the progress from one phase of age and experience to another; there are archetypal attitudes, ideas, ways of assimilating experience, which, set in motion under certain circumstances, emerge from their hitherto unconscious state and become visible, as it were.

Thus the archetype can manifest itself not only in static form, as a primordial image for example, but also in a dynamic process such as the differentiation of a function of consciousness. Actually all typical, universally human manifestations of life, whether biological, psycho-biological, or spiritual-ideational in character, rest on an archetypal foundation. We can even set up a certain 'order of sequence' of the archetypes, corresponding to whether they represent a characteristic of the whole of mankind or of a larger or smaller group. The archetypes, like the founders of a dynasty or family line, are able, as it were, to give birth to children and grandchildren without losing their own primordial form. The archetypes are reflections of instinctive, that is, psychically necessary, reactions to certain situations; with their inborn propensities they circumvent consciousness and lead to modes of behaviour which are psychologically necessary,[3]

---

[1] *Liber de diversis quaestionibus*, XLVI, 2. Translation by Alan Glover.
[2] Cf. 'Nature', pp. 159 ff.   [3] 'Instinct and the Unconscious', p. 133.

though they do not always seem appropriate when considered rationally from without.[1] They play a vital part in the psychic economy for, as Jung says, 'they represent or personify certain instinctive data of the dark, primitive psyche, the real but invisible roots of consciousness'.[2]

This line of thought has often been criticized on the ground that, as far as science can now determine, acquired characteristics or remembered images cannot be inherited. But Jung replies: 'Of course this term is not meant to denote an inherited idea but rather an inherited mode of psychic functioning,

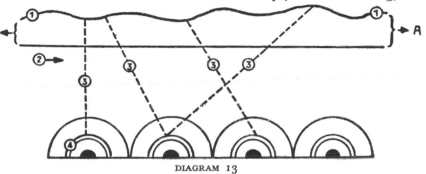

DIAGRAM 13

1. The surface of consciousness.
2. The sphere in which the 'inner order' begins to operate.
3. The paths by which contents sink into the unconscious.
4. The archetypes and their magnetic fields, which often distract the contents from their course, by their power of attraction.
AA. The zone where the purely archetypal processes are rendered invisible by external happenings; where the 'primordial pattern' is overlaid, as it were.

corresponding to that inborn *way* according to which the chick emerges from the egg; the bird builds its nest; a certain kind of wasp stings the motor ganglion of the caterpillar; and eels find their way to the Bermudas. In other words, it is a "pattern of behaviour". This aspect of the archetype is the biological one— it is the concern of scientific psychology. But the picture changes at once when looked at from the inside, that is, from within the realm of the subjective psyche. Here the archetype presents itself as numinous, that is, it appears as an experience of fundamental importance. Whenever it clothes itself with adequate

---

[1] For further detail on the archetype, see my *Complex, Archetype, Symbol*, pp. 31 ff.

[2] 'The Psychology of the Child Archetype', p. 160.

symbols, which is not always the case, it takes hold of the individual in a startling way, creating a condition of "being deeply moved", the consequences of which may be immeasurable.'[1]

Diagram 13[2] is designed to show the stratification of the psyche in regard to the workings of the archetypes. The realm of consciousness is full of the most heterogeneous elements; the archetypal symbols contained in it are often overlaid by other contents or cut off from their context. To a considerable extent we can guide and control the contents of consciousness by our will; the unconscious, however, has a continuity and order that is independent of us and impervious to our influence. The archetypes are its centres and fields of force. Thus the contents that sink into the unconscious are subjected to a new, invisible order that is not accessible to conscious knowledge; their path is often refracted, and frequently their aspect and significance are changed in a manner incomprehensible to us. This absolute inner order of the unconscious is a haven and helper amid the upheavals and accidents of life, provided that we know how to deal with it.[3] The archetype can modify our conscious orientation or even change it into its opposite, as for example when in a dream we see our idealized father as a man with the head of an animal and the hoofs of a he-goat, or as Zeus, the terrible thunderer, and our gentle beloved wife as a maenad, etc. Such dreams may be taken as warning messages from the unconscious, which 'knows better' and is trying to save us from a false evaluation.

The archetypes are also akin to what Plato called the 'idea'. But Plato's idea is a model of supreme perfection only in the 'luminous' sense, whereas Jung's archetype is bipolar, embodying the dark side as well as the light.

Jung also calls the archetype a 'psychic organ',[4] or with Bergson he speaks of *les éternels incréés*. Their 'ultimate core of meaning', he writes, 'may be circumscribed, but not described'.[5]

[1] Introduction to M. Esther Harding, *Woman's Mysteries*. (In C.W. 18.)

[2] The diagram is taken from the English report on Jung's lectures delivered at the Eidgenössische Technische Hochschule in Zurich, in 1934–35.

[3] Yoga exercises, for example, are based on this inner order of the unconscious.

[4] 'The Psychology of the Child Archetype', p. 160.

[5] Ibid., p. 156.

For 'whatever we say about the archetypes, they remain visualizations or concretizations which pertain to the field of consciousness'.[1]

Still another useful analogy is 'Gestalt', in the broadest sense of the word, as employed in Gestalt psychology and recently taken over by biology.[2] The form of the archetypes, says Jung, 'might perhaps be compared to the axial system of a crystal, which, as it were, preforms the crystalline structure in the mother liquid, although it has no material existence of its own. This first appears according to the specific way in which the ions and molecules aggregate. . . . The axial system determines only the stereometric structure but not the concrete form of the individual crystal.' Similarly 'the archetype . . . has an invariable nucleus of meaning—but only in principle, never as regards its concrete manifestation'.[3]

Thus the archetype as a potential 'axial system' (the archetype per se) is pre-existent and immanent in the psyche. The 'mother liquid'—the experience of humanity—in which the precipitate must form represents the images which crystallize around the axial system and which take on increasing sharpness and richness of content in the womb of the unconscious. The image is not 'engendered' at the time when it rises, but is already present in the darkness where it has lain ever since the typical and fundamental experience it reflects was added to the psychic treasure-house of mankind. As it rises to consciousness, it is irradiated with an increasing light, which sharpens and clarifies its contours until it becomes visible in every detail. This process of illumination has not only an individual but also a universally human significance. 'In sleep and in dreams,' said Nietzsche, 'we pass through the whole thought of earlier humanity,'[4] which is not very far from Jung's statement: 'The supposition that there

---

[1] 'Nature', p. 214.

[2] The relations between archetype and Gestalt have been investigated by K. W. Bash, 'Gestalt, Symbol und Archetypus'. Cf. also my *Complex, Archetype, Symbol*, pp. 44 ff., 53 ff.

[3] 'Psychological Aspects of the Mother Archetype', pp. 79 f. Compare with this the striking analogy in J. Killian's *Der Kristall*: 'The crystalline lattice determines what forms are possible; the environment decides which of these possibilities will be realized.'

[4] *Human, All Too Human*, Vol. II (quoted from Jung's *Symbols of Transformation*, p. 23).

may also be in psychology a correspondence between onto-genesis and phylogenesis therefore seems justified.'[1] In line with modern genetics, which in a measure takes its orientation from the Gestalt theory, one might say that the inherited factors are

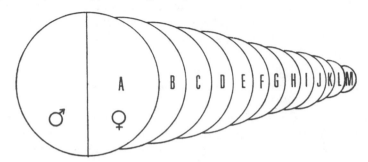

DIAGRAM 14

Developmental Sequence of the 'Archetype of the Feminine'.

♂♀= the two spheres of primordial origin, which one could imagine as being bi-sexual:

♂= *the archetype of the masculine;*
♀= *the archetype of the feminine.*

A = night, the unconscious, the receptive
B = sea, water, etc.
C = earth, mountain, etc.
D = forest, valley, etc.
E = cave, underworld, depths, etc.
F = dragon, whale, spider, etc.
G = witch, fairy, divine maiden, fairy princess, etc.
H = house, box, basket, etc.
I = cow, cat, etc.
J = rose, tulip, plum, etc.
K = ancestral mother
L = grandmother
M = one's own mother

precisely the Gestalten and our structural tendency to perceive in Gestalten, taken both in a literal sense and more broadly as totalities. The figure needs no interpretation; it expounds its own meaning.

The archetypes might be described as 'self-portraits of the instincts', as psychic processes transformed into images, or as primordial patterns of human behaviour. An Aristotelian would

[1] *Symbols of Transformation*, p. 23.

say: The archetypes are ideas rooted in man's experience of his real father and mother. The Platonist would say: Father and mother grew from the archetypes, for these are the primordial images, the prototypes of the phenomena.[1] From the standpoint of the individual, the archetypes exist a priori; they are inherent in the collective unconscious, and hence unaffected by individual growth and decay. 'Whether,' says Jung, 'this psychic structure and its elements, the archetypes, ever "originated" at all is a metaphysical question and therefore unanswerable' by psychology.[2] 'The archetype is metaphysical because it transcends consciousness,'[3] it belongs essentially to the 'psychoid' realm. 'The archetype is, so to speak, an "eternal" presence, and it is only a question of whether it is perceived by consciousness or not.'[4] It may emerge on many psychic levels and in the most diverse constellations; it takes on a form, a 'habitus', adapted to the individual situation and yet remains unchanged in fundamental structure and meaning; like a melody, it can be transposed.[5] This can be illustrated by a diagram showing, however, only a few of the manifold aspects and manifestations of, for example, the 'feminine'. The Gestalt remains constant, its content changes. (Diagram 14.)

When the form of an archetypal image is scanty and poorly defined, it usually springs from a deep stratum of the collective unconscious, a stratum where the symbols are present only as 'axial systems', not yet filled with individual content, not yet differentiated by the endless chain of individual experience, which they precede as it were. The more personal and current a problem is, the more intricate, detailed, and clearly defined is the archetypal figure by which it is expressed; the more impersonal and universal the situation it concretizes, the simpler or more blurred it will be—for the cosmos itself is built on a few simple principles. In its succinct simplicity an archetypal image of this sort contains potentially all the wealth and diversity of life and the world. Thus, for example, the 'mother' archetype in the structural sense we have described precedes and is super-

---

[1] See *Kindertraumseminar*, 1936–37.

[2] 'Psychological Aspects of the Mother Archetype', p. 101.

[3] Introduction to *Woman's Mysteries*. (In C.W. 18.)

[4] *Alchemy*, par. 329.

[5] Here again we note a kinship with Gestalt psychology.

ordinate to every individual manifestation of the 'motherly'. The primordial image of the mother, the 'Great Mother' with all her paradoxical attributes, is the same in the human soul of today as it was in mythical times.[1] The differentiation of the ego from the 'mother' is at the beginning of every 'coming to consciousness'. And coming to consciousness (*Bewusstwerdung*) means building a world by differentiating.[2] To create awareness, to formulate ideas—this is the father principle of the logos, which perpetually struggles to free itself from the primordial darkness of the maternal womb, from the realm of the unconscious. At the beginning both were one, and neither can exist without the other, just as light would be meaningless in a world without darkness. 'The world exists only because opposing forces are held in equilibrium.'[3]

In the language of the unconscious, which is a language of images, the archetypes are manifested in personified or symbolic form. 'An archetypal content,' writes Jung, 'expresses itself, first and foremost, in metaphors. If [it] should speak of the sun and identify with it the lion, the king, the hoard of gold guarded by the dragon, or the power that makes for the life and health of man, it is neither the one thing nor the other, but the un-

[1] The primordial image occupies a different plane in the masculine and in the feminine psyche. The so-called mother complex, which we are only beginning to explore, represents a serious and intricate problem for the man, while in the woman it is a relatively simple matter. The opposite is probably true of the father complex.

[2] *Bewusstwerdung*, as Jung employs the term, means more than mere 'perceiving', 'noticing', or 'becoming aware of' something. It has no specific object and signifies the unfolding of a deeper, wider, more intensive, and more receptive consciousness with an enhanced power of apprehending and elaborating what comes to it from the outer as well as the inner world. The coming to consciousness, or conscious realization, that is the goal of the analytical process does not imply an orientation toward a one-sided predominance of consciousness in the psychic life of the individual, for such a development must be regarded as incompatible with psychic balance and health. *Bewusstwerdung* is not equivalent to 'consciousness' in the usual sense, to the realm of the psyche that is governed exclusively by reason. On the contrary, it refers to a kind of 'higher consciousness' relating to the contents of the unconscious as well as of ego-consciousness; or it might perhaps better be termed a 'deeper and wider consciousness', for a firmly rooted and unobstructed connection with the unconscious is the foundation on which it grows.

[3] 'Psychological Aspects of the Mother Archetype', p. 94.

known third thing that finds more or less adequate expression in all these similes, yet—to the perpetual vexation of the intellect—remains unknown and not to be fitted into a formula. . . . Not for a moment dare we succumb to the illusion that an archetype can be finally explained and disposed of. Even the best attempts at explanation are only more or less successful translations into another metaphorical language.'[1]

The archetypes make up the actual content of the collective unconscious; their number is relatively limited, for it corresponds to 'the number of typical and fundamental experiences' incurred by man since primordial times. Their meaning for us lies precisely in the 'primordial experience' which is based on them and which they represent and communicate. The motifs of the archetypal images correspond to the part of man's make-up that is conditioned by phylogeny, and they are the same in all cultures. We find them recurring in all mythologies, fairy tales, religious traditions, and mysteries. What are the myths of the 'night sea journey', of the 'wandering hero', or of the sea monster, if not the eternal knowledge of the sun's setting and rebirth, transformed into images? Prometheus the stealer of fire, Heracles the dragon slayer, the countless creation myths, the fall from paradise, the mysteries of creation, the virgin birth, the treacherous betrayal of the hero, the dismembering of Osiris, and many other myths and fairy tales represent psychic processes in symbolic images. Similarly, the figures of the snake, the fish, the sphinx, the helpful animals, the Tree of the World, the Great Mother, the enchanted prince, the *puer aeternus*, the Mage, the Wise Man, Paradise, etc., stand for certain motifs and contents of the collective unconscious.[2] In every single

---

[1] 'The Psychology of the Child Archetype', pp. 157, 160.

[2] We can also discern a dominant archetype underlying the doctrines of the various thinkers, particularly the psychologists. When Freud sees the beginning and principle of everything that happens in sexuality, Adler in the striving for power, these two are ideas expressing an archetype, and we find similar archetypal representations at work in the ancient philosophers, gnostics, and alchemists.

Jung's teaching is also based on an archetype which finds its expression particularly in 'tetrasomy', four-bodiedness (cf. the theory of the four functions, the pictorial arrangement of the four, orientation by the four cardinal points, etc.). The number four is often discernible in the arrangement of dream contents, and probably the universal distribution and

individual psyche they can awaken to new life, exert their magic power, and condense into a kind of 'individual mythology',[1] which presents an impressive parallel to the great traditional mythologies of all peoples and epochs, concretizing as it were their origin, essence, and meaning, and throwing new light on them.

Thus for Jung the archetypes taken as a whole represent the

---

magical significance of the cross or of the four-part circle may be explained by the archetypal character of the quaternity (*Alch.*, par. 189). Another archetype is the number three, which from time immemorial, and particularly in the Christian religion, has been regarded as a symbol of the 'pure abstract spirit'. Beside it Jung sets the four as an archetypal expression of the highest significance for the psyche. With this fourth term the 'pure spirit' takes on 'corporeity' and a form adequate to physical creation. Along with the masculine spirit, the father principle which represents only one half of the world, the quaternity comprises the feminine and bodily aspect as its opposite pole—the two are needed to form a whole. In most cultures, the uneven numbers are indeed regarded as symbols of the masculine, the even numbers as symbols of the feminine. This might have some relation to the fact that (as Bash has called to my attention) the number of chromosomes in the male of nearly all biological species (including man) is uneven, while in the female it is even. As Jung writes, 'it is . . . a curious "sport of nature" that the chief chemical constituent of the physical organism is carbon, which is characterized by four valencies; also it is well known that the diamond is a carbon crystal. Carbon is black . . . but the diamond is "purest water". To draw such an analogy would be a lamentable piece of intellectual bad taste were the phenomenon of four merely a poetic conceit on the part of the conscious mind and not a spontaneous production of the objective psyche' (*Alchemy*, par. 327).

Perhaps it is something more than an accident that in this period, which, with its revolutionary discoveries in the natural sciences and above all physics, is in process of transition from three-dimensional to four-dimensional thinking, the most modern trend in depth psychology, that of Jung, should have selected the archetype of the four as its central structural concept. Just as it became necessary for modern physics to introduce time, a fourth dimension, which strikes us as fundamentally different from the three familiar spatial dimensions, if it was to gain a comprehensive view of the physical world, so a comprehensive view of the psyche called for consideration of the fourth, 'inferior', the 'completely other' function, which is diametrically opposed to consciousness. His fundamental innovation with its implications for the understanding and treatment of the psyche ranks Jung's psychology among the sciences that are profoundly modifying our picture of the world and building a new one on lines that are common to them all.

[1] This term was coined by K. Kerényi and first used in *Essays on a Science of Mythology*, p. 31.

sum of the latent potentialities of the human psyche—a vast store of ancestral knowledge about the profound relations between God, man, and cosmos. To open up this store in one's own psyche, to awaken it to new life and integrate it with consciousness, means nothing less than to save the individual from his isolation and gather him into the eternal cosmic process. Thus the conceptions of which we have been speaking become more than a science and more than a psychology. They become a way of life. The archetype as the primal source of all human experience lies in the unconscious, whence it reaches into our lives. Thus it becomes imperative to resolve its projections, to raise its contents to consciousness.

In his recent study, *Synchronicity: An Acausal Connecting Principle*, Jung pointed to a particularly significant aspect of the workings of the archetypes. In so doing he has thrown new light on certain phenomena of ESP (extrasensory perception) such as telepathy, clairvoyance, etc., for which science had hitherto provided no adequate explanation, and applied scientific methods to the investigation of certain strange occurrences and experiences which had previously been ignored, denied, or set down as mere accident. He gives the name 'synchronicity' (in distinction to synchronism, or simultaneity) to a principle of explanation which supplements causality; he defines it as 'a coincidence in time of two or more causally unrelated events which have the same or a similar meaning'. This may take the form of a coincidence of inner perceptions (forebodings, dreams, visions, hunches, etc.) with outward events situated in the past, present, or future. Thus far synchronicity is only a 'formal factor', an 'empirical concept' which postulates a principle necessary to a more comprehensive knowledge and which 'could be added as a fourth to the recognized triad of space, time, and causality'. Jung explains the occurrence of such synchronistic phenomena by an 'a priori, causally inexplicable knowledge', based on an order of the microcosm and macrocosm, which is independent of our will and in which the archetypes play the role of ordering factors. The meaningful coincidence of an inner image with the outward event, which characterizes synchronistic phenomena, reveals the spiritual as well as the material and corporeal aspect of the archetype. It is also the archetype which by its enhanced energic charge (or numinous effect) provokes in the individual who experiences it the increased emotionality or partial *abaissement du niveau mental* which is indispensable if synchronistic phenomena of this kind are to occur and to be perceived. Jung even goes so far as to say: 'The archetype is the introspectively recognizable form of a priori psychic orderedness.'[1] Jung's investigations on synchronicity have raised a number of new problems which demand further investigation and discussion.

'Archetypes,' says Jung, 'were, and still are, living psychic forces that demand to be taken seriously, and they have a strange way of making sure of their effect. Always they were the bringers of protection and salvation, and their violation has as its consequence the "perils of the soul", known to us from the psychology of primitives. Moreover, they are the unfailing causes of neurotic and even psychotic disorders, behaving exactly like neglected or maltreated physical organs or organic functional systems.'[2]

Not without reason have the archetypal images and experiences always formed a central part of all the religions of the earth. And although they have often been overlaid by dogma and stripped of their original form, they are still active in the psyche, their rich meaning is still powerfully at work, especially where religious faith remains a living force. And this is true of the dying and resurrected god as it is of the immaculate conception in Christianity, the veil of Maya among the Hindus, or the prayer of the Mohammedans turned toward Mecca. Only where faith and dogma have frozen into empty forms—and this is largely the case in our ultra-civilized technological, rational-minded Western world—have they lost their magic power and left man helpless and alone, at the mercy of evil without and within.

To relieve the isolation and confusion of modern man, to enable him to find his place in the great stream of life, to help him gain a wholeness which may knowingly and deliberately reunite his luminous conscious side with his dark unconscious side—this is the meaning and purpose of Jungian psychological guidance.

[1] 'Synchronicity: An Acausal Connecting Principle', pp. 441, 447, 511, 512, 516.
[2] 'The Psychology of the Child Archetype', pp. 156 f.

One of the main tasks of this book is to elucidate this form of guidance and the implements and methods employed by Jung. But for a better understanding of the foundation on which it is based, we must first consider briefly the second part of the theory, namely the 'dynamics of the psyche'.

II

THE LAWS OF THE PSYCHIC PROCESSES AND FORCES

THE CONCEPT OF LIBIDO

FOR Jung the psychic system is engaged in a continuous energic movement. By PSYCHIC ENERGY he means the total force which pulses through all the forms and activities of the psychic system and establishes a communication between them. He calls this kind of psychic energy LIBIDO. It is nothing other than the intensity of the psychic process, its *psychological value*,[1] which can be determined only by psychic manifestations and effects. Like the analogous term 'energy' in physics, 'libido' is employed as an abstraction expressing dynamic relations and based on a theoretical postulate which is confirmed in experience.[2]

It is essential that we distinguish between psychic force and psychic energy, 'for energy is really a concept and, as such, does not exist objectively in the phenomena themselves but only in the specific data of experience. In other words, energy is always

[1] We see that the concept 'libido', which Freud used to designate the sexual drive both in its restricted and extended sense, has for Jung a very different and far more comprehensive meaning. Even among psychologists, this distinction has not been sufficiently taken into account.

[2] To avoid misunderstandings of a kind that have been very frequent, it should be stressed at the outset that this concept of energy is fundamentally different from the Aristotelian concept of energy as a 'formative principle'. We have in mind a concept similar to that employed in physics, and Jung uses the term 'libido' merely to distinguish psychic from physical energy. When he speaks of an 'undifferentiated libido', he is stating *not a premise* from which something is supposed to follow but an empirical finding. The concept of energy has nothing to do with metaphysics, for it is only a sign or token for the understanding which makes use of it in ordering *experience*; the same is true of Jung's 'libido'. 'Energy' is metaphysical only when it is not an empirical concept but is presupposed as a substance, the foundation of the world, etc., as with the monists. When an empirical scientist says 'energy', he is postulating nothing, but merely drawing an inference from the facts at hand. There are two kinds of 'concept': first, the concept postulated as an idea (or model), such as the Aristotelian or scholastic concept of 'energy'; and second, the empirical concept as an a posteriori principle of order, an example of which is the Jungian concept of 'libido'.

experienced specifically as motion and force when actual, and as a state or condition when potential.[1] When actualized, psychic energy is reflected in the specific phenomena of the psyche: drives, wishes, will, affect, performance, and the like. But when it is only potential, it is manifested in specific acquisitions, possibilities, aptitudes, attitudes, etc.[2] 'If,' writes Jung, 'we take our stand on the basis of scientific common sense and avoid philosophical considerations which would carry us too far, we would probably do best to regard the psychic process simply as a life process. In this way we enlarge the narrower concept of psychic energy to a broader one of life energy, which includes psychic energy as a specific part.' But this concept of life energy has nothing to do with the so-called vital force. 'I have therefore suggested that, in view of the psychological use we intend to make of it, we call our hypothetical life energy "libido". To this extent I have differentiated it from a concept of universal energy, so maintaining the right of biology and psychology to form their own concepts.'[3]

For Jung, accordingly, the structure of the psyche is not static but dynamic. Just as metabolism maintains a balance in the physical economy of the organism, so—to suggest a rough comparison—psychic energy determines the relations between the various elements of the psyche and, when it is disturbed, pathological phenomena result. The energic view of the psychic process is finalistic, in contrast to the mechanistic view, which is causal.[4] Yet this finalistic conception is not the only one, for as we shall see, Jung examines the problem from many different aspects.

STRUCTURE OF THE OPPOSITES

But it does set its stamp on his theory of energy and is contained in its fundamental principle, the law to the effect that all psychic life is governed by a necessary *opposition*. In Jung's view opposition is a law inherent in human nature. For 'the psyche is . . . a self-regulating system', and 'there is no balance, no

[1] 'Energy', p. 15.
[2] The 'will', for example, is a special case of free psychic energy which can be directed by consciousness. Cf. footnote 1, p. 16.
[3] 'Energy', p. 17.
[4] Ibid , pp. 3 ff.

53

system of self-regulation, without opposition'. It was Heraclitus who discovered the most marvellous of all psychological laws, namely the regulative function of opposites. He called it *enantiodromia*, by which he meant that everything must ultimately flow into its opposite. 'The transition from morning to afternoon,' says Jung, 'means a revaluation of the earlier values. There comes the urgent need to appreciate the value of the opposite of our former ideals, to perceive the error in our former convictions. . . . It is of course a fundamental mistake to imagine that when we see the non-value in a value or the untruth in a truth, the value or the truth ceases to exist. It has only become *relative*. Everything human is relative, because everything rests on the inner polarity; for everything is a phenomenon of energy. Energy necessarily depends on a pre-existing polarity, without which there could be no energy. There must always be high and low, hot and cold, etc., so that the equilibrating process—which is energy—can take place. . . . The point is not conversion into the opposite but conservation of precious values together with recognition of their opposites.'[1]

Everything we have said thus far about the structure of the psyche—about its functions, attitudes, the relation between the conscious and the unconscious, etc.—takes into account this law of opposition, built upon complementary or compensatory factors. But the law also holds good in each of the partial systems. When the unconscious, for example, is left to take its natural course, positive and negative contents alternate. Often a fantasy representing the light principle is immediately followed by an image of the dark principle. In consciousness a great effort of thought often results in emotional reactions of a negative kind. These relations are regulated—the living tension between them is maintained—by the movements and transfers of psychic energy. For all these pairs are opposites not only in content but also in respect to their energetic intensity. The distribution of their energy charge might best be illustrated by the image of communicating vessels. But when this image is transposed to the totality of the psyche, it becomes highly complex, for here we are dealing with a coherent, relatively self-contained system, which in turn comprises many subsidiary systems of similar communicating vessels. In the total system—to a certain

[1] 'Unconscious', pp. 60, 74 f.

degree—the *quantity* of energy is constant and only its distribution is variable.

The physical law of the conservation of energy and the Platonic conception of the 'soul as that which moves itself' are archetypally close together. 'No psychic value can disappear without being replaced by another of equivalent intensity.'[1] The law of the conservation of energy operates not only in the opposition of consciousness and the unconscious, but also in every single element or content of consciousness and the unconscious, for generally speaking the energy with which one element is charged must be withdrawn from the corresponding opposite element.

'The idea of energy and its conservation,' says Jung, 'must be a primordial image that was dormant in the collective unconscious. Such a conclusion naturally obliges us to prove that a primordial image of this kind really did exist in the mental history of mankind and was operative through the ages. As a matter of fact, this proof can be produced without much difficulty; the most primitive religions in the most widely separated parts of the earth are founded upon this image. These are the so-called dynamistic religions whose sole and determining thought is that there exists a universal magical power about which everything revolves. . . . According to the old view, the soul itself is this power; in the idea of the soul's immortality there is implicit its conservation, and in the Buddhist and primitive notion of metempsychosis—transmigration of souls— is implicit its unlimited changeability together with its constant preservation.'[2]

FORMS OF MOVEMENT OF LIBIDO

From the law of conservation of energy it follows that energy can be displaced, that it can flow by a natural gradient from one member of a pair of opposites to the other. This means, for example, that the energy charge of the unconscious increases in proportion as that of consciousness diminishes. Energy can also be transferred from one opposite to the other by a directed act of the will, and in this case its mode of operation and mani-

---

[1] 'The Spiritual Problem of Modern Man', par. 175.
[2] 'Unconscious', pp. 67 f.

festation is transformed. In Freudian terminology this might be designated as 'sublimation', with the difference that in Freud's view it is always 'sexual energy' that is thus transformed.

Displacement of energy occurs only when there is a gradient, a difference in potential—expressed psychologically by the pairs of opposites. This explains why the damming up of libido causes neurotic symptoms and complexes, and why when one side is utterly emptied, the pair of opposites disintegrates—a phenomenon that may occur in all sorts of psychic disturbances from slight neurosis to total dissociation or splitting of the personality. For energy lost by consciousness passes into the unconscious and activates its contents—archetypes, repressions, complexes, etc. —which embark on a life of their own and irrupt into consciousness, often provoking disturbances, neuroses, and psychoses.

But a completely uniform distribution of energy is also dangerous. Here the law of entropy operates very much as in physics. To put it briefly and roughly, the physical law of entropy states that heat is lost in the performance of work, or in other words, that ordered movement is transformed into disordered, dispersed movement, useless for the performance of work. But since movement is based on a gradient, through which more and more potential is lost, the flow of energy necessarily tends towards an equalization which would lead to a total standstill in the form of death from heat or cold.[1] Since the systems accessible to our experience are only relatively self-contained, we nowhere observe absolute psychological entropy, which could occur only in a perfectly self-contained system. But the more the partial psychic systems are closed off from one another and the more extreme the tensions between the poles, the more likely becomes the phenomenon of entropy (cf. the stiff, catatonic posture of many insane persons, their lack of contact with the world, their apathy, and seeming lack of ego, etc.). We often see this law, in a relative form, at work in the psyche. 'The most intense conflicts, if overcome, leave behind a sense of security and calm which is not easily disturbed, or else a brokenness that can hardly be healed. Conversely, it is just

[1] It is this law which determines the temporal direction and irreversibility of the physical process. We cannot here go into the possible implications— manifested in other fields—of the theory of probability for this physical law.

these intense conflicts and their conflagration which are needed in order to produce valuable and lasting results. An involuntary sense of the energic process crops up even in language, when we speak of 'lasting conviction' and the like.[1]

The irreversibility that characterizes energic processes in inanimate nature can be modified only by artificial intervention (e.g. by technical or mechanical means). In the psychic system it is consciousness that can intervene to bring about a reversal. 'Intervention in the natural process is inherent in the creative character of the psyche. This basic intervention consists in the creation, differentiation, and amplification of consciousness,'[2] which is the source of its power to guide and subjugate nature.

PROGRESSION AND REGRESSION

The flow of energy has *direction*, and accordingly we distinguish a PROGRESSIVE and a REGRESSIVE MOVEMENT, in temporal succession.[3] The progressive movement is a process that takes its direction from consciousness and consists in a continuous and unobstructed 'adaptation to the conscious demands of life and the differentiation of the attitude and function type which this necessitates'.[4] This can be accomplished only by adequate solution of conflicts and by making decisions of all sorts of co-ordination of the opposite poles. Regressive movement occurs when the failure of conscious adaptation and the resulting intensification of the unconscious, or a repression, provokes a one-sided accumulation of energy, as a result of which the contents of the unconscious, unduly charged with energy, rise to the surface. If consciousness does not intervene in time, a partial regression can throw the individual back into an earlier stage of development and create a neurosis, while in total regression consciousness is inundated by the contents of the unconscious and a psychosis occurs.

[1] 'Energy', pp. 26, 27.
[2] T. Wolff, *Studien zu C. G. Jungs Psychologie*, p. 188.
[3] These are 'life movements' which should not be confused with 'development' or 'involution'. More satisfactory terms for them might be 'diastole' and 'systole'. In this connection 'diastole is an extraversion of libido spreading through the entire universe; systole is its contraction into the individual, the monad' ('Energy', p. 37, note 52).
[4] T. Wolff, *Studien*, p. 194.

Progression and regression should not be conceived only in these extreme forms, for in countless big and little, important and unimportant variations they make up part of our daily life. Every act of attention or psychic exertion, every conscious act of the will, is an expression of energic progression; every instance of fatigue or distraction, every emotional reaction, and above all sleep are examples of regression. Ordinarily progression is looked upon only as a positive form and regression only as a negative form of psychic functioning. But such a view is inaccurate, for whereas the movement of an ideal, normal psyche would indeed be purely progressive, regression (in contrast to Freud's views on this problem) also has its positive value in the Jungian system. Progression is rooted in the need for adaptation to the outside world and regression springs from the need for adaptation to an inner world, for harmony with the individual's inner law. Thus they are equally necessary forms of natural psychic experience. Progression and regression, looked at energetically, must be thought of only as a means, 'as transitional stages in the flow of energy'.[1] In the individual psyche regression may be a symptom of disturbance, but it can also be a way to restore balance and indeed to broaden the psyche. For it is regression that activates images and raises them from the unconscious, in dreams for example. It makes possible an enrichment of consciousness, because it contains, though in undifferentiated form, the seeds of a new psychic health. It raises up unconscious contents which can act as 'transformers of energy' and turn the psychic process back into a progressive direction.

VALUE INTENSITY AND CONSTELLATION

After the temporal direction or movement of the energic process—and the libido moves not only forward and backward, progressively and regressively, but also inward and outward in line with extraversion or introversion—the second important characteristic of this process is its *value intensity*. The specific form in which energy is manifested in the psyche is the IMAGE, raised up by the formative power of the *imaginatio*, the creative fantasy, from the material of the collective unconscious, the

[1] 'Energy,' pp. 39, 40.

objective psyche. This creative activity of the psyche transforms[1] the chaos of the unconscious contents into such images as appear in dreams, fantasies, visions, and every variety of creative art. It ultimately determines the meaning charge of the images, which is equivalent to their value intensity, and is measured by the individual constellation or context in which each image appears.[2] In a dream, for example, there are always elements whose meaning varies with the context and their position in it. An image or motif may in one case be secondary, while in another it becomes the central figure or vehicle of the complex; the mother symbol, for example, will be charged with more energy and have higher value intensity in a psyche suffering from a mother complex than in one suffering from a father complex.

Direction and intensity are correlative in the dynamic of the psyche; for the gradient which makes possible the movement of psychic energy and determines its direction is caused by the varying energy charge of the diverse psychic phenomena, that is to say the varying importance of their contents for the individual.

Libido or psychic energy in the Jungian sense is the foundation and regulator of all psychic life. The concept is indispensable for a sound description of the psychic processes and the relations between them. But it is perfectly possible to use the concept without deciding whether or not there is such a thing as a specific psychic energy. In setting out to describe the life of the psyche, its processes, and its phenomena, one can proceed from three points of view: first, from the standpoint of its structural characteristics, as we have attempted to do in Chapter I; second, from the standpoint of its functional aspect, in keeping with the libido theory; and third from the standpoint of its contents as we encounter them in psychotherapeutic work. This last aspect will be discussed in the next chapter.

---

[1] 'The psychological mechanism that transforms energy is the symbol' (ibid., p. 45).
[2] Cf. also our discussion of 'conditionalism', pp. 83 f.

III

THE PRACTICAL APPLICATION OF
JUNG'S THEORY

TWO-FOLD ASPECT OF JUNGIAN PSYCHOLOGY

JUNGIAN psychotherapy is not an analytical procedure in the usual sense of the term, although it adheres strictly to the relevant findings of science and medicine. It is a *Heilsweg*, in the twofold sense of the German word: a way of healing and a way of salvation. It has the power to cure man's physic and psychogenic sufferings. It has all the instruments needed to relieve the trifling psychic disturbances that may be the starting point of a neurosis, or to deal successfully with the gravest and most complicated developments of psychic disease. But in addition it knows the way and has the means to lead the individual to his 'salvation', to the knowledge and fulfilment of his own personality, which have always been the aim of spiritual striving. By its very nature, this path defies abstract exposition. Jung's system of thought can be explained theoretically only up to a certain point; to understand it fully one must have experienced or, better still, 'suffered' its living action in oneself. And like every process that transforms man, this experience cannot be described but only adumbrated. Like all psychic experience, it is very personal; its subjectivity is its most effective truth. Often as it may be repeated, this experience of the psyche is unique and only within its subjective limits is it open to rational understanding.

Apart from its medical aspect, Jungian psychotherapy is thus a system of education and spiritual guidance, an aid in the forming of the personality. Only a few are willing and able to travel a path of salvation. 'And these few tread the path only from inner necessity, not to say suffering, for it is sharp as the edge of a razor.'[1]

Jung has devised no general prescription for the infinite variety of sufferers who entrust themselves to his therapy. The method and the intensity with which it is applied vary with the

---

[1] 'Relations', par. 401.

requirements of the individual case, with the patient's psychic make-up. Jung recognizes the importance of sexuality and the striving for power. There are many cases in which the disorder can be traced to one of these factors and must therefore be approached from a Freudian or Adlerian point of view. But while for Freud sexuality, and for Adler the will to power, is the main explanatory principle, Jung believes other psychic motivations to be equally essential and rejects the notion that any one factor is at the source of all psychic disorders. Apart from these two assuredly important factors, he finds other crucial motivations, the first and foremost one which pertains to man alone—the spiritual and religious need that is innate in the psyche. This view is the essential part of his theory that distinguishes it from all others and determines its prospective-synthetic direction. For 'the spiritual appears in the psyche also as an instinct, indeed as a real passion. . . . It is not derived from any other instinct . . . but is a principle *sui generis*, a specific and necessary form of instinctual power.'[1]

To the world of the natural instincts, to the primordial biological nature in us, Jung from the very outset opposes a counterpole of equivalent rank which forms and develops this primordial nature and is given only to man. 'Over against the polymorphism of the primitive's instinctual nature there stands the regulating principle of individuation. . . . Together they form a pair of opposites . . . often spoken of as nature and spirit. . . . This opposition is the expression, and perhaps also the basis, of the tension from which psychic energy flows.'[2] It represents as it were the two basic tones on which the intricate contrapuntal structure of the psyche is built. 'So regarded, psychic processes seem to be balances of energy flowing between spirit and instinct, though the question of whether a process is to be described as spiritual or as instinctual remains shrouded in darkness. Such evaluation of interpretation depends entirely upon the standpoint or state of the conscious mind. . . . Psychic processes therefore behave like a scale along which consciousness "slides". At one moment it finds itself in the vicinity of instinct, and falls under its influence; at another, it slides along to the other end where spirit predominates and even assimilates the instinctual processes most opposed to it.'[3]

---

[1] 'Energy', p. 58.   [2] Ibid., pp. 51, 52.   [3] 'Nature', p. 207.

But the terms 'nature' and 'spirit' should not be taken in their usual philosophical sense. We have no unambiguous definition of the term *Trieb* ('instinct' or 'drive'); Jung always employs it in the sense of an 'instinctual action or process', i.e., an autonomous functioning without conscious motivation. Consequently what he means by the 'tension' between nature and spirit is above all an 'occasional opposition between consciousness and the unconscious or instinctual', since it is only this conflict that can be observed. 'In archetypal conceptions and instinctual perceptions,' says Jung, 'spirit and matter confront one another on the psychic plane. Matter and spirit both appear in the psychic realm as distinctive qualitities of conscious contents. The ultimate nature of both is transcendental, that is, irrepresentable, since the psyche and its contents are the only reality which is given to us *without a medium*.'[1]

RELATIONSHIP TO THE EXACT SCIENCES

Here we come to a crucial idea, which gives direction, tone, and depth to Jung's whole thinking and makes his psychology an open, unprejudiced system that excludes none of the new problems which spring up almost of their own accord where new psychic ground is being explored. An attentive reader may think he has found theoretical contradictions in Jung's books. But the study of the psyche must set down the facts as they are met with. And it meets with them not as an either—or, but rather, as Jung once said, as an 'either *and* or'. Jung's investigation of the truth is at once cognition and vision.

Those who reproach Jung for 'mysticism' are perhaps unaware that theoretical physics, the strictest of the modern sciences, is no more nor less mystical than Jung's psychology, which presents close analogies to it.[2] The dualistic 'either *and* or', which strikes Jung's critics as a contradiction, is accepted in present-day physics, simply because reality demands it. In investigating the nature of light, for example, the modern physicist must work with two contradictory hypotheses, the

[1] 'Nature', p. 216.
[2] Jung draws a certain parallel between 'matter' and 'psyche' and suggests the possibility that they may be two different aspects of the same thing ('Nature', p. 215).

wave theory and the particle theory; and all attempts to establish a logical connection between the field theory of relativity and the quantum theory have failed. Still, no one accuses the modern physicists of logical ineptitude or disorderly thinking, for physical facts actually seem to defy logic. The physicists are forced to admit that certain phenomena appear to be irreconcilable and even paradoxical, though of course they hope to achieve—not force—unity at some future day.

Psychology faces a similar difficulty: starting from and adhering to the empirical facts, it is moving into a realm where the language of experience is by nature inadequate and can provide no more than an approximation. In this sense Jung is as far from being a 'metaphysician' as any natural scientist has ever been, for his statements, like theirs, refer exclusively to empirical data. But here, just as in the modern natural sciences, there is a limit where empirical knowledge ends and metaphysics begins. Planck, Hartmann, Uexküll, Eddington, Jeans, and others admit as much. To be sure, the realm of experience which the Jungian psychology has investigated in accordance with definite scientific principles is by its very nature closed to the old scientific method with its insistence on a purely logical approach. (It might be mentioned in passing that among the modern exact sciences only physics has the possibility of framing its bold hypotheses, which can no longer be verified by concrete facts, in the pure association-free language of mathematics.)

Thus modern depth psychology must inevitably bear a Janus head, one of its faces turned toward living experience, the other toward abstract thought or cognition. It is no accident that many of the profoundest European thinkers—such as Pascal, Kierkegaard, or Jung—have been driven, and fruitfully so, to paradoxes when they concerned themselves with questions to which a single unequivocal answer is not possible—with the dual nature of the psyche.

Jung's great step forward, and the justification of the term 'synthesis' as he uses it, lies in his break with this linear causal thinking of the old psychology—in his insight that the *spirit* must be viewed not as a mere epiphenomenon or 'sublimation' but as a principle *sui generis*, a formative and hence supreme principle which is the indispensable condition of all psychic and perhaps even physical form.[1] Though one should be wary of hasty parallels, it might be mentioned here that it was precisely the logical difficulties encountered by the principle of causality in the face of new experience which brought about the revolutionary upheaval in modern physics. Modern discussion of the concept of causality has shown that in the interpretation of the physical process the strict notion of cause and effect must give way to a conception of mere sequence. Over thirty years ago Jung remarked that in psychology the concept of causality as generally used in natural science was inadequate. In his foreword to the *Collected Papers on Analytical Psychology*[2] he said: 'causality, however, is only *one* principle, and psychology cannot be exhausted by causal methods only, because the mind lives by aims as well.' This purposiveness is grounded in an inner law, inaccessible to our consciousness, a law based on the manifestation and action of the symbols rising up from the unconscious. Since then Jung, as we have seen on p. 49, has devoted a number of studies to the problem of acausality, and proposed it as a special principle of explanation for certain phenomena which he subsumes under the heading of 'meaningful coincidence'.

As a matter of fact, the manifestations of creativity in our psyche can never be demonstrated nor explained on a basis of causality. 'At this crucial point,' says Jung, 'psychology stands

---

[1] 'The microphysical world of the atom,' Jung remarks, 'exhibits certain features whose affinities with the psychic have impressed themselves even on the physicists' ('Education', p. 89). A more detailed treatment of this subject and of the considerations that led to these reflections may be found in C. A. Meier's 'Moderne Physik—Moderne Psychotherapie', which also includes a bibliography on the subject. Special attention is also called to the papers of Niels Bohr (*Naturwissenschaften*, 16, p. 245, 1928, and 17, p. 483, 1929). Recently the physicist Pascual Jordan [Rostock] has also called attention to certain analogies between the findings of modern physics on the one hand and biology and psychology on the other (cf. *Die Physik des 20. Jahrhunderts*; 'Positivistische Bemerkungen über die paraphysischen Erscheinungen'; *Anschauliche Quantentheorie*, pp. 271 ff.; *Die Physik und das Geheimnis des organischen Lebens*, pp. 114 f.; 'Quantenphysikalische Bemerkungen zu Biologie und Psychologie'; and the physicist Max Knoll [Princeton and Munich], 'Transformations of Science in our Age', and 'Quantenhafte Energiebegriffe in Physik und Psychologie'). Cf. also Jung, 'On the Nature of the Psyche'.

[2] *Collected Works*, vol. 4, p. 292.

outside natural science. Although sharing with the latter its method of observation and the empirical verification of fact, it lacks the Archimedean point outside and hence the possibility of objective measurement.'[1] And 'there is no Archimedean point from which to judge, since the psyche is indistinguishable from its manifestations. The psyche is the object of psychology, and—fatally enough—also its subject. There is no getting away from this fact.'[2] For the conclusions drawn by such thinkers as Whitehead and Eddington from physics itself point to primary, form-creating, spiritual forces, which might also be—and have indeed been—called mystical.

Thus we need no longer feel the customary dread of the word 'mystical'; above all, we should not confuse it with a cheap irrationalism, for here reason itself, like modern logic, is honestly striving to ascertain its own limits, not by rejecting the autonomy of the 'mystical', but by according it a kind of sovereignty that follows from a proper definition of 'knowledge'.

In the borderland between cognition and experience which is necessarily the realm of 'depth psychology', and which by its very nature must confront the conceptual language with vast and often insuperable difficulties, Jung strives, with all his power of creative expression, to draw the necessary and legitimate distinctions, though the caprices of the subject matter sometimes bar the way to complete success. The hallmark of the 'metaphysician' is a tendency to confuse cognition and experience, to suppose that experience can always be reduced to conceptual terms. But Jung does his utmost to avoid this fallacy.

It is perhaps something more than an accident that modern logic and Jungian psychology both employ the same term—'transcendent problems'—for the questions that cannot be answered but can only be experienced. Such are the problems that make up the content of Jung's psychology and psychological guidance. Here too, of course—and this must not be forgotten—the personal equation, which applies to all men, even outstanding scientists, plays a role.

---

[1] 'Education', p. 88.
[2] 'Religion', pp. 49 f.

'CAUSALITY' AND 'FINALITY'

If we wish to compare the three leading psychotherapeutic[1] trends of our day from the standpoint of their salient ideas, we may say that Sigmund Freud looks for the effective causes of the subsequent psychic disorder, that Alfred Adler examines the actual situation, which he regards as a 'final cause', and that both look on instincts as material causes. As for Jung, he too takes the material causes into account, he too takes the 'final causes' as the starting point and end,[2] but he makes a highly significant addition: the *formal causes*. These formative forces consist above all in the symbols which mediate between the unconscious and consciousness and in general between the psychic pairs of opposites.

Jungian psychology 'has in mind the end-result of analysis, and it regards the fundamental thoughts and impulses of the unconscious as symbols, indicative of a definite line of future development. We must admit . . . that there is no scientific justification for such a procedure, because our present-day science is based wholly on causality. But causality is only one principle, and psychology cannot be exhausted by causal methods only, because the mind lives by aims as well. Besides this controversial philosophical argument we have another of much greater value in favour of our hypothesis, namely that of vital necessity. It is impossible to live according to the promptings of infantile hedonism or according to a childish desire for power. If these are to be given a place they must be taken symbolically. Out of the symbolic application of infantile trends there evolves an attitude which may be termed philosophic or religious, and these terms characterize sufficiently well the lines of the individual's further development. The individual is not just a fixed and unchangeable

---

[1] A systematic comparison of the three main psychotherapeutic trends is given in W. Kranefeldt, *Secret Ways of the Mind*; Gerhard Adler, *Entdeckung der Seele*; and J. Jacobi, *Two Essays on Freud and Jung*.

[2] 'According to the concept of finality, causes are understood as means to an end. A simple example is the process of regression. Regarded causally, regression is determined, say, by a "mother fixation". But from the final standpoint the libido regresses to the *imago* of the mother in order to find there the memory associations by means of which further development can take place, for instance from a sexual system into an intellectual or spiritual system' ('Energy', p. 23).

complex of psychological facts; he is also an extremely variable entity. By an exclusive reduction to causes the primitive trends of a personality are reinforced; this is helpful only when these primitive tendencies are balanced by a recognition of their symbolic value. Analysis and reduction lead to causal truth; this by itself does not help us to live but only induces resignation and hoplessness. On the other hand, the recognition of the intrinsic value of a symbol leads to constructive truth and helps us to live; it inspires hopefulness and furthers the possibility of future development.'[1]

In his book on *The Structure and Dynamics of the Psyche*, Jung writes: 'When a psychological fact has to be explained, it must be remembered that psychological data necessitate a twofold point of view, namely that of *causality* and that of *finality*. I use the word "finality" intentionally, in order to avoid confusion with the concept of teleology. By finality I mean merely the immanent psychological striving for a goal. Instead of "striving for a goal" one could also say "sense of purpose".'[2] Or putting it somewhat differently one might say: Freud's method is reductive, while Jung's is prospective. Freud treats the material analytically, resolving the present into the past, Jung *synthetically*, building toward the future from the present situation by attempting to create relations between conscious and unconscious, i.e., between the pairs of psychic opposites, in order to provide the personality with a foundation on which a lasting psychic balance can be built.

THE DIALECTICAL PROCESS

Jung's method is 'dialectical', not only because it is a dialogue between two persons and as such an interaction between two psychic systems. It is also intrinsically dialectical, because it is a process which, by confronting the contents of consciousness with those of the unconscious, the ego with the non-ego, provokes an interaction aimed at, and culminating in, a third term, a synthesis which combines and transcends them both. From the therapeutic standpoint it is indispensable for the

[1] Preface to the first edition of *Collected Papers on Analytical Psychology*, in *Collected Works*, vol. 4, pp. 292 ff.
[2] 'General Aspects of Dream Psychology', p. 241.

psychologist to recognize and observe this dialectical principle. He does not analyse an object theoretically, from a distance; rather, he himself is just as much *in* the analysis as is the patient.[1]

For this reason and also because of the autonomous action of the unconscious, the 'transference', or blind projection of all the patient's ideas and feelings upon the analyst, is less indispensable in the Jungian than in other analytical methods. Under certain circumstances Jung even regards it as an obstacle to effective treatment, particularly when it takes an exaggerated form. In any case he believes an 'attachment' to a third person, a love relation for example, to be an equally satisfactory 'basis' for an analytical resolution of neuroses, or for a dialogue with the unconscious that may foster psychic development. The all-important thing is not, as with Freud, to 'relive' the past traumatic emotion suffered in childhood, which is the source of every neurosis, but to 'live through' one's present difficulties with a concrete partner, and so reach an understanding of them. Both persons must 'give' themselves, the analyst as well as the analysand, but both must also as far as possible preserve their objectivity.

Each unconsciously influences the other and this is essential for treatment. The encounter between two personalities is like the mixing of two chemical elements; if any reaction occurs, both are transformed. 'In a dialectical procedure . . . the doctor must emerge from his anonymity and give an account of himself, just as he expects his patient to do.'[2] Thus the role of the analyst in the Jungian method is not largely passive as in Freudian analysis; he takes an active part, guides, encourages, and participates in a personal give and take. In this form of intervention, which particularly stimulates the process of psychic transformation, because in it one living process is acting on another, the personality of the physician, its stature and scope, purity and strength, is obviously of the greatest import-

---

[1] Here and in the following, the term 'patient' (or occasionally 'analysand') is applied to sick and healthy persons alike. It refers to all those in search of cure or salvation—psychotics, neurotics, as well as those who undertake a course of Jungian psychotherapy for the sake of its help in building character and personality.

[2] 'Principles of Practical Psychotherapy', p. 18.

ance, far more so than in other techniques of depth psychology. It is for this reason that Jung insists that every analyst himself undergo a thorough analysis as *conditio sine qua non* for the practice of psychotherapy. For here it is particularly true that a spiritual guide can lead his patient no farther than he himself has gone. Nor can the most expert psychotherapist get more out of his patient than what is potentially there; no treatment can stretch the constitutional limits of the psyche. A man's psychic development is always conditioned by his individual structure, and the therapist can only do his best.

WAYS TO THE UNCONSCIOUS

'There are,' says Jung, 'four methods of investigating the unknown in a patient.

'1. The first and simplest is the *association method*. . . . Its principle is to discover the main complexes through disturbances in the association experiment. As an introduction to analytical psychology and to the symptomatology of complexes, this method is recommended for every beginner.

'2. The second method, *symptom analysis*, has a merely historical value. . . . By means of hypnotic suggestion it was attempted to get the patient to reproduce the memories underlying certain pathological symptoms. The method works very well in all cases where a shock, a psychic injury, or a trauma is the chief cause of the neurosis. It was on this method that Freud based his earlier trauma theory of hysteria. . . .

'3. The third method, *anamnestic analysis*, is of greater importance as a method both of investigation and of therapy. In practice it consists in a careful anamnesis or reconstruction of the historical development of the neurosis. . . . Very often this procedure by itself is of great therapeutic value, as it enables the patient to understand the chief factors of his neurosis and may eventually bring him to a decisive change of attitude. It is of course as unavoidable as it is necessary for the doctor not only to ask questions, but to give hints and explanations in order to point out important connections of which the patient is unconscious. . . .

'4. The fourth method is the *analysis of the unconscious*. . . . [It] only begins when the conscious material is exhausted. . . . The anamnestic method often serves as an introduction to the fourth method. . . . This personal contact is of prime importance, because it forms the only safe basis from which to tackle the unconscious. . . . It is by no means easy to establish such a contact, and you cannot achieve it at all except by a careful comparison of both points of view and by mutual freedom from prejudice. . . . From now on we are concerned with the living psychic process itself, namely with dreams.'[1]

DREAMS

The easiest and most effective way of investigating the mechanism and contents of the unconscious is through DREAMS, the material of which consists of conscious and unconscious, known and unknown elements. These elements occur in all sorts of mixtures and may derive from all sources, ranging from the so-called 'vestiges of the day' to the deepest contents of the unconscious. According to Jung, the way they are ordered in dreams is not determined by causality, space, or time. The language of dreams is archaic, symbolic, prelogical—a language of images, whose meaning can only be laid bare by a special interpretive method. Jung attaches the greatest importance to dreams, which he regards not only as the road to the unconscious, but also as a function through which the unconscious carries on the greater part of its *regulative activity*. For dreams express the 'other side', the counterpart of the conscious attitude.

'When I attempted to express this behaviour in a formula,' writes Jung, 'the concept of *compensation* seemed to me the only adequate one, for it alone is capable of summing up all the various ways in which a dream behaves. Compensation must be strictly distinguished from *complementation*. The concept of "complement" is too narrow and too restricting; it does not suffice to explain the function of dreams, because it designates a relationship in which two things supplement one another more or less mechanically. Compensation, on the other hand, as the term implies, means balancing and comparing different data or

---

[1] 'Education', pp. 94 ff.

points of view so as to produce an adjustment or a rectification.'[1] This innate compensatory function of the psyche, which works toward individuation, i.e., the development of the psyche toward 'wholeness', seems to be given to man alone; perhaps one may even designate it as the psychic activity that is specifically human.

In regard to this highly significant compensatory function of dreams, which not only express anxieties and wishes but affect all psychic behaviour, Jung refuses to set up 'standard symbols'. The unconscious contents are always polyvalent; their meaning depends on the context in which they occur and on the specific external and internal situation of the dreamer. Some dreams even go beyond the personal concerns of the individual dreamer, expressing problems which recur over and over again in the history of mankind and concern the whole human collectivity. They often have a prophetic character and for this reason primitive peoples still regard them as the business of the whole tribe, in whose presence they are interpreted with great ceremony.[2]

In addition to dreams, Jung designates FANTASIES and VISIONS as manifestations of the unconscious. Related to dreams, they occur in states of diminished consciousness. They carry a latent as well as a manifest meaning and they may spring either from the personal or the collective unconscious. Thus for purposes of psychological interpretation they are in the same class as dreams. They present an unlimited variety, deeply significant, ranging from common daydreams to ecstatic visions.

For Jung the DREAM is thus the main instrument of the therapeutic method. It is the psychic phenomenon which offers the easiest access to the contents of the unconscious, and its compensatory function makes it the clearest indicator of hidden relationships. For the 'problem of dream-analysis stands or falls with such a hypothesis' (the hypothesis of the unconscious). 'Without it, the dream is a mere freak of nature, a meaningless conglomeration of fragments left over from the day.'[3] Jung uses the patient's fantasies and visions in the same way as his

[1] 'On the Nature of Dreams', pp. 287 f.
[2] See pp. 72 ff. for a detailed account of the theory and interpretation of dreams.
[3] 'Dream Analysis', p. 139.

dreams. If in the following we speak only of dreams, it is for the sake of brevity and simplicity; the word should be taken to include also fantasies and visions.

DREAM INTERPRETATION

Along with the discussion and elaboration of the relevant material on the basis of the context and of associations provided not only by the patient but by the therapist as well, the interpretation of dreams, visions, and all manner of psychic images occupies a central position in the dialectical process of the analytic method. However, the patient alone can decide how the material he furnishes is ultimately to be interpreted. His individuality is the decisive factor. His assent must be more than rational, it must be experienced, lived, before the interpretation may be held to be truly confirmed. 'The analyst who wishes to rule out conscious suggestion must therefore consider every dream interpretation invalid until such a time as a formula is found which wins the assent of the patient.'[1] Otherwise the next dream or vision will inevitably bring up the same problem. And this will go on until the patient's 'experience' of the problem has brought about a new attitude. It is often argued that a therapist might influence the patient with his interpretation, but only by those unfamiliar with the workings of the unconscious. The possibility and danger of such suggestion are greatly overestimated, for experience shows that the objective psyche, the unconscious, is extremely independent. If this were not so, it could not perform its characteristic function, the compensation of consciousness. Consciousness can be trained like a parrot, but not the unconscious.[2] If physician and patient are mistaken in their interpretation, they will be sternly corrected in time by the unconscious, which unceasingly furthers the dialectic process by its autonomous action and continual contribution of new materials.

The basic difference between the Jungian and the other analytical methods is that in these phenomena—dreams, etc.— Jung finds not only reflections of personal conflicts but also in many cases manifestations of the collective unconscious, which transcend individual conflicts and offset them with the primordial experience of universal human problems. Here we can only

[1] Ibid., p. 147.   [2] *Alchemy*, par. 51.

sketch briefly the theory and method of Jungian dream analysis.

'The dream,' says Jung, 'cannot be explained with a psychology taken from consciousness. It is a definite functioning which is independent of willing and wishing, of the intentions and conscious aims of the ego. It is involuntary, like everything that happens in nature. . . . It is very probable that we dream continually, only our consciousness makes such a noise in the waking state that we no longer hear it. . . . If we could keep a continuous record we should see that the whole process follows a definite trend.' In other words the dream is a natural manifestation of the psyche, but it is autonomous and pursues purposes unknown to consciousness. It has its own language and its own laws, which we cannot approach subjectively with the psychology of consciousness. For 'one does not dream, one is dreamt. We "suffer" the dream, we are its objects.'[1] One might almost say that in dreams we experience myths and fairy tales, not as when we read them in the waking state, but as though they were real happenings in our life.

THE ROOTS OF DREAMS

Dreams, as far as we can ascertain, are rooted partly in conscious contents—fragmentary impressions left over from the day—and partly in the constellated contents of the unconscious, which in turn may result from conscious contents or from spontaneous processes of the unconscious. These latter processes, which reveal no relation to consciousness, may derive from all manner of sources: somatic incidents, physical or psychic reactions to the environment, past or future events—for there are dreams which recapitulate historic events from the remote past or which (as sometimes happens in the case of markedly archetypal dreams) anticipate future events. There are dreams which originate in a conscious context that has been lost, as though it had never existed, so that nothing remains but disconnected, incomprehensible fragments; and there are others which represent unconscious psychic contents of the individual, unrecognized as such.

We have seen that for Jung the *order* of dream images is outside of space, time, and causality. The dream, he writes, is an

[1] *Kindertraumseminar*, 1938–39. Specially translated by R. F. C. Hull.

'enigmatic message from the nocturnal realm of the psyche'.[1]

A dream is never—not even when it seems so to us—a mere repetition of preceding experiences or events. The only exception to this rule is a certain category of shock or reaction dreams that occur when objective events—the war, for example—have brought about a psychic trauma. These dreams, which are essentially a reproduction of the trauma or shock experience, can therefore not be interpreted as compensatory. Nor can one dispel the shock that has caused them by raising it to consciousness. 'The dream calmly goes on "reproducing"; that is to say, the content of the trauma, now become autonomous, goes on working and will continue to do so until the traumatic stimulus has exhausted itself.'[2]

The dream, says Jung, is always 'knit together or altered according to its aim, even if only in inconspicuous ways, but in a different way from that which would correspond to the aims of consciousness and to causality'.[3]

THE DIFFERENT TYPES OF DREAMS

In regard to their *significance* dreams may be reduced to the following three types:

1. A certain conscious situation is followed by a dream which is a reaction of the unconscious. Supplementing or complementing, it points clearly to impressions of the day; quite obviously this dream would never have occurred without a definite impression of the immediate past.

2. The dream has not been provoked by a definite conscious situation, but springs from a spontaneous action of the unconscious which creates a situation so different from the conscious situation of the moment that a conflict arises between the two. While in the first type the conscious component was the stronger factor, from which the energic potential flowed toward the unconscious component, here there is a balance between the two.

3. But when the contrary position of the unconscious is the stronger, the gradient runs from the unconscious to conscious-

---

[1] 'Dream Analysis', p. 151.
[2] 'General Aspects of Dream Psychology', p. 261.
[3] *Kindertraumseminar*, 1938–39.

ness. It is then that we have the significant dreams which can sometimes utterly change and even reverse the orientation of consciousness.

The third type, where the activity, the weight of meaning, is concentrated in the realm of the unconscious, comprises the strangest dreams, those that are most difficult to interpret but convey the most important content; they reflect unconscious processes disclosing no relation whatever to consciousness. The dreamer does not understand them and usually wonders why he is dreaming such things, for he cannot discern even the most indirect relation to his conscious concerns. These, precisely because they are archetypal, are the overpowering, often oracular dreams. Sometimes they appear before the onset of mental illness and grave neurosis; a suddenly erupting content makes a profound impression on the dreamer even if he does not understand it.[1]

The frequent opinion that the more archetypal dreams a person has the better it is for him is quite unsound. On the contrary, the frequent occurrence of such dreams indicates an excessive mobility of the collective depths of the unconscious, which in turn involves the danger of sudden explosions and upheavals. In such cases an analysis must proceed slowly and with the utmost caution. For beneficial as an archetypal dream may be if its content can be understood correctly and integrated at the proper moment, it can also prove extremely dangerous and lead to psychosis if the dreamer's ego is still too narrow to confront it and come to terms with it.

In distinguishing between dreams of the different types, we must ask: How are the reactions of the unconscious related to the conscious situation? The most diverse shadings may be found, ranging from a reaction to purely conscious contents to the spontaneous manifestation of the unconscious depths.[2]

PATTERN AND ARRANGEMENT IN DREAMS

How, by what methods, do we interpret dreams?

Every interpretation is a hypothesis, a mere attempt to

[1] An illuminating example may be found in C. A. Meier's 'Spontanmanifestationen des kollektiven Unbewussten'. See also the child's dream of the 'Bad Animal', related and interpreted in detail in my *Complex, Archetype, Symbol*, pp. 139-89.

[2] *Kindertraumseminar*, 1938-39.

decipher an unknown text. Seldom can an isolated dream be interpreted with even an approximation to certainty. Interpretation can become relatively certain only in a series of dreams: each successive dream corrects the mistakes made in interpreting its predecessors. Jung was the first to investigate whole series of dreams. He started from the assumption that 'dreams continue like a monologue beneath the cover of consciousness',[1] although their chronological order does not always coincide with their inner order of meaning. Dream *B* does not necessarily follow dream *A*, or dream *C* follow dream *B*. For the actual order of dreams is *radial*; they cluster round 'a centre of meaning' from which the dreams radiate, roughly diagrammed as follows:

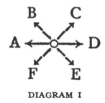

DIAGRAM I

Dream *C* may perfectly well occur before dream *A*, and dream *B* may equally well be dreamed before or after *F*. If this centre is disclosed and raised to consciousness, it ceases to operate, the dreams begin to spring from a new centre, and so on. Thus it is extremely important to have the patient keep a record of his dreams and the interpretations, thereby providing a certain continuity; 'in this way the patient learns how to deal correctly with his unconscious without the doctor's help.'[2] The psychotherapist does not remain passive but actively guides the patient. He participates in the development by indicating the possible meaning of the dream and suggesting the *direction* the patient may take. It is only then that the patient can consciously work through the interpretation and assimilate it.[3] 'The actual interpretation of the dream,' says Jung, 'is as a rule a very exacting task. It needs psychological empathy, ability to

[1] Ibid.   [2] 'Dream Analysis', p. 150.
[3] See our discussion of the 'dialectical process' above, p. 67.

co-ordinate, intuition, knowledge of the world and of men, and above all a special "canniness" which depends on wide understanding as well as on a certain "intelligence du cœur".[1]

MANIFOLD MEANING OF DREAM CONTENT

Every dream content may have manifold meanings and is, as we have said, conditioned by the individuality of the dreamer. Interpretation by standard symbols that can be 'looked up in the dictionary' is utterly incompatible with Jung's view of the nature and structure of the psyche. In order to interpret a content correctly and effectively, one must approach it with a thorough knowledge of the dreamer's situation in life and his manifest, conscious psychology. Moreover, one must carefully establish the context of the dream, and this is what analysis sets out to accomplish by its methods of association and amplification. The context we are looking for is a 'tissue of relationships in which the dream content is naturally embedded. Theoretically one can never know this tissue in advance, and the meaning of every dream and of each of its parts must be postulated as unknown.'[2] It is only after the context has been carefully reviewed that an interpretation may be attempted. Only when the meaning derived from the context has been checked with the record of the dream and the dreamer's meaning-reaction (i.e. his relative acceptance or rejection of a proposed meaning) has been determined can one speak of a result. But under no circumstances may we accept a meaning because it seems to fit in with what we expected. For the correct meaning is often startlingly different from our subjective anticipations. A solution that is 'just what one expected' is very much subject to suspicion. For the unconscious is usually surprisingly 'different'. Parallel dreams, the meaning of which coincides with the dreamer's conscious orientation, are extremely rare.[3]

---

[1] 'On the Nature of Dreams', p. 286.

[2] *Kindertraumseminar*, 1938–39.

[3] An example of the compensatory function of a dream might be the following: Someone dreams that it is spring, but that his favourite tree in the garden has only dry branches. This year it bears no leaves or blossoms. What the dream is trying to communicate is this: Can you see yourself in this tree? That is how you are, although you don't want to recognize it. Your nature has dried up, no green grows within you. Such dreams are a

Jung holds that on the basis of a single dream one can seldom bare the general psychic situation but at most can infer a momentarily acute problem or aspect of a problem. Thus it is only by observing and interpreting a relatively long series of dreams that we can obtain a complete picture of the cause and nature of a disturbance. The series may be said to replace the context which Freudian analysis tries to disclose by 'free association'. With Jung 'directed association', encouraged and guided by the analyst and manifested in dream series, etc., helps to reveal and regulate the psychic process.

COMPENSATORY ASPECT OF DREAMS

As a rule the orientation of the unconscious is complementary or compensatory to the conscious attitude. 'The more one-sided [the] conscious attitude is, and the further it deviates from the optimum, the greater becomes the possibility that vivid dreams with a strongly contrasting but purposive content will appear as an expression of the self-regulation of the psyche.'[1] The character of the compensation, of course, is closely connected with the whole nature of the individual. 'Only in the light of this knowledge (of the individual's conscious situation) is it possible to make out whether the unconscious content carries a plus or a minus sign. . . . In reality the relation between the conscious mind and the dream is strictly causal, and they interact in the subtlest ways. . . . In this sense we can take the theory of compensation as a basic law of psychic behaviour.'[2]

In addition to compensating the conscious situation, which is the rule for the normal individual under normal inward and outward conditions, the dream contents can also exert a reductive or prospective function. They may compensate negatively, reducing 'the individual to his human nullity and to his dependence on physiological, historical, and phylogenetic condi-

---

lesson to persons whose consciousness has become autonomous and over-emphasized. Of course the dreams of an unusually unconscious person, living entirely by his instincts, would correspondingly emphasize his 'other side'. Irresponsible scoundrels often have moralizing dreams while paragons of virtue frequently have immoral dream images.

[1] 'General Aspects of Dream Psychology', p. 253.
[2] 'Dream Analysis', pp. 153, 154.

tions' (this material was brilliantly investigated by Freud), or else positively by providing a kind of 'guiding image' which corrects a self-devaluating attitude and brings about a 'better' direction of consciousness. Both forms may be salutary. The dream's prospective function must be distinguished from its compensatory function. The latter means primarily that the unconscious, viewed as relative to consciousness, contributes to consciousness all the elements that are repressed or disregarded and lacking to its completeness. 'Compensation, considered as a self-regulation of the psychic organism, must be called purposive. The prospective function, on the other hand, is an anticipation in the unconscious of future conscious achievements, something like a preliminary exercise or sketch, or a plan roughed out in advance.'[1]

As is evident from Jung's whole conception of dream structure, from the importance he attributes to the dreamer's conscious situation and to the contextual and positional value of dream motives, from the spaceless and timeless character he attributes to dreams, etc., the principle of causality can be applied only in a restricted sense to his—in contrast to Freud's —interpretation of dreams. 'Considering a dream from the standpoint of finality . . . does not,' says Jung, 'involve a denial of the dream's causes but rather a different interpretation of the associative material gathered round the dream.'[2] And as we shall soon see, it also involves a different *method* of interpretation. For Jung does not look primarily for effective causes; he even believes that 'dreams are often anticipatory and would lose their specific meaning completely if considered from a purely causalistic view. They afford unmistakable information about the analytical situation, the correct understanding of which is of the greatest therapeutic importance.' This is particularly true of 'initial dreams', that is, the dreams of a patient at the beginning of analysis. For 'every dream is an organ of information and control'.[3]

---

[1] 'General Aspects of Dream Psychology', pp. 255, 258.
[2] Ibid., p. 243.
[3] 'Dream Analysis', pp. 144–45, 153 (modified).

DREAMS AS THE 'LAND OF CHILDHOOD'

In analysis the path leads to the 'land of childhood', the time before the rational present-day consciousness separated from the historical psyche, the collective unconscious; not only to the land where the complexes of childhood have their origin, but to a prehistoric country which was the cradle of all our psyches. Departure from the 'land of childhood' is inevitable, but too often the individual travels so far from the primordial twilight psyche that his natural instincts are lost. 'The result is instinctual atrophy and hence disorientation in everyday human situations. But it also follows from the separation that the "land of childhood" will remain definitely infantile and become a perpetual source of childish inclinations and impulses. These intrusions are naturally most unwelcome to the conscious mind, and it consistently represses them for that reason. But the very consistency of the repression serves to bring about a still greater alienation from the fountainhead, thus increasing the lack of instinct until it becomes lack of soul. As a result, the conscious mind is either completely swamped by childishness or else constantly obliged to defend itself in vain against the inundation, by means of a cynical affection of old age or embittered resignation. We must therefore realize that despite its undeniable successes the rational attitude of present-day consciousness is, in many human respects, childishly unadapted and hostile to life. Life has grown desiccated and cramped, crying out for the rediscovery of the fountainhead. But the fountainhead can only be rediscovered if the conscious mind will suffer itself to be led back to the "land of childhood", there to receive guidance from the unconscious as before. To remain a child too long is infantile, but it is just as childish to move away and then assume that childhood is no longer visible because we do not see it. But if we return to the "land of childhood" we succumb to the fear of becoming infantile, because we do not realize that everything psychic in origin has a double face. One face looks forward, the other back. It is ambivalent and therefore symbolic, like all living reality.

'We stand on a peak of consciousness, believing in a childish way that the path leads upward to yet higher peaks beyond.

That is the chimerical rainbow bridge.[1] In order to reach the next peak we must first go down into the land where the paths begin to divide. . . . The resistance of the conscious mind to the unconscious and the depreciation of the latter were historical necessities in the development of the human psyche, for otherwise the conscious mind would never have been able to differentiate itself at all.' But the consciousness of modern man has moved somewhat too far from its origins, from the unconscious; we have forgotten that the unconscious does not function in accordance with our conscious purposes, but autonomously. 'Consequently,' says Jung, 'the approach of the unconscious induces a panic fear in civilized people, not least on account of the menacing analogy with insanity. The intellect has no objection to "analysing" the unconscious as a passive object; on the contrary such an activity would coincide with our rational expectations. But to let the unconscious go its own way and to experience it as a reality is something beyond the courage and capacity of the average European. He prefers simply not to understand this problem. For the spiritually weak-kneed this is the better course, since the thing is not without its dangers. The experience of the unconscious is a personal secret communicable only to a very few.'[2]

In the psyche of modern man the conscious side has been overemphasized; consequently the repressed, dammed-up, unconscious side threatens to burst forth and inundate the conscious mind. That is why the need to integrate the unconscious into the psyche as a whole has become specifically Western and modern problem, crucial not only for the individual but for whole peoples as well. In Eastern man, and probably in the African, we seem to find a very different relation between consciousness and the unconscious.

Jung holds that before dealing with the material of the collective unconscious we must first raise the infantile contents to consciousness and integrate them. The ' "personal unconscious",' he says, 'must always be dealt with first, that is, made conscious.'[3] Otherwise the gateway to the collective unconscious is closed. Every conflict must first be considered in its personal

---

[1] See below, p. 87.
[2] *Alchemy*, pars. 74–75, 60–61.
[3] Ibid, par. 81.

aspect and examined in the light of individual experience. The accent must be placed on the most intimate life of the individual and the psychic contents acquired in connection with it, before the individual can begin to deal with the universal problems of human existence. This path, which leads to the activation of the archetypes and the unification of consciousness and the unconscious or a proper balance between them, is the path of 'healing' and, from the technical point of view, it is also the way followed by dream interpretation.

THE STAGES OF DREAM INTERPRETATION

Thus, to sum up once again, the technique of analysing a dream may be divided into the following stages: description of the present situation of consciousness; description of preceding events; investigation of the subjective context and, where archaic motives appear, comparison with mythological parallels; finally, in complicated situations, comparison with objective data obtained from third persons.

On the other hand, the course taken by the contents of the unconscious consists roughly of the following seven stages: (1) lowering of the threshold of consciousness, permitting the contents of the unconscious to emerge;[1] (2) rising up of the contents of the unconscious in dreams, visions, fantasies; (3) perceiving the contents and holding them fast by consciousness; (4) investigation, clarification, interpretation, and understanding of the meaning of the contents; (5) integration of this meaning with the general psychic situation of the individual; (6) acquisition, incorporation, and elaboration of the meaning thus found; (7) integration of the 'meaning', its organic incorporation in the psyche becoming so complete that it 'enters the bloodstream' as it were, becomes a *knowledge secured by instinct*.

THE STRUCTURE OF DREAMS

Jung found that most dreams show a certain similarity of structure. Unlike Freud, he believes that they form a self-con-

[1] Some patients find it very hard to allow this; secret anxiety at the prospect of exposing contents from the unconscious is a frequent cause of insomnia.

tained whole, a dramatic action which can meaningfully be broken down into the elements of a Greek play. (1) *Place, time, dramatis personae*: this is the beginning of the dream, which often indicates the scene of action and the cast of characters; (2) *Exposition* or statement of the problem. Here is presented the central content: the unconscious frames the question to which it will reply in the course of the dream; (3) *Peripety*: this is the 'backbone' of the dream; the plot is woven, the action moves toward a climax, transformation, or catastrophe; (4) *Lysis*, the solution, the outcome of the dream, its meaningful conclusion and the disclosure of its compensatory message.

This rough pattern, on which most dreams are constructed, forms a suitable basis for interpretation.[1] Dreams that reveal no lysis suggests a tragic development in the dreamer's life; but these are very specific dreams and should not be confused with those which have no lysis because the dreamer remembers or relates them incompletely. It goes without saying that the psychotherapist can seldom obtain a full account of a dream all at once. A careful investigation is often needed before its whole structure is revealed to him.

CONDITIONALISM

Jung has brought the theory of CONDITIONALISM to the interpretation of dreams.[2] 'Under conditions of such and such a

---

[1] The following dream of a six-year-old child from the *Kindertraumseminar*, 1938–39, may serve as an example: 'A beautiful rainbow springs up before the little girl. She climbs up on it until she reaches the sky. From there she calls down to her friend Marietta to come up. But Marietta hesitates so long that the rainbow passes and the little girl falls down.' The place is that of a natural event: a beautiful rainbow springs up before the little girl. The *exposition* also refers to this event: she climbs up on it until she reaches the sky. The *peripety* or weaving of the plot: she calls down to her friend to come up. But Marietta hesitates and the *lysis* follows: the rainbow passes and the little girl falls down to earth.

[2] Max Verworn, the physiologist and philosopher (1863–1921) who originated the concept of conditionalism, defined it as follows: 'A state or process is determined by the totality of its conditions: (1) similar states or processes are always the expression of similar conditions; dissimilar conditions find their expressions in dissimilar states and processes; (2) a state or process is identical with the totality of its conditions. From this it follows that a state or process is fully known to science if the totality of its conditions is established' (*Kausale und konditionale Weltanschauung*).

kind,' he writes, 'such and such dreams can occur.'[1] The crucial factor is always the situation of the moment with its actual conditions. In the conditionalist view, the same problems, the same causes, have different meanings according to the context; one can no longer ignore situation and circumstances and say that the same phenomenon always has the same meaning.

Conditionalism is a broader form of causality, a polyvalent interpretation of causal relations. It is an attempt 'to conceive strict causality by means of an interplay of conditions, to enlarge the simple significance of the relation between cause and effect by means of the manifold significance of the relations between effects. Causality in the general sense is not thereby abolished, but only accommodated to the many-sided living material,'[2] and so broadened and complemented. Accordingly, the meaning of a particular dream motif is not explained solely by its causal connections, but also by its 'positional value'[3] within the total dream context.

THE AMPLIFICATION METHOD

Jung does not work with 'free associations' but employs a method he calls *amplification*. Free association, he believes, 'always leads to a complex, but we can never be certain whether it is precisely this one that constitutes the meaning of the dream. . . . We can, of course, always get to our complexes somehow, for they are the attraction that draws everything to itself.'[4] But sometimes the dream points in exactly the opposite direction from the content of the complex, indicating on the one hand the natural function that may be able to free the dreamer from the complex and on the other hand a way the dreamer may follow. Thus amplification, in contrast to the Freudian method of *reductio in primam figuram*, is not an unbroken chain of causally connected associations leading backward, but a process by which the dream content is broadened and enriched with the help of analogous images. The associations—and here again it differs from the 'free association' method—are not provided only by the patient or dreamer but also by the analyst. Indeed, the analogies contributed by the

---

[1] *Kindertraumseminar*, 1938–39.   [2] *Kindertraumseminar*, 1938–39.
[3] See also p. 59.   [4] *Kindertraumseminar*, 1938–39.

analyst often determine the direction of the patient's associations. With all their rich variety, these images and analogies will be reasonably close to the dream content that is to be interpreted, whereas there is no way of controlling free association and preventing it from straying too far from the dream content.

Thus amplification is a limited, controlled, and directed association process which circles round the dream nucleus and so helps the analyst to put his finger on it. 'The *amplificatio*,'

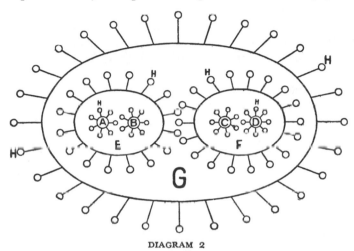

DIAGRAM 2

A,B,C,D. The individual dream motifs.
    E,F. Two elements of meaning (dream motifs), are combined into
        a whole; e.g., A = horn, B = animal, E = horned animal.
    G. The whole dream as a meaningful unit, e.g., considered as
        an analogy to a mythologem.
    H. The individual points of correspondence.

writes Jung, 'is always appropriate when dealing with some obscure experience which is so vaguely adumbrated that it must be enlarged and expanded by being set in a psychological context in order to be understood by all. That is why, in analytical psychology, we resort to amplification in the interpretation of dreams, for a dream is too slender a hint to be understood until it is enriched by the stuff of association and analogy and thus amplified to the point of intelligibility.'[1]

In the amplification method, analogies are not selected on the

_____
[1] *Alchemy*, par. 403.

basis of temporal coincidence or any scientific, historical criterion, but because their nucleus of meaning is identical with, or similar to, that of the dream content under investigation. If we assume that everything man has ever expressed in word or picture possesses absolute psychic reality, regardless of when it was produced and regardless of whether it originated as a unique inspiration, as the product of a long tradition, or of scientific inquiry, every analogy, in so far as it embodies an archetypal aspect of the dream motif in question, helps to refine, explain, and corroborate our interpretation. In this form amplification represents a new and fruitful scientific method for the investigation of psychologems, mythologems, and psychic structures of all kinds.

It must be applied to all the elements of the dream if we are to form a total picture from which the 'meaning' can be deciphered. In Jung's amplification method the various dream motifs are enriched by analogous, related images, symbols, legends, myths, etc., which throw light on their diverse aspects and possible meanings, until their significance stands out in full clarity. Each element of meaning thus obtained is linked with the next, until the whole chain of dream motifs is revealed and the whole dream as a unit can be subjected to a final verification. Diagram 2 gives an idea of the process.

REDUCTIVE INTERPRETATION

Diagrams 3 and 4 show a rough comparison between the amplification method and the *reductio in primam figuram*. Both start with four different elements, dream contents A, B, C, D. Amplification combines them in all directions, taking account of all possible analogies, extending their field of implication and baring their meaning as far as possible. If, for example, the figure of the real father appears as an element in a dream, amplification may enrich and broaden it into the idea of the fatherly as such. The reductive method, in which it is assumed that the various dream elements are a 'distortion' of contents that were originally different, carries the four points back along a chain of free association until, trapped in causal connections, they culminate in the *one* point X from which they started and which it was their function to 'distort' or 'conceal'. Thus amplification illuminates all the possible meanings of the four points for the dreamer in his actual situation, while reduction merely carries them back to a complex point. Freud with his reduction asks 'Why?' and 'Whence?' Jung in his method of interpreting dreams asks primarily 'To what end?' What did the unconscious intend, what did it wish to tell the dreamer by

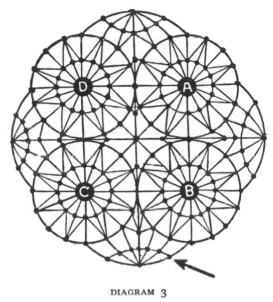

DIAGRAM 3

A,B,C,D. The dream elements.
      The nodal points of the net of connections indicated by the small arrow represent the individual parallels or amplifications.

sending him just this dream and not another? An intellectual dreams, for example, that he is passing under a great rainbow bridge. Under, not over it, and this surprises him greatly. The dream aims to point out that this man has been trying to solve his problems in an unreal way, and to show him the right way— not over the bridge but under it.[1] For intellectuals who suppose that they can simply exclude their instinctual nature, that they can 'think away' or somehow 'rationalize' their life, subjugate it with their intellect, such a hint is often very necessary. This

[1] Example from *Kindertraumseminar*, 1938–39.

dream, as we see, served as a warning that would open the dreamer's eyes to his real situation.

THE DYNAMIC ASPECT OF DREAMS

Of course the actual meaning of the dream in all its particulars can be disclosed only by a detailed process of analysis as described above. But from the little that has been said here it is already evident that the dream had a certain 'purpose', namely to disclose a fact of which the dreamer was not or

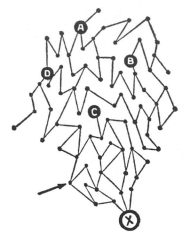

DIAGRAM 4. A,B,C,D. The dream elements. X. The original figure. The various associations are indicated by the nodal points, shown by the arrow.

did not want to be aware.[1] Such dreams are relatively easy to interpret, for they are 'parables' which can be translated directly into a warning. Such a warning is the expression of a dynamic tendency in the unconscious. This dynamic tendency, the force behind the dream and its utterances, sends new contents into consciousness which in turn—if they have been assimilated by the personality—react upon and modify the un-

[1] Of course we must not attribute 'conscious purpose' to a dream. Such formulation as: the unconscious, or the dream, 'expressed the opinion' or 'pursued the purpose', are intended to mean only that the manifestations of the unconscious realm of the psyche are also meaningfully guided by the self-regulative activity of the psyche.

conscious field of forces. The dynamic process that is invisible in a single dream but can easily be followed in a series prevents interruption and loss between analytic sessions, and makes it possible to carry out an analysis with meetings at fairly long intervals. And since, as we have shown, the dynamic has aim and meaning, it makes certain that when a dream is falsely interpreted other dreams will follow which will correct the error and lead the analysis back into the right path.

In line with the above-mentioned principle of the conservation of energy, nothing is lost in the psyche; an exchange of energy occurs between all the elements; all are encompassed in a definite and meaningful but continuously evolving whole. 'The unconscious,' says Jung, 'is continually active, combining its material in ways which serve the future. It produces, no less than the conscious mind, subliminal combinations that are prospective; only, they are markedly superior to the conscious combinations both in refinement and in scope. For these reasons the unconscious can serve man as a unique guide, provided that he can resist the lure of being misguided.' In dreams we can discern not only the momentary situation of the dreamer but also the progress or obstruction of the analytic process. Recorded without the context or detailed information about the dreamer, they do not seem very meaningful. But once understood and elaborated, they can exert an extraordinary and even liberating effect on the dreamer whose problem they express and illuminate. 'On paper the interpretation of a dream may look arbitrary, muddled, and spurious; but the same thing in reality can be a little drama of unsurpassed realism.'[1]

INDIVIDUAL AND COLLECTIVE MEANING

The subjective, individual meaning of the dream is supplied by *subjective amplifications*; i.e., the analyst asks the dreamer what each dream element means to him personally. Then the collective meaning is obtained by *objective amplification*; i.e., the dream elements are enriched with the universal, symbolic material of fairy tales, myths, etc., which illuminate the universal aspect of the problem that concerns every human being.

Dreams rich in pictorial detail seem to relate primarily to

---

[1] 'Unconscious', pp. 114, 115 (slightly modified).

individual problems; they belong to the realm of the personal unconscious and their sharply drawn images represent a response, a counterpart, to the waking consciousness; they embody the repressed 'other side'. On the other hand, the dreams characterized by scant detail and simple images communicate insights into great, universal contexts; they represent aspects of the cosmos, the eternal laws of nature and the truth. From them we can usually infer an overdifferentiated or even autonomous consciousness that has very largely split off from the unconscious, for these dreams usually signify a striving to compensate such a consciousness through the images of the collective unconscious.

The dream is a statement, uninfluenced by consciousness, expressing the dreamer's inner truth and reality 'as it really is: not as I conjecture it to be, and not as he would like it to be, but *as it is*'.[1] Thus for Jung the manifest content of a dream is not a façade but a fact which always reveals what the unconscious has to say about the situation and which always says exactly what the unconscious means. When, for example, a snake appears in a dream, the significant fact is precisely that it is a snake and not a bull or something else. The snake has been selected by the unconscious because its specific aspect and rich implications can convey to the dreamer exactly what the unconscious 'intended'. We establish what snake means to the dreamer *not* by a chain of association but by amplification, in which we supplement the snake symbol with all the allusions and connections, myths for example, which are relevant to its character as a snake and which correspond to the subjective constellation of the dreamer. Precisely because we do not—with Freud for example—regard the snake as a 'cover figure', but hold that as a snake it has something definite to say to the dreamer, we do not attempt to interpret the dream by trying to find out what the symbol may hide. On the contrary, the whole context surrounding the symbol is drawn into the question and examined. Just as the representational value of a colour results only from the context in which it is placed (e.g. whether a grey spot represents a patch or shadow or a reflection of light, a spot of dirt or a strand of hair, depends entirely on the forms and colours of the entire picture), so the role and meaning of a dream symbol can be

[1] 'Dream Analysis', p. 142.

discerned only in context. If in addition we consider the specific psychic structure of the dreamer, his general situation and conscious psychological orientation, the meaning of the figure in its subjective reference will emerge of its own accord.

Without personal associations and consideration of the context, we can hope to interpret only dream contents of a collective nature, representing universal human problems. In other words, purely archetypal themes can be investigated and interpreted in this way, but they alone. That is why it is so absurd to suppose that we can say anything of decisive importance for the life of the dreamer when a dream is submitted all by itself, without its personal setting. In such cases only the archetypal meaning of the dream can be elucidated and we must forego any concrete interpretation of the dream in personal reference to the dreamer. For no interpretation is contained in the archetypes themselves, the reflections of our instincts, or as Jung calls them, the 'organs of our psyche', the images of nature itself. In order to arrive at a correct interpretation or reject a false one, we must always take the individual human being as our point of departure. It is perfectly obvious that the same motif will have very different meanings according to whether it is dreamed by a child or by a man of fifty.

FORMS OF INTERPRETATION

Jung distinguishes two forms or planes of interpretation: the SUBJECT LEVEL and the OBJECT LEVEL. On the subject level the figures and events of a dream are interpreted *symbolically*, as reflections of the dreamer's intrapsychic factors and situations. Here the figures in the dream represent psychic tendencies or functions of the dreamer, and the dream situation reflects his attitude toward himself and his psychic reality. Thus conceived, the dream points to inner data.

In interpretation on the object level, however, the dream figures are taken not symbolically but *concretely*. They then represent the dreamer's attitude toward the outward facts or persons of his environment. They aim to show, in a purely objective way, how something that the dreamer in his conscious mind has seen only from one side looks from the other side, or to reveal something that he has not yet observed. Let us suppose for example that a man's father, whom he has always regarded as noble and kindly, appears to him in a dream as domineering, cruel, selfish, and violent. Interpreted on the subject level, this would mean that the dreamer harbours such qualities in his own psyche but is unaware of them or puts an unrealistic construction on them. Interpreted on the object level, the dream would represent the man's real father, revealing his true character that had hitherto been unknown to or unrecognized by the dreamer.

When persons vitally connected with the dreamer occur in a dream, they must—aside from their possible significance as partial aspects of the psyche, which would cause them to be interpreted on the subject level—always be interpreted on the object level as well. On the subject level we must interpret the dream contents as representations of subjective images, as embodiments or projections of complexes in the unconscious of the patient himself. Thus a certain figure in the dream of a woman patient, that of a male friend for example, may be interpreted as an image of the masculine element in her. Unrecognized by her consciousness, it lies in her unconscious and appears as projected upon a person outside her. The meaning of this dream figure is that it calls the patient's attention to her own masculine side, to qualities whose presence she had not known or at least not accepted. This may be extremely important for a woman who mistakenly regards herself as eminently frail, sensitive, and feminine, the familiar type of fussy old maid for example.

PROJECTION

'Everything unconscious is projected; i.e., it appears as a property or activity of an object. Only by an act of self-knowledge are these contents integrated with the subject, detached from the object and recognized as psychic phenomena.'[1] The phenomenon of projection is an integral part of the mechanism of the unconscious, and since the unconscious plays a considerable part in every psyche, there can be no psychic life without a certain amount of projection. In dreams or waking, in individuals or groups, in relation to persons, things, or conditions, it stands wholly outside the conscious will. 'Projection,' says

---

[1] T. Wolff, *Studien*, pp. 99 f.

Jung, 'is never made; it happens.'[1] He defines it as the 'expulsion of a subjective content into an object', in contrast to introjection, which 'consists in taking an object into the subject'.[2]

Inability to differentiate oneself from the object is a state characteristic of primitive peoples and also of children. In the naïve—primitives as well as children—the contents of the individual psyche are not yet differentiated from those of the collective psyche; they are not yet set off from one another, but are always in a kind of 'participation'. For, as Jung says, 'the gods and demons were not regarded as psychic projections and hence as contents of the unconscious, but as self-evident realities. Only in the age of enlightenment did people discover that the gods did not really exist, but were simply projections. Thus the gods were disposed of. But the corresponding psychological function was by no means disposed of; it lapsed into the unconscious, and men were thereupon poisoned by the surplus of libido that had once been laid up in the cult of divine images.'[3]

If consciousness is not sufficiently consolidated, or if the core of the personality is not strong enough to assimilate, understand, and elaborate the unconscious contents and their projections, consciousness may be flooded and even submerged by the then activated and swollen unconscious materials. In this case the psychic contents not only take on a character of reality but reflect the conflict in a crudely primitive or in a magnified, mythological form, and the road to psychosis lies open. For this reason interpretation on the subject level is one of the most important 'instruments' of Jung's dream analysis. It enables us to understand the difficulties and conflicts of the individual in

---

[1] *Alchemy*, par. 346.

[2] *Types*, par. 783. The psychological attitude of the German Romantics and their way of experiencing the world may be characterized as introjection; for they turned away from the ugly outside world which they felt to be inadequate, but of whose reality they were nevertheless fully aware, to an arbitrary, ideal world of their own fancy through which they transformed the outside world or adapted it to their subjective feelings. It is obvious that where the subjective standpoint is so overvalued the conscious ego is in constant danger of being engulfed by a superabundance of inner images and thus of losing its objective point of reference.

[3] 'Unconscious', par. 150.

his relation to the outside world as a mirroring of his intra-psychic processes and may thus help him to take back his projections and to solve his problems within his own psyche. When we consider what the perpetual projection of our own qualities and complexes upon others leads to in this world we can fully appreciate the importance of this Jungian method.

THE SYMBOL

In the Jungian interpretation of dreams a central role is played by the psychic phenomenon which is generally designated by the term SYMBOL.[1] Jung calls the symbol a 'libido analogue', because it is a transformer of energy. By symbol he means a representation that can supply an equivalent expression of the libido and so canalize it into a new form.[2] The psychic images in dreams, fantasies, etc. are products and expressions of psychic energy, just as a waterfall is a product and expression of physical energy. For without energy (though the physical concept is only a working hypothesis) there would be no waterfall; and without such concrete manifestations as the waterfall the energy could not be observed and verified. This may sound paradoxical; but paradox is the very essence of all psychic life.

Symbols have at once an *expressive* and *impressive* character; on the one hand they express the intrapsychic process in images; but, on the other hand, when they have become image, 'incarnated' as it were in a pictorial material, they 'make an impression', that is, their meaning content influences the intrapsychic process and furthers the flow of psychic energy. Thus the symbol of the withered Tree of Life, signifying an excessively intellectualized life that had lost its natural roots in instinct,[3] expresses this meaning in an image which discloses it to the dreamer while, at the same time, it impresses him by the disclosure and influences the direction of his psychic process. Thus symbols are the true transformers of energy in the psychic process.

In the course of an analysis one can repeatedly note how one

[1] A detailed definition of the symbol is given in my *Complex, Archetype, Symbol*, pp. 74 ff.

[2] 'Energy', p. 48.

[3] See the dream related on p. 77.

pictorial motif conditions and leads to another. At first the motifs are cloaked in the material of personal experience, marked by childhood recollections or other more recent memories. But the deeper the analysis penetrates, the more clearly the effects of the archetypes appear; the symbol becomes increasingly dominant, for it encloses an archetype, a nucleus of meaning that is not representable in itself but charged with energy. It is very much as when we print an engraving: the first print is extremely sharp, its slightest details are discernible and its meaning is clear; the following prints become poorer in detail and definition; and in the last perceptible image the outlines and details are quite blurred, though we can still distinguish the basic form which leaves all the possible aspects open or combines them. The first dream of a series, for example, gives a detailed image of the real mother in her limited diurnal role; but gradually the meaning becomes wider and deeper, until the image is transformed into a symbol of Woman in all her variations as the contrasexual partner; then, rising up from a still deeper stratum, the image discloses mythological features, becomes a fairy or a dragon; in the deepest stratum, the storehouse of collective, universally human experience, it takes the form of a dark cave, the underworld, the ocean, and finally it swells into the one half of creation, chaos, the darkness that receives and conceives.

These symbols from the unconscious, whether manifested in dreams, visions, or fantasies, embody a kind of 'individual mythology' that finds its closest analogies in the typical figures of myths, legends, fairy tales, etc.[1] 'We must therefore assume that they correspond to certain *collective* (and not personal) structural elements of the human psyche in general, and, like the morphological elements of the human body, are *inherited*.'[2]

'Symbols were never *devised consciously*, but were always produced out of the unconscious by way of revelation or intuition.'[3] Symbols can stand for the most diverse contents. Natural as well as intrapsychic processes may appear in symbolic dress. To a primitive, for example, the course of the sun may symbolize the concrete, eternal process of nature while in the eyes of the

[1] Cf. p. 47.
[2] 'The Psychology of the Child Archetype', p. 155.
[3] 'Energy', p. 48.

psychologically oriented modern man it may stand for a similar, equally regular process in his inner world. The symbol of 'rebirth' always stands for the primordial idea of psychic transformation, whether it takes the form of a primitive initiation rite, of baptism in its early Christian connotation, or of a modern individual's dream image. But the way this rebirth is achieved varies with the historical and individual situation of consciousness. For this reason it is necessary to evaluate and interpret every symbol both collectively and individually if we wish to be sure of its actual significance in a given case. 'Mythological images,' as Kerényi has written, 'never occur in isolation. Originally they were always part of an objective and a subjective context: the inner context of the product itself and its connection with the person producing it.' However, the personal context and the particular psychological situation must remain dominant factors in any interpretation.

SYMBOL AND SIGN

The content of a symbol can never be fully expressed in rational terms. It stems from the 'intermediate realm of subtle reality which can only be adequately expressed by the symbol'.[1] An allegory is a sign for something, a way of expressing a known content; but a symbol always means something more, something that cannot be expressed by rational concepts. Freud is therefore unjustified in defining symbols as 'those contents of consciousness which give us a clue to the unconscious background', for in his theory they are merely 'signs or symptoms of the background processes'. When on the other hand Plato, for example, 'expresses the whole problem of the theory of knowledge in his allegory of the cave, or when Christ expresses the idea of the Kingdom of Heaven in his parables, these are genuine and true symbols; that is, attempts to express something for which no verbal concept yet exists.'[2] The German word for symbol is *Sinnbild*, a compound which strikingly denotes the two realms of which the symbol partakes: the *Sinn*, or meaning, pertains to the conscious, rational sphere, the *Bild*, or image, belongs to the irrational sphere, the unconscious. It is this twofold origin and

---

[1] *Alchemy*, par. 400.
[2] 'On the Relation of Analytical Psychology to Poetry', par. 105.

Plate 1. Symbolic Representation of the Psyche. Torn between its four functions this is the 'inward perception' of a psyche striving towards the conscious realization of its totality but held prisoner in a circle of snakes, symbols of the primordial instincts. The four functions are symbolized by the four colours—blue, yellow, red, and green—of the circle of rays, while the striving towards conscious realization is represented by the four burning torches.

Plate 2. The Snake of Passion. Symbol of the undifferentiated
instinctual world in man, the 'snake of passion' has here emerged
from the chest floating on the ocean of the unconscious, in which
it had been rigorously enclosed by repression, and has risen
above it. A sheaf of glowing, searing rays of fire issues from its
gullet, but its head is marked with the cross of redemption, thus
symbolizing its dual aspect as a power both of destruction and
of healing. The saturation and strength of the colours indicate
the intense emotion which produced the picture and which it
released in the patient.

Plate 3. The Helpful Shadow. This picture was produced by a woman who was unaware of having a hidden 'other' side, a 'shadow' who stood helpfully by her, making it easier for her to bear the heavy burden, the 'stone of her problems'. The moon and the two stars indicate that the problem in question is an eminently feminine one. (N.B.: As this picture, like the others reproduced here—except Plates 8, 9, 10, 17, 19—was done by a woman, it must be understood and interpreted from the standpoint of feminine psychology.)

Plate 4. The Mountain as a Symbol of Emergent Consciouness.
This picture represents a mountain arising out of the collective
unconscious and symbolizes a newly attained, higher, and more
solid situation of consciousness, the birth of a 'new world'. Parallels
to this figure are found in numerous cosmologies, mythological
images, and religious conceptions. The sun as symbol of consciousness forms the peak of the mountain but is organically embedded
in it. The sun has captured the over-bold, high-soaring eagle,
symbol of the animus, the ambitious feminine intellect, which
suffers and bleeds. Earth and water are fertilized with the blood,
and life puts forth its green shoots.

Plate 5. An example of the numerous forms taken by the archetype
of the Wise Old Man. His face is marked by age-old, boundless
knowledge and understanding. The eyes are turned inward, the
immobile features and the closed mouth express an extreme
spirituality which has become one with nature, which indeed has
become nature. Chest and shoulders have turned to earth, overgrown
with grass and moss which provide food for the doves, the birds of
Aphrodite, goddess of kindness and love. The sun disk behind
his head indicates his logos character, and the crystal in his hands, a
symbol of wholeness, points to the highest goal of psychic development, the 'Self'; for the Wise Old Man is one of the archetypal
figures which represent the Self—he is its masculine half.

Plate 6. The Great Mother, the all-encompassing inexorable
'world' clad in the starry mantle of heaven, seated beneath golden
fruit in the soft light of the crescent moon, looks down compas-
sionately at the poor creature whom she herself is tearing in two
with her rough hands, gouging out a deep wound from which the
blood drips down. Torn between the two opposites, the upper
and lower realms of being, caught up in their tension, the woman's
life is a martyrdom, but this martyrdom is indispensable if she
is to be reborn in the child symbolizing the Self and if the sun is to
shine forth in the unfathomable womb of the world.

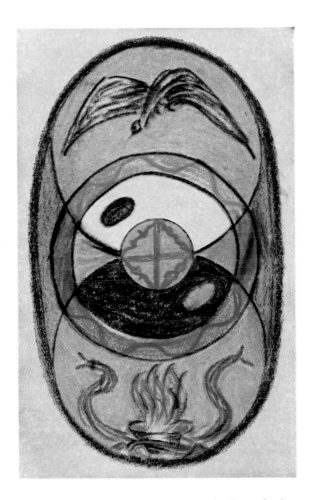

Plate 7. This crayon drawing presents the inward picture of psychic totality that manifested itself in the course of the analytic treatment of a woman patient. The blue bird symbolizes the sphere of consciousness, the fire with the snakes the realm of the unconscious; the small yellow circle in the middle is the centre, the Self, which is situated between the feminine part of the psyche, the black field with the white egg, and the masculine part, the white field with the black egg. Round it flows the stream of life, which connects and waters all the spheres.

Plate 8. Mandala from Tantric Buddhism, from Jung's private collection. It is finely painted in soft colours, on parchment, and probably dates back to the beginning of the eighteenth century.

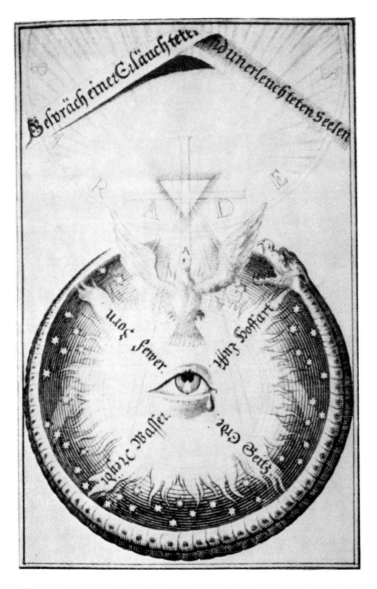

Plate 9. Mystic vision from J. Boehme's *Theosophische Werke*. It shows a sinful world of creation, surrounded by the Serpent of Eternity, the Uroboros, and characterized by the four elements and the sins corresponding to them; the whole circle relates to the centre, the weeping eye of God, i.e. the point where salvation, symbolized by the dove of the Holy Ghost, may be achieved through compassion and love.

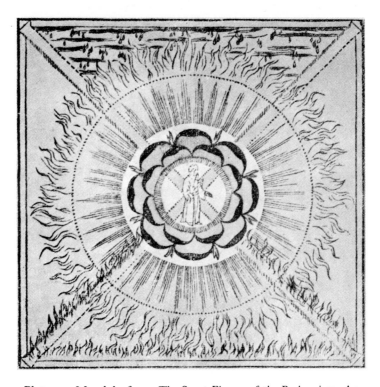

Plate 10. Mandala from *The Secret Figures of the Rosicrucians*. An eighteenth-century drawing, this mandala shows the Saviour at the centre of a flower with a double row of eight petals, surrounded by a fiery garland of rays. It is divided into four parts by a cross, whose lower shafts are burning in the fire of the instincts and whose upper shafts are sprinkled with tears of heavenly dew.

Plate 11. The Peacock Wheel. The eyes, symbolizing the forever
changing dynamic aspects and qualities of the psyche, revolve
around the central eye. The wheel is enclosed in a circle of flame,
forming a protective wall of 'burning emotions' around the
mysterious process of self-realization and shuts it off from the
outside world. In its arrangement, motifs, and entire dynamic
structure, this mandala shows a striking resemblance to Plate 9,
which was not known to the analysand who painted this 'picture
from the unconscious'.

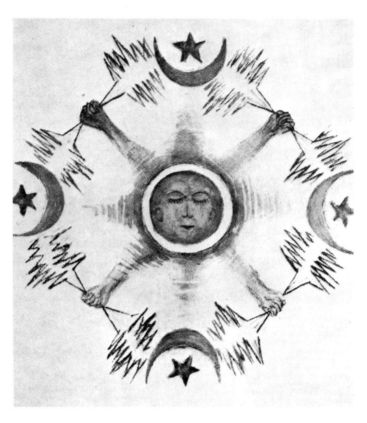

Plate 12. The Four-armed Sun God. As symbol of the dynamic aspect of the Self, the whole revolves around the sun which is ringed by the 'river of life'. Arms and lightning are 'masculine', the moon-sickle is feminine in character. The five-pointed stars symbolize what is still imperfect and nature-bound in man.

Plate 13. Mandala Composition. More formal and abstract, this is also an attempt to relate a variety of lines and forms to the centre.

Plate 14. Mandala of Awakening Consciousness. Around the four-leafed calyx in the middle, the figure shows varied arrangements of form and colour: blue, red, green, yellow, standing for the four functions of consciousness.

Plate 15. The Face of Eternity surrounded by the serpent of
eternity, the uroboros, and the zodiac.

Plate 16. The Eye of God, symbolizing universal awareness, penetrating the flower-like mandala in which it is embedded with its quadruple rays.

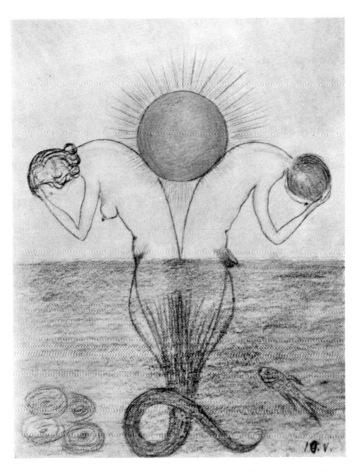

Plate 17. The False *Coniunctio*. The man and the woman have
grown together into a snake at the base of the spine, the instinctual level. In the conscious world, the area above the water
(water symbolizing the unconscious) they turn their backs to
each other. They carry the sun, symbol of illuminating consciousness, as a heavy burden and are unable to turn it to their
enlightenment.

Plate 18. The Right *Coniunctio*, a 'picture from the unconscious' which attempts to symbolize the individual's relation to the contra-sexual. It represents the true, creative union. The unconscious, animal sides of the man and woman have not grown inseparably together as in the case of blind infatuation, but are joined by the 'snake of salvation', which helps them to lift the precious stone, the symbol of the Self, without which true communion between them, represented as the tree of life with many branches, could never thrive.

PHILOSOPHORVM.

ſeipſis ſecundum ęqualitatē inſpiſſentur. Solus
enim calor tēperatus eſt humiditatis inſpiſſatiuus
et mixtionis perſectiuus, et non ſuper excedens.
Nā generatiões et procreationes rerū naturaliū
habent ſolū fieri per tēperatiſsimū calorē et ęqua
lē, vti eſt ſolus ſimus equinus humidus et calidus.

Plate 19. The alchemical conception of one of the stages of the
coniunctio. Here the 'king' and 'queen', who may be taken as Sol
and his sister Luna, appear as symbols of the primordial psychic
opposites, masculine and feminine. Their 'marriage' is meant
primarily in the spiritual sense, as is made clear not only by the
words of the middle band: *spiritus est qui vivificat,* but also by the
dove as symbol of the spirit and (according to the ancients) of
amor coniugalis. The primordial opposites confront one another in

continued

Plate 19 *continued*

their naked, unfalsified truth and essence, without conventional covering; the difference between them is evident and 'essential'; it can be bridged in fruitful union only through the intermediary of the spirit symbol, the dove, the 'unifier' which intervenes from 'above'. The branches held to form a cross, the *flores mercurii*, and the flower hanging down from the dove's beak—all these symbols of the process of growth illustrate the common effort of man and woman in the living work of the *coniunctio*. (From *Rosarium Philosophorum, Secunda pars Alchemiae de Lapide Philosophico*, Frankfurt, 1550, first edition, from the collection of Dr. C. A. Meier.)

nature which make the symbol the most faithful expression of the psychic totality, and which enable it not only to represent but also to influence the most antithetical and complex psychic situations.

'Whether or not something is a symbol,' says Jung, 'depends primarily on the attitude of the consciousness that contemplates it.'[1] The question is whether the individual has the aptitude or the right momentary disposition to perceive an object, a tree for example, not merely as a concrete phenomenon but also as a symbol for something more or less unknown and vitally meaningful, a symbol of human life. It is perfectly possible that the same fact or object will represent a symbol for one man and a mere sign for another. But in Jung's opinion there are certain objects or forms that impose themselves as symbols on every beholder, one of them being a triangle enclosing an eye. Yet by and large it is the individual's type which determines whether he will see facts as nothing more than facts or approach them with a feeling for the symbolical.

The symbol is not an allegory and not a sign, but an image of a content that largely transcends consciousness. Yet symbols can 'degenerate' into signs and become 'dead symbols' when the meaning hidden within them is fully revealed, when it loses its richness of implication because its whole content has been made accessible to reason. For an authentic symbol can never be fully explained. We can open up the rational part of it to our consciousness, but the irrational part can only be 'brought home to our feeling'. For this reason a symbol always addresses the whole psyche, its conscious and unconscious parts and all its functions as well. That is why Jung insists so emphatically that his patients should not only frame their 'inner images' in speech or writing, but also reproduce them just as they originally appeared. In this connection he attaches as much importance to colour and design as to what the images represent.[2] This method

---

[1] Cf. *Types*, par. 818.

[2] The correlation of the colours with the diverse functions varies according to the different cultures, groups, and even individuals. But as a rule (to which there are numerous exceptions) for the psychology of the European, blue, the colour of the empty air, of the clear sky, is the colour of thought; yellow, the colour of the sun which brings the light out of the unfathomable darkness and vanishes again into the darkness, is that of intuition, the function which, as though by sudden illumination, apprehends the origins and

enables the therapist to appreciate their full significance for the patient and to utilize them as the most important factor in his progress toward conscious realization (*Bewusstwerdung*).[1]

PICTORIAL EXPRESSIONS

Plate 1 may serve as an example. It is the 'inwardly perceived' symbolic representation of a psyche which, torn between its four psychic functions, strives toward conscious realization but is held prisoner in the circle of snakes, symbols of the primordial instincts. The four functions are symbolized by the four colours—blue, yellow, red, green—of the circle of rays, while the striving toward conscious realization is symbolized by the four burning torches.

This explanation, like that of the following pictures, should not be taken literally. It is only a rough attempt to put into words the feelings and thoughts of the individual whose unconscious expressed them in images. All these images are symbols and nothing more, and it is the very essence of the symbol that its content can never be fully rationalized and set down in words. A vital part defies discursive formulation and can only be apprehended by intuition, and this is true even where a gifted artist succeeds in framing such symbols in 'word images'. The present explanations are intended solely to give the reader a sort of introduction to the 'intermediate realm of subtle realities' which speaks to us in symbols.

A second example of the expressive character of such images is provided in Plate 2. In the course of the psychic process, the 'snake of passion', symbol of the undifferentiated instinct world in man, has emerged from the chest floating on the ocean of the unconscious, in which it had hitherto been rigorously enclosed by repression, and risen above it. A sheaf of glowing, searing rays of fire issues from its gullet, but its head is marked with the cross of redemption, so symbolizing its twofold aspect as a power of destruction and of healing. The saturation and force of

---

tendencies of things; red, the colour of the throbbing blood and of fire, is that of the burning, surging emotions; while green, the colour of earthly, tangible, directly perceptible vegetation, represents the function of sensation.

[1] See footnote 2, p. 46.

the colours indicate the intense emotion which produced the picture and which it released in the patient.

In considering such pictures we should think, not 'of art, but of something more and other than mere art, namely the living effect upon the patient himself',[1] that is, the producer of the picture, whether he be sick or healthy. It makes no difference whether such a picture is good or bad from an artistic standpoint. For in this portraiture of the unconscious a skilled artist has been known to draw or paint as awkwardly as a child and to turn out pictures which as representations are poorer than those of a patient who has never held a pencil or brush but whose inner images are so intense that he is able to 'reproduce' them completely.[2] For what he is depicting are his 'active fantasies—that which is active within him. And that which is active within him is himself, but no longer in the guise of his previous error, when he mistook the personal ego for the self; it is himself in a new and hitherto alien sense, for his ego now appears as the *object of that which works within him*.'[3]

'The mere execution of the pictures,' Jung goes on, 'is not enough. Over and above that, an intellectual and emotional understanding is needed; they require to be not only rationally integrated with the conscious mind, but morally assimilated. They still have to be subjected to a work of synthetic interpretation. Although I have travelled this path with individual patients many times, I have never yet succeeded in making all the details of the process clear enough for publication. . . . The truth is, we are here moving in absolutely new territory, and a ripening of experience is the first requisite. . . . We are dealing with a process of psychic life outside consciousness, and our observation of it is indirect. As yet we do not know to what depths our vision will plumb.'[4] But anyone who in profound mental anguish has succeeded in expressing, in capturing and holding fast, an inward image that it seemed impossible to frame in words knows what a wonderful sense of liberation this can provide. In the course of an analysis persons who had never taken up pencil or brush have achieved a remarkable skill in

---

[1] 'The Aims of Psychotherapy', p. 48.

[2] In such a case the dissociation between the conscious work of the painter and the images that he brings up from the unconscious is obvious.

[3] 'The Aims of Psychotherapy', p. 49.   [4] Ibid., p. 51.

portraying psychic contents that could not be expressed in words, sharing in a measure the ecstasy of the artist who consciously fixates and gives form to an image he has raised up from the depths of his unconscious.

Such fixation of a symbol is a kind of objectivization; it lends form to what is otherwise indeterminate and inexpressible and enables one, up to a certain point, to penetrate to its true meaning, to understand it, and, by drawing or painting it, to assimilate it into one's consciousness. Thus fixated, the symbol possesses a kind of magic power, which indeed is the psychological foundation of most of the magical objects, amulets, and omens of former times, and of the equally magic formulas, slogans, and images that still bewitch us today, though their magic quality is seldom recognized. In this category we may also include emblems, banners, heraldic devices, and trademarks, with their often magical form and colour symbolism and their appeal to the masses. Such 'magic' plays a significant role even in the worlds of politics and business today (ultramodern advertising techniques based on it have been perfected with the help of so-called 'motivational research').

BASIC PRINCIPLES OF THE ANALYSIS

Thus we may say that the analytical situation has a fourfold aspect: (1) the analysand describes his conscious situation in words; (2) the dreams or fantasies of the analysand give the psychotherapist a supplemental picture from the unconscious; (3) the relation between the analysand and the psychotherapist adds an objective side to the other two, subjective, sides; (4) elaboration of the material provided by 1, 2, and 3 and by the therapist's amplifications and clarifications round out the picture of the psychic situation, which usually contrasts sharply with the standpoint of the ego personality, so leading to all sorts of intellectual and emotional reactions and problems which press for an answer and solution.

With Freud and Adler, Jung believes that to raise the conflicts to consciousness and maintain them in consciousness is the *sine qua non* of therapeutic success. In the main, however, he does not carry the conflicts back to a single instinctual factor but attributes them to a disturbance in the harmony of the total psyche: that is to say, an imbalance between the conscious and unconscious, the personal and the collective factors which taken together make up our psychic totality. Another fundamental difference is that Jung tries to solve most conflicts on the basis of their *present* meaning and not of their significance at the time of their origin, regardless of whether it is recent or far in the past. For in his opinion every life situation and every age level demands its own solutions; the significance of one and the same conflict varies with the actual situation though the origin· of course remains the same. A man of fifty will have to solve his parent complex in an entirely different way from a man of twenty, though in both the conflict may be rooted in the same childhood experience.

Jung's method is *finalistic*, his eyes are always turned toward the totality of the psyche, so that the most limited conflict is seen in terms of the whole. And within the psychic totality the unconscious is not merely a cesspool for the repressed contents of consciousness; it is also the 'ever-creative mother of consciousness'.[1] It is not, as Adler calls it, a 'trick of the psyche', but on the contrary, it is the primary and creative factor in man, the never failing source of all art and all human endeavour.

This view of the unconscious and its archetypal forms as symbolic images of the 'union of opposites' enables Jung to approach the interpretation of dream contents both from a reductive and a prospective, constructive standpoint, for he 'is concerned not only with the sources or basic materials of the unconscious product, but tries to find a generally comprehensible expression for the symbolic end result. The free associations to the unconscious product are thus evaluated with respect to where their goal lies and not with respect to their origin. . . . This method takes its departure from the unconscious product as from a symbolic expression representing a piece of psychological development in anticipatory form.[2] Thus it was inevitable that Freud, for whom the unconscious was limited to the data of 'individual biography', should regard symbols as nothing more than signs or allegories, whose purpose it was to conceal something else. Whereas Jung, by viewing symbols as expressions of the paradoxical 'double face', looking both for-

---

[1] 'Education', p. 115.   [2] Cf. *Types*, par. 702.

ward and backward, of the 'either *and* or' that characterizes all psychic activity, was able for the first time to devise an analysis of the psyche which is not merely—like Freudian analysis—designed to normalize the psychic process by removing blocks, but which also strives by consciously promoting the formation of symbols and exploring their meanings, to enrich the psyche with seeds of growth and so open up a source of energy that will play a creative role in the future life of the patient.

ON THE MEANING OF NEUROSIS

This approach enables Jung to regard neurosis not only as a negative factor, a troublesome disorder, but also as a positive, salutary force that can contribute to the formation of personality. For whether we are compelled to recognize our shallowness through awareness of our attitude or function type, or whether we are obliged to compensate our overdeveloped consciousness by drawing on the depths of the unconscious, the process always involves a *broadening and deepening of our consciousness*,[1] in other words, a broadening of our personality. Thus a neurosis can serve as a warning issued by a higher authority, a reminder that our personality is urgently in need of broadening and that this can be accomplished only if we deal correctly with our neurosis. Jungian guidance helps the neurotic out of his isolation by fostering a confrontation with the unconscious and so activating within him the archetypes which stir 'that faraway background . . . of the human mind . . . inherited from the dim ages of the past. If this supra-individual psyche exists,' Jung goes on, 'everything that is translated into its picture-language will be depersonalized, and if this becomes conscious will appear to us *sub specie aeternitatis*. Not my sorrow, but the sorrow of the world; not a personal isolating pain, but a pain without bitterness that unites all humanity. The healing effect of this needs no proof.'[2]

Jung would not by any means deny that there are also neuroses of traumatic origin, based essentially on childhood experiences, and that these must be treated accordingly, that is, according to Freudian principles. In many cases he employs

[1] See footnote 2, p. 46.
[2] The Structure of the Psyche', pp. 149 f. (slightly modified).

this method, which is particularly suited to neuroses of young people which spring from traumatic causes. But he emphatically denies that all neuroses are of this type and that all can be treated in this way. 'As soon as we speak of the collective unconscious,' he writes, 'we find ourselves . . . concerned with a problem which is altogether precluded in the practical analysis of young people or of those who have remained infantile too long. Wherever the father and mother imagos have still to be overcome, wherever there is a little bit of life still to be conquered which is the natural possession of the average man, then we had better make no mention of the collective unconscious and the problem of opposites. But once the parental transferences and the youthful illusions have been mastered, or are at least ripe for mastery, then we must speak of these things. We are here outside the range of Freudian and Adlerian reductions; we are no longer concerned with how to remove the obstacles to a man's profession, or to his marriage, or to anything that means a widening of his life, but are confronted with the task of finding a meaning that will enable him to continue living at all—a meaning more than blank resignation and mournful retrospect.'[1] Accordingly, we usually employ a reductive method in cases involving illusions, fictions, and exaggerations. On the other hand, a constructive method is advisable in cases where the conscious attitude is relatively normal but susceptible of greater completeness and refinement, or where promising unconscious tendencies are misunderstood and repressed by consciousness. 'The reductive standpoint . . . always leads back to the primitive and elementary. The constructive standpoint, on the other

[1] 'The Psychology of the Unconscious', par. 113. In his 'Commentary on the *Tibetan Book of the Dead*' (1935) Jung shows very impressively how aware the Tibetans seemed to be that personal as well as suprapersonal realms are contained in the human psyche. If as Westerners we interpret the dead man's path to a new incarnation (as seen by the Tibetans) as a process of psychic growth to be travelled during our lifetime, it leads through three main realms. The first represents the land of the personal unconscious, which is a kind of gateway leading to the second realm, that of the collective images, of the numinously charged, suprapersonal figures of the archetypes (the 'blood-drinking demons' as they are called in the Tibetan funeral ritual). After passing through this realm, or confronting its 'inhabitants', the psyche comes to the 'place' where the opposites are transcended and peace is achieved, where reigns exclusively the central 'power', the self, the ordering authority which embraces and enhances all psychic processes.

hand, tries to synthesize, to build up, to direct one's gaze forward.'[1]

The causes of a neurosis, particularly at a more advanced age, may be entirely contained in the actual situation. In youth an unconsolidated, undeveloped ego-consciousness is quite natural, and at the onset of manhood a one-sided preponderance of consciousness is an actual necessity. But if both these forms persist into advanced age they can produce neuroses. An individual may be unable to adapt to his situation because he has not yet achieved a 'natural' bond with his instincts, his unconscious, or else has lost it. Sometimes the roots of this state of affairs are to be sought in childhood, but sometimes they reside wholly in the actual situation. In this case the images and symbols which rise up to broaden the psyche and further the psychic process should be considered from the prospective, finalistic view, which starting from the actual situation sets out to create a new equilibrium in the patient's psyche.

THE 'PROSPECTIVE' ASPECT

Neurosis tends toward something positive; this is the cornerstone of Jung's view. It is not just an ailment for its own sake as it may sometimes appear. For 'thanks to the neurosis contrived by the unconscious, [people] are shaken out of their apathy, and this in spite of their own laziness and often desperate resistance'. In the course of the years neurosis may result from the energy dammed up by the one-sidedness of consciousness as well as from a state of unconsciousness poorly adapted to the demands of the environment. However, relatively few individuals succumb to neurosis, though the number is on the rise, especially among so-called intellectuals; particularly in the years before World War II the figure assumed terrifying proportions. 'The few who are smitten by such a fate,' says Jung, 'are really persons of the "higher" type who, for one reason or another, have remained too long on a primitive level,' no doubt because, under the pressure of the mechanized outside world, they could no longer do justice to the claims of the inner realities. But it should not be supposed that there is any 'plan' of the unconscious behind all this. 'A perfectly understandable urge toward self-realization

[1] 'Education', p. 105.

would provide a quite satisfactory explanation. We could also speak of a retarded maturation of the personality.'[1]

Thus under certain circumstances a neurosis can touch off the struggle for the wholeness of the personality, which for Jung is at once a task, a goal, and the highest good to which man can attain on earth, a goal quite independent of all medico-thera-peutic considerations.

In order to cure a neurosis or a general disturbance of the psychic balance, we must activate certain contents of the uncon-scious and assimilate them to consciousness. For the more the unconscious is repressed, the more it threatens the psychic balance as one grows older. By assimilation or integration we mean not an evaluation of conscious and unconscious contents, but an interchange in which both sides are shaped into a coherent psychic totality. Above all, no essential values of the conscious personality, that is, the ego, must be impaired, for if this happens, there is no one left to do the integrating. For 'unconscious compensation is only effective when it co-operates with an integral consciousness'.[2] A practising analyst must 'believe implicitly in the significance and value of conscious realization, whereby hitherto unconscious parts of the per-sonality are brought to light and subjected to conscious discri-mination and criticism. It is a process that requires the patient to face his problems and that taxes his powers of conscious judgement and decision. It is nothing less than a direct challenge to his ethical sense, a call to arms that must be answered by the whole personality.'[3]

THE DEVELOPMENT OF THE PERSONALITY

Wholeness of the personality is achieved when the main pairs of opposites are relatively differentiated, that is, when both parts of the total psyche, consciousness and the unconscious, are linked together in a living relation. But the dynamic gradient, the flow of psychic life, is not endangered, for the unconscious can never be made wholly conscious and always has the greater store of energy. The wholeness is always relative and *gives us something to work on as long as we live*. 'Personality, as the complete

[1] 'Relations', par. 291.
[2] 'Dream Analysis', par. 338.
[3] Ibid., par. 315.

realization of our whole being, is an unattainable ideal. But unattainability is no argument against the ideal, for ideals are only signposts, never the goal.'[1]

The development of the personality is at once a blessing and a curse. We must pay dearly for it and the price is isolation and loneliness. 'Its first fruit is the conscious and unavoidable segregation of the single individual from the undifferentiated and unconscious herd.' But to stand alone is not enough, above all one must be faithful to one's own law: 'Only the man who can consciously assent to the power of the inner voice becomes a personality.'[2] And only a personality can find a proper place in the collectivity; only personalitities have the power to create a community, that is, to become integral parts of a human group and not merely a number in the mass. For the mass is only a sum of individuals and can never, like a community, become a living organism that receives and bestows life. Thus self-realization, both in the individual and in the extrapersonal, collective sense, becomes a moral decision, and it is this moral decision which lends force to the process of self-fulfilment that Jung calls INDIVIDUATION.

Self-scrutiny and self-fulfilment are therefore—or rather they should be!—the absolute prerequisite for the assumption of any higher obligation, even of the obligation to lend the best possible form and the greatest possible scope to the fulfilment of one's own individual life, as nature always does, though without the responsibility which is the divine burden of man. 'Individuation means becoming a single, homogeneous being, and, in so far as "individuality" embraces our innermost, last, and incomparable uniqueness, it also implies becoming one's *own self*.'[3] But individuation is far from meaning individualism in the narrow, egocentric sense, for all that individuation does is to make a man the individual that he really is. By individuation he does not become 'selfish'; he fulfils his individual nature, which is something very different and must not be confused with egoism or individualism. He becomes not only an individual but also a member of a collectivity, and the wholeness he has achieved is in contact, through consciousness and the uncon-

---

[1] 'The Development of Personality', par. 291.
[2] Ibid., pars. 294, 308.
[3] 'Relations', par. 266.

scious, with the whole world. The accent is not on his supposed individuality as opposed to his collective obligations but, as stated above, on the fulfilment of his own nature as it is related to the whole. For 'an actual conflict with the collective norm takes place only when an individual way is raised to a norm, which is the real aim of extreme individualism'.[1]

THE INDIVIDUATION PROCESS

Taken as a whole, individuation is a spontaneous, natural process within the psyche; it is potentially present in every man, although most men are unaware of it. Unless it is inhibited, obstructed, or distorted by some specific disturbance, it is a process of maturation or unfolding, the psychic parallel to the physical process of growth and aging. Under certain circumstances, in practical psychotherapy for example, it can in one way or another be stimulated, intensified, made conscious, consciously experienced, and elaborated; the individual can thus be helped to 'complete' or 'round out' his personality. In such cases it requires an intensive analytical effort, a conscious and absolutely honest concentration on the intraphysic process. By activating the contents of the unconscious, such an effort eases the tension between the pairs of opposites and makes possible a living knowledge of their structure. Leading through all the hazards of a psyche thrown off balance, cutting through layer after layer, it finally penetrates to the centre that is the source and ultimate foundation of our psychic being, to the SELF.[2]

This path, as we have said above, is not advisable for all men, nor is it open to all. It is not without its perils, and the strictest control by the partner or therapist and by the patient's own consciousness as well is needed to safeguard the ego against the violently irrupting contents of the unconscious and to integrate these contents into the psychic totality in a manner consonant with the end in view. Consequently it takes two to undertake this journey. Whatever may be accomplished in other parts of the world under entirely different circumstances, any attempt to travel it alone is extremely dangerous, particularly for an Occidental, and success is more than doubtful.

Exclusive self-reliance makes for spiritual pride, sterile

[1] Cf. *Types*, par. 761.
[2] Cf. p. 126 and Jolande Jacobi, *The Way to Individuation* (1967).

brooding, and isolation within one's own ego. Man needs an opposite to concretize his experience. Without the presence of someone other and different, question and answer merge into a formless mass. This is one of the reasons why the confessional with its 'dialogue' between believer and priest is so wise an institution, though for the practising Catholic the Church has other instrumentalities that reach far deeper. But for the many who do not attend confession and for the unbeliever to whom it is not available, work with a psychotherapist provides a useful expedient. The difference, to be sure, is considerable, for the therapist is not a priest or an absolute moral authority, speaking in the name of a higher power, and should not set himself up as one; he is at most a trusted individual with a certain experience of life and a specialized knowledge of the nature and laws of the human psyche. 'He does not admonish to penitence except in so far as the patient himself does so; he does not mete out penance, except in so far as the patient—which to be sure is most often the case—has got himself into a frightful mess; and he gives no absolution, unless God proves indulgent.'[1] The 'wholeness', the fulfilment of the analysand's potential personality which is the aim of the process, should develop naturally, but the psychotherapist may lend a helping hand. If, however, the personality does not grow spontaneously, no one can conjure it up by an act of will.

In its broad outlines the individuation process is inherent in man and follows regular patterns. It falls into two main, independent parts, characterized by contrasting and complementary qualitities. These parts are the first and the second halves of life. The task of the first half is 'initiation into outward reality'. Through consolidation of the ego, differentiation of the main function and of the dominant attitude type, and development of an appropriate persona, it aims at the adaptation of the individual to the demands of his environment. The task of the second half is a so-called 'initiation into the inner reality', a deeper self-knowledge and knowledge of humanity, a 'turning back' (*reflectio*) to the traits of one's nature that have hitherto remained unconscious or become so. By raising these traits to consciousness the individual achieves an inward and outward

[1] From an interview with C. G. Jung, 'Depth Psychology and Self-knowledge', originally in the journal *Du*, September 1943; in C.W. 18.

bond with the world and the cosmic order. Jung has devoted the greater part of his effort to the second half of the process and has offered persons in their middle years the possibility of attaining a broader personality that may be regarded as a preparation for death. When he speaks of the 'individuation process', it is this latter part that he has primarily in mind.

Signposts and milestones in such an individuation process as observed and described by Jung are provided by certain archetypal symbols, whose form and manifestation vary with the individual. Here too the personal factor is decisive. For 'the method . . . is only the way and direction laid down by a man in order that his action may be the true expression of his nature'.[1]

To describe these symbols in all their many forms would require a thorough knowledge of every conceivable mythology and order of symbolism throughout human history. Without that they cannot be described and explained in detail. In the following therefore we shall have to content ourselves with a brief sketch, in which we shall cite only those symbolic figures and forms which are characteristic for the principal stages of the process. In addition to these, of course, many other archetypal images and symbols appear, some of which illustrate secondary problems and some of which represent variants of the main figures.

THE SHADOW

The first stage leads to the experience of the SHADOW, symbolizing our 'other side', our 'dark brother', who is an invisible but inseparable part of our psychic totality. For 'the living form needs deep shadow if it is to appear plastic. Without shadow it remains a two-dimensional phantom.'[2]

The shadow is an archetypal figure which among primitive peoples still makes its appearance in a wide range of personifications. It is a part of the individual, a split-off portion of his being which nevertheless remains attached to him 'like his shadow'. Accordingly, it is a 'bad omen' to a primitive man when someone steps on his shadow, and the damage can only be repaired by a set of magic ceremonies. The shadow-figure is also a

---

[1] Cf. *Golden Flower*, par. 3.   [2] 'Relations', par. 400.

frequent theme in art. For in his creative activity and choice of themes the artist draws very largely on the depths of his unconscious; with his creations he in turn stirs the unconscious of his audience, and this is the ultimate secret of his effectiveness. The images and figures of the unconscious rise up in him and carry their powerful message to other men, although these do not know the source of their 'rapture'. Shakespeare's Caliban, Mrs. Shelley's *Frankenstein*, Oscar Wilde's *The Fisherman and His Soul*, Stevenson's Mr. Hyde, Chamisso's *Peter Schlemihl*, Hermann Hesse's *Steppenwolf*, Aldous Huxley's *Grey Eminence*, not to mention Mephisto, Faust's dark tempter, are examples of the artistic use of this motif.

Encounter with the shadow often coincides with the individual's conscious realization of the functional and attitudinal type to which he belongs. The undifferentiated function and underdeveloped attitude type are our 'dark side', the inborn collective predisposition which we reject for ethical, aesthetic, or other reasons, and repress because it is in opposition to our conscious principles. For as long as an individual has differentiated only his main function and apprehends outward and inward reality almost exclusively with this side of his psyche, his other three functions remain inevitably in the darkness or 'shadow', from which they must be reclaimed, as it were, piece by piece— disengaged from their contamination with the various figures of the unconscious. The development of the shadow runs parallel to that of the ego; qualitities which the ego does not need or cannot make use of are set aside or repressed, and thus they play little or no part in the conscious life of the individual. Accordingly, a child has no real shadow, but his shadow becomes more pronounced as his ego gains in stability and range. And because in the course of our lives we are constantly having to inhibit or repress one quality or another, the shadow can never be fully raised to consciousness. Nevertheless it is important that at least its most salient traits should be made conscious and correlated with the ego, which thereby gains in strength and vigour and comes to feel more firmly anchored in our nature.

Despite the shift of accent, the resolution of the shadow is closely related to what the psychoanalysts try to accomplish by unearthing biographical data, particularly those of childhood. Consequently Jung has largely retained the Freudian principles in dealing with the shadow qualities of persons in the first half of life, for in their case it usually suffices for purposes of treatment to raise these qualities to consciousness.

The shadow may be manifested in an inward, symbolic figure or in a concrete figure from the outside world. In the first case it is embodied in the material of the unconscious, perhaps as a dream figure personifying one or more of the dreamer's psychic qualities; in the second case, we project one or more of our latent unconscious traits upon someone in our environment who is suited to this role by certain structural qualities. It is in ourselves that we most frequently and readily perceive shadow qualitities, provided we are willing to acknowledge them as belonging to ourselves; for example, when an outburst of rage comes over us, when suddenly we begin to curse or behave crudely, when quite against our will we act antisocially, when we are stingy, petty, or choleric, cowardly, frivolous, or hypocritical, so displaying qualities which under ordinary circumstances we carefully hide or repress and of whose existence we ourselves are unaware. When the emergence of such traits of character can no longer be overlooked, we ask ourselves in amazement: how was it possible? Is it really true that things like this are me?

Jung distinguishes between two different forms of the shadow, although he uses the same term for both. The first form is that of the 'personal shadow', containing psychic features of the individual which are unlived from the beginning of his life or only scarcely lived. The second is the 'collective shadow'. It belongs together with the other figures of the collective unconscious and corresponds to a negative expression of the 'Old Wise Man' or the dark aspect of the Self. It symbolizes, as it were, the 'back' of the prevailing *Zeitgeist*, its hidden antithesis. Both forms of the shadow are operative in the human psyche.

Whether the manifestation is of a personal or collective nature depends on whether the shadow pertains to the realm of the ego and the personal unconscious or to that of the collective unconscious. Thus it may appear to us as a figure from our sphere of consciousness, as our elder brother or sister, our best friend, or, for example, as that person who represents our opposite, such as Faust's famulus, Wagner, or—when the projected contents spring from the collective unconscious—it may appear in mythical form, for example, as Mephistopheles, a faun, Hagen, Loki, etc.[1] Consequently it may equally well appear as a twin brother or a close friend or as a figure from a work of art, e.g. Virgil in the Divine Comedy, who accompanies Dante to Hell as his faithful friend. 'Ego and shadow' is a well-known archetypal motif. As examples we may cite Gilgamesh and Enkidu, Castor and Pollux, Cain and Abel, etc.

But paradoxical as it may seem at first sight, the shadow as 'alter ego' may also be represented by a positive figure, for example, when the individual whose 'other side' it personifies is living 'below his level', failing to fulfil his potentialities, for then it is his positive qualities that lead a dark shadow existence (Plate 3). In its individual aspect the shadow stands for the 'personal darkness', personifying the contents (sometimes positive) of our psyche that have been rejected and repressed or less lived in the course of our conscious existence; in its collective aspect, is stands for the universally human dark side within us, for the tendency toward the dark and inferior that is inherent in every man. In analysis we encounter the shadow primarily in figures belonging to the realm of the personal unconscious; for this reason we must always start by interpreting the purely personal aspect, and only then turn to the collective aspect.

The shadow stands, as it were, on the threshold of the realm of the 'Mothers', the unconscious. It is the counterpart of our conscious ego, growing and crystallizing in pace with it. This dark mass of experience that is seldom or never admitted to our conscious lives bars the way to the creative depths of our unconscious. That is why persons who strive convulsively, with a frightening effort of the will that is far beyond their strength, to remain 'on the peak', who can admit their weaknesses neither to themselves nor to others, often succumb, sometimes suddenly, sometimes gradually, to a deep-seated sterility. The spiritual and moral tower they live in is not a natural growth but an artificial scaffolding erected and sustained by force, hence in danger of collapsing under the slightest weight. Such persons find it difficult or impossible to face up to the inner truth, to enter into a genuine relationship, to do any really vital work; and as more and more repressions accumulate in their shadow,

[1] What we have said above about the 'archetype of the feminine' is equally applicable here (cf. p. 95).

they become increasingly entangled in neurosis. In youth the shadow stratum is relatively thin and easy to bear; but as life goes on and more and more material collects, it becomes a serious and often unsupportable burden.

'Everyone carries a shadow,' says Jung, 'and the less it is embodied in the individual's conscious life, the blacker and denser it is. . . . If the repressed tendencies, the shadow as I call them, were obviously evil, there would be no problem whatever. But the shadow is merely somewhat inferior, primitive unadapted, and awkward; not wholly bad. It even contains childish or primitive qualities which would in a way vitalize and embellish human existence.' The individual runs up against prejudice, custom and all sorts of considerations of respectability and prestige which, because they are closely connected with the problem of the persona, can often play a disastrous role and block all psychic development. 'Mere suppression of the shadow is as little of a remedy as beheading would be for headache. . . . If an inferiority is conscious, one always has a chance to correct it. Furthermore, it is constantly in contact with other interests, so that it is continually subjected to modifications. But if it is repressed and isolated from consciousness, it never gets corrected.'[1]

To confront the shadow thus means to take a mercilessly critical attitude towards one's own nature. But like everything of which we are unconscious, the shadow is experienced in projection upon an object outside us. That is why the 'other fellow is always to blame' as long as we are not aware that the darkness is in ourselves. For this reason, the exposure of the shadow in analysis usually encounters great resistance; frequently the analysand cannot bring himself to accept all this darkness as a part of himself, fearing that the painstakingly erected and maintained edifice of his conscious ego will collapse under the weight of this insight.[2] And indeed many analyses fail at this stage; unable to confront the contents of his unconscious, the analysand breaks off in the middle and crawls back into the shelter of his illusions or neurosis. An outsider should bear all this

---

[1] 'Religion', pp. 76–78.

[2] The primary importance Jung attaches to making the shadow conscious is one of the principal, though often unconscious, reasons why so many persons are afraid to undergo a Jungian analysis.

in mind when passing judgement on an 'unsuccessful analysis'.

Bitter as the cup may be, no one can be spared it. For only when we have learned to distinguish ourselves from our shadow by recognizing its reality as a part of our nature, and only if we keep this insight persistently in mind, can our confrontation with the other pairs of psychic opposites be successful. For this is the beginning of the objective attitude toward our own personality without which no progress can be made along the path of wholeness. 'If you imagine someone who is brave enough to withdraw all[1] these projections,' writes Jung, 'then you get an individual who is conscious of a considerable shadow. Such a man has saddled himself with new problems and conflicts. He has become a serious problem to himself, as he is now unable to say that *they* do this or that, *they* are wrong, and *they* must be fought against. . . . Such a man knows that whatever is wrong in the world is in himself, and if he only learns to deal with his own shadow he has done something real for the world. He has succeeded in shouldering at least an infinitesimal part of the gigantic, unsolved social problems of our day.'[2]

ANIMUS AND ANIMA

The second stage of the individuation process is characterized by the encounter with the 'soul-image', which in the man Jung calls the ANIMA and in the woman, the ANIMUS. The archetypal figure of the soul-image always stands for the complementary, contrasexual part of the psyche, reflecting both our personal relation to it and the individual human experience of the contrasexual. It represents the image of the other sex that we carry in us as individuals and also as members of the species. Every man has his own Eve within him, says a German proverb. As we have said, the latent, undifferentiated, still unconscious contents of the psyche are always projected, and this applies to the man's Eve as well as the woman's Adam. Just as we experience our

---

[1] The word 'all' in this quotation should not be taken literally, for *all* projections can never be made conscious and withdrawn; if this were possible, nothing would be left behind in the unconscious. Thus it always depends on the psychic situation of the individual what share of his projections he can deal with and in what measure.

[2] 'Religion', p. 83.

own shadow through someone else, so also do we experience our basic contrasexual components through another. We choose, we become attached to, someone who represents the qualities of our own psyche.

Here again, as in dealing with the shadow and all unconscious contents, we must distinguish between an inner and an outward manifestation. We encounter the inner form of animus or anima in our dreams, fantasies, visions, and other expressions of the unconscious when they disclose contrasexual traits of our own psyche;[1] we are dealing with the outward form when we project a part or the whole of our unconscious psyche upon someone in our environment and fail to realize that this other person who confronts us is in a way our own inner self.

The soul-image is a more or less solidly constituted functional complex, and inability to differentiate oneself from it leads to such phenomena as the moody man, dominated by feminine drives, buffeted by emotions, or the animus-possessed woman, opinionated and argumentative, the female know-it-all, who reacts in a masculine way and not instinctively.[2] 'Sometimes an alien will makes itself felt within us, which does the opposite of what we want and what we approve of. What this other will does is not necessarily evil; it can also desire the good, and then we feel it to be a higher source of guidance or inspiration, a tutelary spirit similar to the Socratic daemonion.'[3] In such cases we have the impression that another, strange person has 'taken possession' of an individual, that 'an alien spirit has got into him'. We see the man who blindly succumbs to a certain type of woman— how frequently a highly cultivated intellectual, for example, will become hopelessly entangled with the worst sort of strumpet because his feminine, emotional side is utterly undifferentiated; and equally familiar is the woman who for no apparent reason ties herself to a swindler or adventurer. The character of our soul-image, the anima or animus of our dreams, is a natural

[1] Although there is no absolute, scientific definition of what constitutes a 'masculine' or 'feminine' trait, we do possess generally accepted ideas on the subject, based on our cultural tradition, which perhaps goes back to the simple biological qualities of the sex cells.

[2] Cf. T. Wolff, *Studien*, pp. 155 ff.

[3] Emma Jung, 'Ein Beitrag zum Problem des Animus', p. 297.

index to our internal psychological situation. The seeker after self-knowledge will do well to accord it the utmost attention.

The variety of forms in which the soul-image may appear is well-nigh inexhaustible. It is seldom unequivocal, almost always complex and ambiguous; the traits belonging to it must be typical of one or the other sex, but otherwise may embody all sorts of contradictions. The anima can equally well take the form of a sweet young maiden, a goddess, a witch, an angel, a demon, a beggar woman, a whore, a devoted companion, an amazon, etc. Highly characteristic anima figures, for example, are Kundry in the Parsifal legend, or Andromeda in the myth of Perseus; typical anima figures in literature are Helen of Troy in the Homeric legend, Beatrice in the *Divine Comedy*, Don Quixote's Dulcinea, etc. The animus can also assume a variety of forms. Typical animus figures might be Dionysus, the Pied Piper, the Flying Dutchman, and on a lower, more primitive plane a famous film star or boxing champion, or in particularly troubled times like ours, an outstanding political or military leader. But the animus and anima can also be symbolized by animals and even by objects of a specifically masculine or feminine character, particularly when the animus or anima has not yet reached the level of the human figure and appears in purely instinctual form. Thus the anima may take the form of a cow, a cat, a tiger, a ship, a cave, etc., and the animus may appear as an eagle, a bull, a lion, a lance, a tower, or as some kind of phallic shape.

Plate 4 represents a mountain rising out of the collective unconscious, symbolizing a newly attained, higher, and more solid situation of consciousness, the birth of a 'new world'. We find parallels to this figure in numerous cosmologies, mythological images, and religious conceptions (e.g., the 'mountain of the adepts' in alchemical symbolism and Mount Meru in Hindu mythology). The sun as symbol of consciousness forms the peak of the mountain but is organically embedded in it; the sun has captured the over-bold, high-soaring eagle, symbol of the animus, the ambitious feminine intellect, which suffers and bleeds. Earth and water are fertilized with the blood, and life puts forth its green shoots.

'The first bearer of the soul-image,' says Jung, 'is always the mother; later it is borne by those women who arouse the man's feelings, whether in a positive or a negative sense.' The detachment from the mother is one of the most important and most delicate problems in the development of the personality, particularly for the male. To help in this process, primitive peoples possess a wide range of ceremonies, initiations to manhood, rites of rebirth, etc., in which the initiand receives instruction intended to wean him from his mother's tutelage. Only after such a course of instruction can he be recognized as an adult in his tribe. The European, however, must make the 'acquaintance' of his contrasexual component by raising this part of his own psyche to consciousness. If the figure of the soul-image, the contrasexual element in our own psyche, has sunk so deep into the unconscious, if accordingly it plays so crucial and often disastrous a role in Western man, our patriarchally oriented culture is largely to blame. For 'a man counts it a virtue to repress his feminine traits as much as possible, just as a woman, at least until recently, considered it unbecoming to be "mannish". The repression of feminine traits and inclinations naturally causes these contrasexual demands to accumulate in the unconscious. No less naturally, the imago of woman (the soul-image) becomes a receptacle for these demands, which is why a man, in his love choice, is strongly tempted to win the woman who best corresponds to his own unconscious femininity—a woman, in short, who can unhesitantly receive the projection of his soul. Although such a choice is often regarded and felt as altogether ideal, it may turn out that the man has manifestly married his own worst weakness.'[1] And the same may be said of the woman.[2]

For in consequence of the patriarchally oriented development of our Western culture, the woman too tends to think that the masculine as such is more valuable than the feminine, and this attitude does much to increase the power of the animus. Birth control, the reduction of household duties through modern techniques and appliances, and an unquestionable increase in the intellectual aptitudes of the modern woman, are other contributory factors. But just as the male by his very nature is uncertain in the realm of Eros, so the woman will always be

---

[1] 'Relations', pars. 315, 297.
[2] See also Jung's essay 'Psychological Aspects of the Mother Archetype'.

insecure in the realm of Logos. 'What woman has to overcome in respect to the animus is not pride but inertia and lack of self-confidence.'[1]

Both the animus and the anima have two basic forms: light or dark, 'upper' or 'lower', positive or negative. In the animus as mediator between consciousness and the unconscious, 'the accent, in accordance with the nature of the logos, is on knowledge and particularly on understanding. What it communicates is more meaning (*Sinn*) than image (*Bild*).'[2] The quaternity which, in Goethe's Faust for example, determines the principle of the logos presupposes an element of consciousness.[3] 'The image is transferred to a real man resembling the animus, who now takes over its role; or it appears as a figure in dream or fantasy.' Ultimately, since it represents a living psychic reality, it can impart a distinct coloration to the individual's whole behaviour, for the 'coloration' of the unconscious is always contrasexual. Consequently it is 'an important function of the higher, that is, suprapersonal animus, to act as a psychopompos, guiding and accompanying the movements and transformations of the soul.' To be sure, an archetype such as the animus or anima will never fully coincide with the concrete reality of an individual man; and the more individual a man is, the less he will correspond to the image projected on him. For the individual is the exact opposite of the archetypal. 'The individual is precisely not what is in any way typical; he is a unique mixture of particular traits which may themselves be typical.'[4] This disparity which is at first obscured by the transference becomes more evident as time goes on; as the carrier of the projection reveals his true nature, conflicts and disappointments are inevitable.

[1] Emma Jung, 'Ein Beitrag zum Problem des Animus', p. 329.

[2] Ibid., p. 332.

[3] In her fine study, 'Ein Beitrag zum Problem des Animus', Emma Jung expresses the belief that the gradation 'word, meaning, power, act', which has been said to define the Greek logos, seems to define the quintessence of the masculine character, and that each of these steps is represented in a man's life as in the development of the animus figure. Modifying the order, she assigns the 'strong' or 'strong-willed' man to the first step, the 'man of action' to the second, the 'man of the word' to the third, and finally, to the fourth, the man who has lived according to 'meaning'.

[4] Emma Jung, op. cit., pp. 302, 312, 342.

The soul-image stands in a direct relation to the persona. 'If the persona is intellectual, the soul-image is quite certainly sentimental.'[1] For the persona corresponds to a man's habitual outward attitude, while the animus or anima reflects the habitual inner attitude. We may term the persona the mediating function between the ego and the outside world and the soul-image the corresponding mediating function between the ego

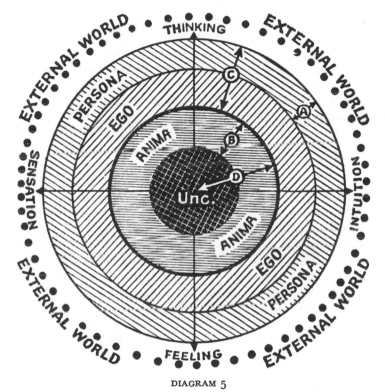

DIAGRAM 5

and the inner world. Diagram 5 is an attempt to clarify what has been said. A represents the persona mediating between the ego and the outside world; B is the animus or anima, mediating between the ego and the inner world of the unconscious; C is at once the ego and the persona, which represent our phenotypical, outwardly visible psychic disposition; D is the genotypical element, our invisible, latent, unconscious inner nature.

[1] *Types*, par. 804.

Persona and soul-image stand in a compensatory relation to one another; the more rigidly the mask, the persona, cuts off the individual from his natural, instinctual life, the more archaic, undifferentiated, and powerful becomes the soul-image. It is extremely difficult to free oneself from either of them. Yet such liberation becomes an urgent necessity when the individual is unable to distinguish himself from persona and soul-image.

As long as the different aspects and traits of the unconscious psyche are not yet differentiated from one another and integrated with consciousness (e.g., as long as an individual does not know his shadow), a man's whole unconscious will be predominantly feminine, and the converse is true for a woman; everything in it seems to be coloured by contrasexual qualities. Accordingly, when Jung wishes to stress this characteristic, he refers to this area of the unconscious simply as the animus or anima. When the persona becomes too rigid, that is to say, when only one main function is differentiated while the other three remain more or less undifferentiated, the anima will of course represent a mixture of the three. But when the two accessory functions have developed, in the course of an analysis for example, the anima will stand out more and more as an 'embodiment' of the darkest, the fourth, the inferior function.[1] If the shadow is also still undifferentiated, i.e., if it remains in the unconscious depths, it is often contaminated by the features of the anima. In such cases one can initially meet with a triad of shadow figures in the dreams. These figures belong, as it were, to the still unconscious functions. Equally, we may meet with a triad of anima or animus figures. The contamination may be recognized in the dreams as a sort of 'pair situation', a kind of 'marriage' between a shadow figure and an anima or animus figure. For the more one is dominated by the persona, the more the anima remains in the 'darkness'. It 'is at once projected, so that our hero comes under the heel of his wife's slipper'. For 'the absence of resistance outwardly against the lure of the persona means a similar weakness inwardly against the influence of the unconscious'.[2] A man obsessed by the anima is in danger of losing his 'well-fitting' persona and succumbing to effeminacy, just as the usual feminine persona of the animus-possessed

---

[1] See Diagram 5 on p. 14.
[2] 'Relations', pars. 308, 309.

woman may be unable to withstand the 'arguments' of her animus. One of the most typical products of both figures is what has long since been known as 'animosity'.[1]

The animus seldom appears as a single figure. As we know, the contents of the unconscious compensate our conscious attitude; since the male tends to be rather polygamous in his outward life, his anima usually appears singly, combining the most diverse and contradictory feminine types into one image.[2] This accounts for the 'glamorous' or 'elfin' character of the true anima figure. The woman, on the other hand, tends toward monogamy in her real life and thus reveals a polygamous trait in her soul image; her masculine complement will be personified in a series of the most diversified figures. This is why the animus appears so often in the plural. It 'is rather like an assembly of fathers or dignitaries of some kind who lay down incontestable, "rational", *ex cathedra* judgements'.[3] These often take the form of uncritically accepted opinions, prejudices, principles, which make women argue and bicker. This happens most often to those whose main function is that of feeling and whose thinking function is undifferentiated. They seem to make up a fairly high percentage of their sex, though there may have been some change since the turn of the century, perhaps as a result of the emancipation of woman.

Since the soul-image coincides with the function that has been least elucidated and still rests in the unconscious, it is antithetical to the main function, and this contrast will be manifested in the figure symbolizing it. Therefore in principle an abstract scientist's anima will be primitive, emotional, and romantic, while that of the intuitive, sensitive artist will be a down-to-earth, sensual type. And it is no accident that effemi-

---

[1] 'Religion', p. 30.

[2] However, this is essentially true only for the very 'male' type of man. The more pronounced a man's feminine side is—that is, the more strongly his mother complex is developed (and this is rather frequently the case today)—the more numerous will be the feminine figures that represent his anima characteristics in dreams and visions. Often there will be a whole series of feminine figures of the same type (e.g., from a group of ballet dancers, or of uniformed nurses, etc.) and only with the progressive development of the personality do these coalesce into a single image embodying all the different characteristics of the anima.

[3] 'Relations', par. 332.

nate emotional men usually bear in their hearts the image of an Amazon, disguised in our time as a feminist or bluestocking. Similarly, a woman's animus, according to the nature of her main function, will take the form of a dangerous Don Juan, a bearded professor, a brawny hero, whether embodied in a soldier, a horseman, a football player, a chauffeur, a pilot, or a film star, to mention only a few of the possibilities.

But just as the anima is not only an expression of the 'serpent', of the instinctual temptations lurking in wait in the darkness of the unconscious, but also of the man's wise, luminous guide— that is, of the other aspect of the unconscious—which leads him not down but onward, so too the animus is not only the 'opinion-ated devil' hostile to all logic, but also a productive, creative being, though not in the form of masculine endeavour but as fructifying word, *logos spermatikos*. And just as the well-rounded man gives birth to his work through his inner 'femininity', his anima becoming his inspiring Muse, 'so the inner masculine side of a woman brings forth creative seeds which have the power to fertilize the feminine side of the man'.[1] Thus there is a natural complementarity between the sexes, not only on the physical level where it gives birth to the 'bodily child', but also in the mysterious stream of images which flows through the depths of their souls and joins them together to engender the 'spiritual child'. Once a woman has become aware of this, once she knows how to 'handle' her unconscious and let herself be guided by her inner voice, then it will be up to her whether in her dealings with the man she becomes a *femme inspiratrice* or a self-righteous harridan, a Beatrice or a Xanthippe.

When in their ripe years men become effeminate and women belligerent, this is always an indication that a part of the psyche which should be turned inward is directed toward the outside world, that these persons have failed to accord their inner life its due recognition. For we are at the mercy of a contrasexual partner, unprepared for the surprises he has in store, only so long as we have not recognized his true nature. But we can only per-ceive this true nature *in ourselves*, for as a rule we choose a partner who stands for the unconscious part of our psyche. If this part of our personality is made conscious, we cease to im-pute our own faults to our partner; in other words, the projec-

[1] 'Relations', par. 336.

tion is withdrawn. We recover the psychic energy that was bound up in the projection and are able to put it to work for the benefit of our own ego. This withdrawal of the projection must not be confused with narcissism. In both cases the individual 'comes to himself', but there is a big difference between self-knowledge and self-complacency.

Once we have perceived the contrasexual element in ourselves and raised it to consciousness, we have ourselves, our emotions, and affects reasonably well in hand. Above all we have achieved a real independence and with it, to be sure, a certain isolation. In a sense we are alone, for our 'inward freedom' means that a love relation can no longer fetter us; the other sex has lost its magic power over us, for we have come to know its essential traits in the depths of our own psyche. We shall not easily '*fall* in love', for we can no longer lose ourselves in someone else, but we shall be capable of a deeper love, a conscious devotion to the other. For our aloneness does not alienate us from the world, but only places us at a proper distance from it. By anchoring us more firmly in our own nature, it even enables us to give ourselves more unreservedly to another human being, because our individuality is no longer endangered. To be sure, it usually takes half a lifetime to arrive at this stage. Probably no one can do so without a struggle. It also takes a full measure of experience, not to mention disappointment.

Accordingly, confrontation with the soul-image is not a task of youth but of mature years. And usually there is no need to tackle the problem until later life. In the first half of life contact with the opposite sex aims above all at physical union with a view to the 'bodily child' as fruit and continuation; in the second half the essential becomes the psychic *coniunctio*, a union with the contrasexual both in the area of one's own inner world and through the carrier of its image in the outer world. Thus the encounter with the soul-image always means that the first half of life with its necessary adaptation to the outside world and the resulting extraverted orientation of consciousness is ended, and that we must begin to take the most important step of our adaptation to the inner world, namely to confront our own contrasexual aspect. 'The activation of the archetype of the soul-image is therefore an event of fateful importance, for it is the most unmistakable sign that the second half of life has begun.'[1]

Goethe's *Faust* provides us with a magnificent example of this development. In the first half Gretchen carries the projection of Faust's anima. But the tragic end of this relationship compels him to withdraw the projection from the outside world and to seek this part of his psyche in himself. He finds it in another world, in the 'underworld' of his unconscious, symbolized by Helen of Troy. The second part of *Faust* portrays an individuation process with all its archetypal figures; Helen is the typical anima figure, Faust's soul-image. He wrestles with it in different transformations and on different levels up to its supreme manifestation, the Mater Gloriosa. Only then is he redeemed, permitted to enter the world of eternity where all the opposites are transcended.

As the conscious realization of the shadow makes possible the knowledge of our other, dark side in so far as it pertains to our own sex, so realization of the soul-image enables us to know the contrasexual aspect of our own psyche. Once the image is recognized and revealed, it ceases to operate from out of the unconscious. At last we can differentiate this contrasexual part of the psyche and integrate it with our conscious attitude. The result is an extraordinary enrichment of the contents of consciousness and a great broadening of our personality (Plate 4).

THE ARCHETYPES OF 'SPIRIT' AND 'MATTER'

One more stretch of the way has been opened up. When all the perils of confrontation with the soul-image have been overcome, new archetypal figures arise. We shall have to come to terms with them and once more take our bearings. As far as one can see, the whole process is implicitly purposive. Although the unconscious is pure nature without particular or explicit aim we may say that it has a kind of 'potential directedness'. It has an invisible inner order of its own, an inherent striving toward a goal. Thus 'when the conscious mind participates actively and experiences each stage of the process, or at least understands it intuitively, then the next image always starts off on the higher

---

[1] T. Wolff, *Studien*, p. 159.

level that has been won, and purposiveness develops'.[1] This process does not consist of a simple sequential presentation of symbols, but resumes its movement whenever a definite problem is made conscious, mastered, and integrated.

Thus it is no accident that the next step after the confrontation with the soul-image should be characterized by the appearance of the archetype of the WISE OLD MAN (Plate 5), the personification of the *spiritual principle*. Its counterpart in the woman's individuation process is MAGNA MATER (Plate 6), the great earth mother who represents the cold, impersonal truth of nature.[2] For now the time has come to throw light upon the most secret recesses of the individual's own being, upon what is most specifically masculine or feminine, or in other words, to elucidate the 'spiritual' principle in man and the 'material' principle in woman. Here we shall not, as in dealing with the animus and the anima, be exploring the contrasexual part of the psyche, but pursuing the innermost essence of the psyche of either sex back to its source, back to the primordial image from which it was formed. To venture a somewhat daring formulation, we might say that the man is materialized spirit whereas the woman is matter saturated with spirit; thus in man the essential determinant is spirit while in woman it is matter. At this stage we shall endeavour to raise as many as possible of the latent figures within us to consciousness, from the crudest primordial image to the highest, most diversified, and most perfect symbol.

Both figures, the Wise Old Man as well as the Magna Mater, can appear in an infinite variety of forms; and their good and bad, luminous and dark aspects are frequently encountered in the conceptions of primitive peoples and in all mythologies: we encounter them as magician, prophet, mage, helmsman of the dead, guide, and as fertility goddess, sibyl, priestess, Mother Church, Sophia, etc. Both figures emanate a powerful fascination, which unfailingly lures the individual who confronts them into a kind of self-glorification and megalomania, unless he is able, by making them conscious and distinguishing them, to

---

[1] 'Relations', par. 386.

[2] Plates 5 and 6 represent examples of the numerous forms taken by these two archetypes. Both show the tension of opposites inherent in all archetypal figures.

free himself from the danger of an identification with their delusive image. An example of this is Nietzsche, who fully identified himself with the figure of Zarathustra.

Jung calls these archetypal figures of the unconscious 'mana personalities'.[1] *Mana* means 'extraordinary power'. To possess mana means to have power over others, but it also involves the danger of becoming arrogant and vainglorious. Thus conscious realization of the contents making up the archetype of the mana personality means, 'for the man the second and real liberation from the father, and, for the woman, liberation from the mother, and with it comes the first genuine sense of his or her true individuality'.[2] It is not until a man has progressed to this point that he can enter on his career as the 'spiritual child of God', and then only if he refrains from puffing up his widened consciousness and so succumbing to an inflation which, 'paradoxically enough, is a regression of consciousness into unconsciousness'.[3] But in view of the profound insights he has obtained, there is nothing surprising about this sort of hubris; everyone succumbs to it for a while in the course of a deliberately deepened individuation process. But the forces that have been activated in the individual by these insights become really available to him only when he has learned in all humility to distinguish himself from them.

THE SELF

We are now not far from the goal. The dark side has been made conscious, the contrasexual element in us has been differentiated, our relation to spirit and primordial nature has been clarified. The essentially double face of the psychic depths has been recognized and spiritual arrogance has been put aside.

---

[1] Obviously an impressive and fascinating dream figure, a 'mana personality' of a given sex, will have different meanings in the dreams of a man and in those of a woman. In a man's dream we shall probably have to interpret a feminine image of this kind as an anima figure, while in a woman's dream it will probably stand for the figure of the Great Mother, which must be considered as one of the 'uniting symbols', that is, those symbols most closely related to the self. *Mutatis mutandis*, the same applies to the figure of the Wise Old Man, or of the *puer aeternus* in a man's dream (cf. Jung, 'The Psychological Aspects of the Kore').

[2] 'Relations', par. 393.

[3] *Alchemy*, par. 563.

We have penetrated deep into the realms of the unconscious, we have brought a good deal of their contents to light, and we have learned to orient ourselves in its primordial world. Our consciousness as vehicle of our personal uniqueness has been confronted with the whole of the unconscious as vehicle of our share of the collective and universal. The way has not been devoid of crises. For the influx of unconscious contents into the realm of consciousness, the dissolution of the persona, and the reduction of the ruling power of consciousness bring with them a state of psychic imbalance. This imbalance has been induced artificially for the purpose of removing an obstacle to the further development of the personality. For this loss of balance leads, with the help of the autonomous, instinctive activity of the unconscious, to the creation of a new balance, provided that consciousness is able to assimilate and elaborate the contents arising from the unconscious. For 'the victory over the collective psyche alone yields the true value, the capture of the hoard, the invincible weapon, the magic talisman, or whatever it be that the myth deems most desirable'.[1]

The archetypal image which leads from this polarity to a union of the two psychic systems—consciousness and the unconscious—through a midpoint common to both is the SELF. It is the last station on the path of individuation, which Jung also calls *self-realization*. Only when this midpoint is found and integrated, can one speak of a well-rounded man. For only then has he solved the problem of his relation to the two realms which make up every man's life, the outward and the inner reality. Both ethically and intellectually, this is an extremely difficult task, which can be successfully performed only by the fortunate few, those elected and favoured by grace.

For the conscious personality the birth of the self means a shift of its psychic centre, and consequently an entirely different attitude toward, and view of, life—in other words a 'transformation' in the fullest sense of the word. 'If the life-mass is to be transformed,' says Jung, 'a *circumambulatio* is necessary, i.e. exclusive concentration on the centre, the place of creative change. During this process one is "bitten" by animals; in other words, we have to expose ourselves to the animal impulses of the unconscious without identifying ourselves with them and

_____
[1] 'Relations', pars. 261, 274.

without "running away"; for flight from the unconscious would defeat the purpose of the whole proceeding. We must hold our ground, which means here that the process initiated by the dreamer's self-observation must be experienced in all its ramifications and then articulated with consciousness to the best of his understanding. This often entails an almost unbearable tension because of the utter incommensurability between conscious life and the unconscious process, which can only be experienced in the innermost soul and cannot touch the visible surface of life at any point.'[1] For this reason Jung insists that whatever his inner turmoil the patient should not interrupt his normal life and daily work for so much as a single day. For it is precisely the endurance of tension, the ability to hold out in the midst of psychic disorder, that provides the possibility of a new psychic order.

The widely prevailing view that psychic development leads ultimately to a state in which there is no more suffering is of course utterly false. Suffering and conflict are a part of life; they must not be regarded as 'ailments'; they are the natural attributes of all human existence, the normal counterpole, so to speak of happiness. Only when from weakness, cowardice, or lack of understanding the individual tries to evade them do ailments and complexes arise. For this reason we must distinguish sharply between repression and suppression. 'Suppression,' says Jung, 'amounts to a conscious moral choice, but repression is a rather immoral "penchant" for getting rid of disagreeable decisions. Suppression may cause worry, conflict, and suffering, but it never causes a neurosis. Neurosis is always a substitute for legitimate suffering.'[2] Fundamentally it is an 'inauthentic' suffering which we feel to be meaningless and hostile to life, while suffering from an 'authentic' cause always bears with it an

---

[1] *Alchemy*, par. 186.

[2] 'Religion', p. 75. This statement by Jung must be properly understood. When he speaks of an 'immoral penchant', he does not of course mean that this 'immorality' springs from a conscious decision. We know that repression begins with early childhood and in part represents a necessary defence mechanism. What Jung has in mind is more the fact that out of weakness and inability to endure difficulties and tensions, one man, even late in life, will make far more use of this defence mechanism than another. The explanation may lie either in his constitution or in events that have inhibited his development.

intimation of future fulfilment and spiritual enrichment. In this light, conscious realization may be interpreted as the transformation of an inauthentic into an authentic suffering.

'But the more we become conscious of ourselves through self-knowledge, and act accordingly, the more the layer of the personal unconscious that is superimposed on the collective unconscious will be diminished. In this way there arises a consciousness which is no longer imprisoned in the petty, oversensitive, personal world of the ego, but participates freely in the wider world of objective interests. This widened consciousness is no longer that touchy, egotistical bundle of personal wishes, fears, hopes, and ambitions which has always to be compensated or corrected by unconscious countertendencies; instead, it is a function of relationship to the world of objects, bringing the individual into absolute, binding, and indissoluble communion with the world at large.'[1] Such a 'renewal of personality . . . is a subjective state whose reality cannot be validated by any external criterion; any further attempt to describe and explain it is doomed to failure, for *only those who have had this experience* are in a position to understand and attest its reality'.[2] Thus an objective criterion for it is no more possible than, say, for 'happiness', which nevertheless has absolute reality. For 'everything about this psychology is, in the deepest sense, experience; the entire theory, even when it puts on the most abstract airs, is the direct outcome of something experienced'.[3]

'The self is a quantity that is supraordinate to the conscious ego. It embraces not only the conscious but also the unconscious psyche, and is therefore, so to speak, a personality which we *also* are.'[4] We know that the unconscious processes usually stand in a compensatory relation to consciousness, but such a relation is not always one of contrast, for the unconscious and consciousness are not necessarily in opposition. They complement one another to form the self. Although we can conceive of partial psyches, we cannot form an equally clear picture of what the self actually is, for the part can never fully understand the whole. Diagram 6 is an attempt to represent the total psyche. The self is in the middle between consciousness and the

---

[1] 'Relations', par. 275. [2] *Alchemy*, par. 188 (my italics).
[3] 'Unconscious', par. 199. [4] 'Relations', par. 274.

unconscious partaking of both but encompassing them both in the sphere of its rays, for 'the self is not only the centre but also the whole circumference which embraces both conscious and unconscious; it is the centre of this totality, just as the ego is the centre of the conscious mind.'[1] The various parts of the total

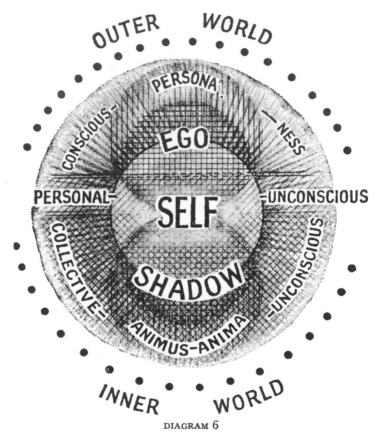

DIAGRAM 6

psyche that we have already discussed here are shown in the diagram, though we do not claim to show their actual order or positional value. For only the roughest idea of anything so complicated can be given in a diagram. Our aim is to provide a hint, a suggestion, of a context that can be properly understood only on the basis of one's own experience (see Plate 7).

[1] *Alchemy*, par. 44.

The only content of the self that we know is the ego. 'The individuated ego senses itself as the object of an unknown and superordinate subject.' Concerning its contents we cannot say more. In any such attempt we come up against the limits of our knowledge. For we can only *experience* the self. If we are determined to characterize it, we can only say with Jung that it is 'a kind of compensation for the conflict between inside and outside. ... So too the self is our life's goal, for it is the completest expression of that fateful combination we call individuality, the full flowering not only of the single individual but of the group, in which each adds his portion to the whole.'[1] And here again we have a reference to something that cannot be defined in conceptual terms but apprehended only in experience.

This self of ours, our 'midpoint', is a centre of tension between two worlds and their forces which we *know* only dimly but *feel* all the more strongly. It 'is strange to us and yet so near, wholly ourselves and yet unknowable, a virtual centre of mysterious constitution. ... The beginnings of our whole psychic life seem to be inextricably rooted in this point, and all our highest and ultimate purposes seem to be striving toward it. This paradox is unavoidable, as always when we try to define something that lies beyond the bourn of our understanding.'[2] ... 'But if the unconscious can be recognized as a codetermining factor along with the conscious, and if life can be lived in such a way that conscious and unconscious (i.e. instinctive) demands are accepted as far as possible, the centre of gravity of the total personality shifts in position. ... This new centre might be called the self. ... If such a transposition succeeds ... there develops a personality who, so to speak, suffers only in the lower story of himself, but in the upper story ... is singularly detached from painful as well as from joyful events.'[3]

The idea of the self, which is solely a limiting concept comparable to Kant's 'Ding an sich',[4] is thus essentially a transcendental postulate, 'which, although justifiable psychologically, does not allow of scientific proof.'[5] But this postulate serves only to formulate the processes that have been empirically

---

[1] 'Relations', par. 404.   [2] Ibid., pars. 398–99.
[3] Cf. *Golden Flower*, par. 67.
[4] *Alchemy*, par. 247.   [5] 'Relations', par. 405.

established and to link them together.[1] For the self is simply a
indication of the primal, unfathomable ground of the psyche
But taken as an aim, it is also an ethical postulate, a goal to b
realized—and what distinguishes the Jungian system from othe
systems is precisely that it presents an ethical challenge an
guides us to ethical decisions. But the self is also a psychi
category and can be experienced as such; to depart for th
moment from the language of psychology, we might call it th
'central fire', our individual share in God, or Meister Eckhart'
'little spark'. It is the early Christian ideal of the Kingdom c
God that is 'within you'. It is the ultimate in psychic experienc
and in man's knowledge of the psyche.

THE REALIZATION OF THE SELF

Here we have been able to give only a brief sketch of th
individuation process as elaborated by Jung. This way to th
broadening of the personality consists, as we have seen, in
gradual exploration of the contents and functions of the tota
psyche and of their effect on the ego. It leads the individual t
know himself for what he naturally is, as distinguished fron
what he would like to be—and probably nothing is mor
difficult for a human being. This process is not accessible t
consciousness without *specific psychological knowledge and techniqu*
and without a particular psychological attitude. It should there
fore be stressed that the phenomena and experiences of th
collective psyche were first *scientifically* observed and describe
by Jung. He himself says of them: 'A scientific term like "in
dividuation" . . . merely indicates an as yet very obscure fiel
of research much in need of exploration: the centralizing pro
cesses in the unconscious that go to form the personality.'[2]

In his treatment Jung investigates and correlates all th
potentialities of the psyche, taking the present psychic situatio
as a starting point and aiming to create a psychic totality. Thi
justifies him in calling his method a *prospective* one in contrast t
a retrospective one which seeks to cure by disclosing pas
causes. Accordingly, it is a way to self-knowledge and self

[1] This is exactly the role played in other sciences by postulates or heuristi
maxims that cannot be justified by logic.

[2] *Alchemy*, par. 564.

regulation, a means of activating the ethical function, and by no means limited to the cure of mental sickness or neurosis. Often, to be sure, the impulsion to undertake the course of treatment is provided by an illness, but just as often it comes from a desire to find a meaning in life, to restore one's lost faith in God and oneself. As Jung himself says, 'About a third of my cases are not suffering from any clinically definable neurosis, but from the senselessness and aimlessness of their lives.'[1] But just this seems to be the form of the universal neurosis of our time—a time in which all the fundamental values are dangerously wavering and a total spiritual and psychic disorientation has taken hold of mankind. In view of this situation, the way of individuation, as postulated by Jung, may be regarded as a serious endeavour to counter the disorientation of modern man by activating the creative forces of his unconscious and by consciously integrating them into the whole of the psyche. It means a 'liberation' from the snares of instinctual nature, an *opus contra naturam* which, however, is meant primarily for the second half of life.

To deepen and broaden consciousness by raising unconscious contents to consciousness is an 'enlightenment', a spiritual act. 'For the same reason,' says Jung, 'most heroes are characterized by solar attributes, and the moment of birth of their greater personality is known as illumination.'[2] This means nothing other than what is so wonderfully symbolized in the Christian sacrament of baptism. 'In the primitive world,' says Jung, 'everything has psychic qualities. Everything is endowed with the elements of man's psyche—or let us say, of the human psyche, of the collective unconscious, for there is as yet no individual psychic life. Let us not forget, in this connection, that what the Christian sacrament of baptism purports to do is of the greatest significance for the psychic development of mankind. Baptism endows the human being with a unique soul. I do not mean, of course, that the baptismal rite in itself as a magical act is effective at one performance. I mean that the idea of baptism lifts a man out of his archaic identification with the world and changes him into a being who stands above it. The fact that mankind has risen to the level of this idea is baptism in

[1] 'The Aims of Psychotherapy', p. 41.
[2] 'The Development of Personality', p. 184.

the deepest sense, for it means the birth of spiritual man who transcends nature.'[1]

To such a consciousness still sheltered in faith and the symbolism of dogma, Jung has nothing to add; and indeed, he does everything in his power to encourage those who seek their way back to the Church. He too believes that *Anima naturaliter christiana*; and that, precisely on the road to self-realization, a man 'knowing the significance of what he does . . . can become the higher type of man who . . . becomes a symbol of the true Christ.'[2]

Thus self-realization is also and above all a way to meaning in life, to character formation, and hence to a *Weltanschauung*. As Jung puts it: 'Consciousness determines *Weltanschauung*. All conscious awareness of motives and intentions is a *Weltanschauung* in the bud; every increase in experience and knowledge means a further step in the development of a *Weltanschauung*. And with the picture that the thinking man fashions of the world he also changes himself. The man whose sun still moves round the earth is essentially different from the man whose earth is a satellite of the sun.'[3]

The sufferer from mental illness or the man for whom life has lost its meaning is beset by problems with which he struggles in vain. For 'the greatest and most important problems of life are all fundamentally insoluble; they must be so, because they express the necessary polarity inherent in every self-regulating system. They can never be solved, but only *outgrown*. . . . This outgrowing, as I called it previously, revealed itself on further experience to be the raising of the level of consciousness. Some higher or wider interest arose on the person's horizon, and through this widening of his view, the insoluble problem lost its urgency. It was not solved logically in its own terms, but faded out before a new and stronger life tendency. It was not repressed and made unconscious, but merely appeared in a different light, and so became different itself. What on a lower level had led to the wildest conflicts and to emotions full of panic, viewed from the higher level of the personality now seemed like a storm in a valley seen from a high mountain top.

[1] Cf. 'Archaic Man', par. 136.
[2] Cf. *Golden Flower*, par. 81.
[3] 'Analytical Psychology and *Weltanschauung*', p. 361.

This does not mean that the thunderstorm is robbed of its reality; it means that, instead of being in it, one is now above it.'[1]

THE UNITING SYMBOL

The archetypal image of this *coincidentia oppositorum*, this transformation of the opposites into a third term, a higher synthesis, is expressed by the so-called UNITING SYMBOL[2] which represents the partial systems of the psyche as *united* on a *superordinate*, higher plane. All the symbols and archetypal figures in which the process is embodied are vehicles of the *transcendent function*,[3] that is, of the union of the different pairs of psychic opposites in a synthesis which transcends them both. The uniting symbol makes its appearance only when, in the course of psychic development, the intrapsychic 'is experienced as just as real, just as effective and psychologically true, as the world of outward reality'.[4] Whenever this symbol, which can manifest itself in the most divergent forms, makes its appearance, the balance between the ego and the unconscious is restored. Symbols of this kind, representing a primordial image of psychic totality, always exhibit more or less abstract form, because their basic law and essence demand a symmetrical arrangement of the parts round a midpoint. Such symbolic figures have been fashioned from time immemorial in the orient; the most significant examples being the so-called MANDALAS, or 'magic circles'. We are not trying to say that the symbol of the self always has the form of a mandala. According to an individual's conscious situation and degree of psychic development, everything in creation, whether big or little,

[1] Cf. *Golden Flower*, par. 17.

[2] Actually all symbols represent a *coincidentia oppositorum*, but this is expressed most sharply in the so-called 'uniting symbol'. Jung has described the various aspects of this symbol in *Aion*, *Mysterium Conjunctionis*, and in Chapter 5 of *Psychological Types*.

[3] 'Here I do not mean a basic function, but a complex one, composed of various other functions; and by "transcendent" I do not wish to designate any metaphysical quality, but merely the fact that by this function a transition is made possible from one attitude to another.' Cf. *Types*, par. 828. Jung gives a detailed definition and description of this concept in 'The Transcendent Function'.

[4] T. Wolff, *Studien*, p. 134.

lowly or sublime, abstract or concrete, can become a symbol of the self, of this 'effective centre'. But it is the mandalas which most eloquently and aptly symbolize a united synthetic view of the psyche.

MANDALA SYMBOLS

Mandalas are among the oldest religious symbols of mankind; we have examples from as far back as the paleolithic age. They occur among all peoples and in all cultures, even in the form of sand paintings, as among the Pueblo Indians. Perhaps the most impressive mandalas, showing the greatest artistic finish, are those of the East, particularly the Tibetan Buddhists (of these Plate 8 is an especially fine example). In Tantric Yoga, mandala pictures were employed as instruments of contemplation. 'The mandalas used in ceremonial,' says Jung, 'are of great significance, because their centres usually contain one of the highest religious figures: either Shiva himself . . . or Buddha.'[1] We have also numerous mandalas from the Western Middle Ages and Renaissance, most of which show Christ at the centre of the circle, surrounded by the four Evangelists or their symbols at the four cardinal points.[2] The high value set upon the mandala in different cultures, says Jung, 'accords very well with the paramount significance of individual mandala symbols, which are characterized by the same qualities of a—so to speak —"metaphysical" nature.'[3] Jung studied these symbols for fourteen years before he ventured to interpret them. But today they belong to a highly important domain of psychological experience, which he opens up and interprets to those who entrust themselves to his guidance.

The mandalas all show the same typical arrangement and symmetry of the pictorial elements. Their basic design is a circle or square (most often a square) symbolizing 'wholeness', and in all of them the relation to a centre is accentuated. Many have the form of a flower, a cross, or a wheel, and there is a distinct inclination toward the number four. 'As the historic parallels

[1] *Alchemy*, par. 125.

[2] Here I should like to mention the particularly fine mandalas of the mystic Jacob Boehme (1575–1642) published in his *Theosophische Werke* (Amsterdam, 1682). One of them is reproduced here as Plate 9.

[3] *Alchemy*, par. 126.

show,' says Jung, 'the symbolism of the mandala is not just a unique curiosity; we can well say that it is a regular occurrence.'[1] Plate 8 shows an arrangement of this sort: in the centre the main figure is surrounded by a stylized lotus with eight petals; the background on which the circle is inscribed consists of triangles in four different colours, which open out into four gates representing the four directions. The triangles are joined to form a large square, which is surrounded by another circle, the 'river of life'. Below this great circle, which also contains numerous symbolic figures, the underworld is represented with its demons; above the circle, the heavenly gods sit enthroned.

Plate 10 is an eighteenth-century Rosicrucian mandala, showing the Saviour in the centre of a flower with a double row of eight petals, surrounded by a fiery garland of rays. It is divided into four parts by a cross, whose lower shafts are burning in the fire of the instincts and whose upper shafts are sprinkled with tears of heavenly dew. Plates 11, 12, 13, 14, 15, and 16 are mandalas produced by patients of Jung on the basis of inner experiences. They were done spontaneously, without model or outside influence. Here again we find the same themes in similar arrangement. The circle, the centre, the number four, the symmetrical distribution of motifs and colours express the same psychic law.[2] The aim is always to combine a number of colours and forms in a balanced organic whole.

Plate 11 represents the turning peacock wheel with its play of colours and its many eyes. The eyes, which symbolize the forever changing dynamic aspects and qualities of the psyche, revolve around the central eye. The wheel is enclosed in a circle of flame, which forms a protective wall of 'burning emotions'

[1] Ibid., par. 331.

[2] Dream figures may also compose themselves into a mandala-like arrangement. At the beginning of the individuation process, for example, the first vision of the self appears. Often it takes the form of three persons seated at a round table with the dreamer, two of them characterized as male or female; or four female figures are centred round a male dreamer. In this second case the self is still 'veiled', obscured in the totality of the four aspects of the anima or soul-image which, as we know, mediates between conscious and unconscious. Only when the confrontation with it has come to a relative conclusion can the image of the self reveal itself directly, in an appropriate uniting symbol.

around the mysterious process of self-realization and shuts it off from the outside world.[1]

Plate 12 represents the four-armed Sun God as symbol of the dynamic aspect of the self. Arms and lightning are 'masculine', the moon sickle 'feminine' in character; the five-pointed stars symbolize what is still imperfect and nature-bound in man; the whole revolves round the sun ringed by the 'river of life' and symbolizing the self.

Plate 13 is more formal and abstract, but is also an attempt to relate a variety of lines and forms to a centre. Plate 14 shows many different forms and colours (blue, red, green, yellow stand for the four functions of consciousness) in varied arrangements around the four-leafed calyx in the middle. The heads still sleeping like buds in their green sheaths look toward the centre as the nascent self, not toward the periphery where, as the psychological development already attained comes to full flower, the fruits cradled in the calyxes shine forth as mature accomplishments and the birds, ready to take flight, as intuitions.

Plate 15 represents a vision of the Face of Eternity, surrounded by the Serpent of Eternity, the Uroboros, and the zodiac. Plate 16 represents the Eye of God, which symbolizes universal awareness, penetrating the flower-like mandala in which it is embedded with its quadruple rays.

It would be quite mistaken to regard all the mandalas as 'pictures' of completed individuation, i.e., the successful union of all the pairs of psychic opposites. For the most part the mandalas produced in the course of analysis are only preliminary sketches, more or less successful steps towards ultimate perfection and wholeness. To strive for this goal is our destiny and highest calling, but in view of our human limitations, the attainment is always relative. In principle mandalas can appear during the whole individuation process, and it would be a mistake to interpret their appearance as an indication of a particularly advanced stage of development. In line with the psychic trend towards self-regulation, they will always appear when a 'disorder' in the realm of consciousness calls for them as

[1] In its arrangement, motifs, and whole dynamic structure, this mandala shows a striking resemblance to Plate 9, which was unknown to the analysand who painted this 'picture from the unconscious'.

compensating factors. The mandalas with their mathematical structure are pictures, as it were, of the 'primal order of the total psyche', and their purpose is to transform chaos into cosmos. For these figures not only express order, they also bring it about.

Meditation on Yantra images, which usually have the form of mandalas, aims precisely at the creation of an intrapsychic order in the meditator. Naturally the mandalas of analysands can never achieve the artistic perfection and finish, the 'traditionally established harmony', of the mandalas of the East, which are not spontaneous products of the psyche but works of conscious artistry. We have cited them only as parallels in order to show that they rest on the same psychic foundations and therefore disclose striking similarities.[1] They are all representations of the 'middle way', which in the East was called Tao and which for Western man lies in the task of uniting the opposites, his inner and outward reality—of consciously striving, in awareness of the primordial forces of nature, to shape his personality into a whole.

Although most people can say little about the meaning of the mandalas they have drawn, they are fascinated by them and find them expressive and effective in connection with their psychic state. 'Very ancient magical effects are associated with this symbol,' says Jung, 'because it comes originally from the "protecting" or "charmed circle", the magic of which has been preserved in countless folk customs. The picture has the obvious purpose of drawing a magical furrow around the centre, the *templum* or *temenos* (sacred precincts) of the innermost personality, in order to prevent "emanation", or to guard by apotropaic means against distraction by external influences.' That is why, in the East, the centre of the mandalas is occupied by the 'golden flower'—which Westerners under analysis often employ with the same meaning. It is also named the 'heavenly heart', the 'empire of the greatest joy', the 'boundless land', the 'altar upon which consciousness and life are created'. The circulation symbolized by the round form of the pictures 'is not merely movement in a circle; it means, on the one hand, the marking off of the sacred precinct, and, on the other, fixation

---

[1] Further details may be found in *Golden Flower*, in 'The Psychology of Eastern Meditation', pp. 558 ff., in 'A Study of the Process of Individuation' and in 'Concerning Mandala Symbolism'.

and concentration. The sun-wheel begins to run; that is to say, the sun is activated and begins on its course, or, in other words, Tao begins to be effective and to take the lead.' Tao is hard to define briefly. R. Wilhelm translates it as 'meaning', others as 'way', and still others as 'God'. 'If,' says Jung, 'we interpret Tao as a method or a conscious way intended to unite what is divided, we shall, I believe, come close to the psychological content of the concept.'[1]

'Unfortunately,' he says elsewhere, 'our Western mind, lacking all culture in this respect, has never yet devised a concept, not even a name, for *the union of opposites through the middle path*, that most fundamental item of inward experience which could respectably be set against the Chinese concept of Tao.'[2] In terms of Jungian psychology this concept might roughly be defined as a 'revolving around oneself' in which all sides of the personality are drawn into the movement. The circular movement, which from a psychological point of view may be compared with the consciously experienced individuation process, is never 'made' but is 'passively' experienced. In other words, it is an autonomous movement of the psyche. 'Thus the circular movement has also the moral significance of activating all the light and dark forces of human nature, and with them, all the psychological opposites of whatever kind they may be.. That means nothing else than self-knowledge by means of self-incubation (Hindu *tapas*). A similar primordial concept of an absolutely complete creature is that of the Platonic man, round on all sides and uniting within himself the two sexes.'[3] This unity, this union of the two sexes to form a whole is symbolized in the corresponding pictures by a *coniunctio* between two contrasexual figures (Plates 17, 18, and 19), e.g., Shiva and Shakti or Sol and Luna, or by a hermaphroditic figure.

'The achievement of such symbolic unity is beyond the power of the conscious will because, in this case, the conscious is partisan. Its opponent is the collective unconscious, which does not understand the language of the conscious. Therefore it is necessary to have the "magically" effective symbol which contains those primitive analogies that speak to the unconscious. . . . Coming from these depths they can unite the uniqueness of

[1] Cf. *Golden Flower*, pars. 36, 38, 30.
[2] 'Relations', par. 327.   [3] Cf. *Golden Flower*, par. 39.

present-day consciousness with the age-old past of life.'[1] The emergence of these mandala symbols from the depths of the psyche is always a spontaneous phenomenon; they come and go of their own accord. But their effect can be amazing, for they can lead to a solution of various psychic complications and a liberation of the inner personality from its emotional and intellectual involvements and entanglements, so producing a unity that can rightly be called a 'rebirth of man on a transcendental plane'.

'All that can be ascertained at present about the symbolism of the mandala,' says Jung, 'is that it portrays an autonomous psychic fact, characterized by a phenomenology which is always repeating itself and is everywhere the same. It seems to be a sort of nucleus, about whose innermost structure and ultimate meaning we know nothing.'[2]

PARALLELS TO THE INDIVIDUATION PROCESS

This common psychic structure is not only revealed in the mandalas of different cultures. We find countless historical parallels to the whole individuation process. The psychic transformation revealed to Western man by Jung's analytical psychology is, fundamentally, a 'natural analogue of the religious initiation ceremonies'[3] of all ages, the only difference being that the rites of initiation use traditional prescriptions and symbols, while the Jungian individuation process tries to achieve its goal by a natural production of symbols, that is, a spontaneous movement of the psyche. The analogy is illustrated by the innumerable initiation rites of primitive peoples, by the Buddhist and Tantric forms of Yoga, or the exercises of Ignatius Loyola. Of course all such endeavours bear the stamp of their times and the people to whom they belong. All have their own cultural premises and accordingly their relevance to the present is only that of a historical and structural parallel. They cannot be directly applied to the modern man, and it is only in their basic principles that they are comparable to Jung's conception of individuation. But what distinguishes most of them from his method is chiefly this: either they were religious acts or else

[1] Ibid., pars. 44, 45.   [2] *Alchemy*, par. 249.
[3] 'Psychological Commentary on *The Tibetan Book of the Dead*', par. 854.

they were expected to lead to a particular *Weltanschauung* which was represented in them, whereas in the Jungian individuation process the work on the psyche paves the way for a spiritual–ethical–religious order which is the *consequence* and *not* the content of the preparation, and which must be chosen consciously and freely by the individual.

Jung found a particularly illuminating parallel to the individuation process in the field of medieval Hermetic philosophy, or alchemy.[1] As products of their times and cultural environments, alchemy and the individuation process differ greatly, but both are attempts to lead man to self-realization. The same 'transcendent function', as Jung calls the process of symbol formation, 'is the principal object of late medieval alchemistic philosophy'. Thus it would be a great mistake to reduce the alchemistic current of thought to crucibles and alembics. Jung went so far as to call it 'the groping precursor of the most modern psychology'. Of course this philosophy, 'hampered by the inevitable concretizations of the still crude and undifferentiated intellect, never advanced to any clear psychological formulation'. But 'the secret of alchemy was in fact the transcendent function, the transformation of personality through the blending and fusion of the noble with the base components, of the differentiated with the inferior functions, of the conscious with the unconscious'.[2] For in all probability alchemy was not concerned at all with chemical experiments, but rather 'with something resembling psychic processes expressed in pseudochemical language'. The gold sought for was not 'the ordinary gold (*aurum vulgi*), it is the philosophical gold or even the marvellous stone, the *lapis invisibilitatis* (the stone of invisibility)'[3] the *alexipharmakon*, the 'red tincture', the 'elixir of life'.

The number of terms employed for this 'gold' is endless. Often it was a mysterious essence consisting of body, soul, and spirit, appearing in winged and hermaphroditic form. It is another image for the symbol which in the Orient was termed the Diamond Body or the Golden Flower. 'First and foremost, as a parallel to the collective spiritual life of the times, [it was]

[1] A detailed treatment of the subject with plentiful illustrations from old alchemical treatises may be found in Jung's *Psychology and Alchemy*.
[2] 'Relations', par. 360. [3] *Alchemy*, pars. 342–43.

the image of the spirit imprisoned in the darkness of the world. In other words, the state of relative unconsciousness in which man found himself, and which he felt to be painful and in need of redemption, was reflected in matter and accordingly dealt with in matter.'[1] Thus from the chaos of the unconscious state, represented by the disorder of the *massa confusa* which was the basic raw material of alchemy, the *corpus subtile*, the 'body of resurrection', the 'gold', was produced by division, distillation, etc., and through ever new combinations.

But this gold, the alchemists believed, could not be made without the intervention of divine grace, for God himself is manifested in it. In Gnosis the man of light is a spark of the eternal light that has fallen into the darkness of matter and must be redeemed from it. Thus the result of the process may be designated as a uniting symbol which almost always has a numinous character. As Jung puts it, 'the Christian *opus* is an *operari* in honour of God the Redeemer, undertaken by man who stands in need of redemption, while the alchemical *opus* is the labour of Man the Redeemer in the cause of the divine world-soul slumbering and awaiting redemption in matter'.[2] It is only in this light that we are able to understand how it was possible for the alchemists to experience the transformation of their own psyche in projection on chemical substances. And it is only when we have found the key that we perceive the deeper meaning of those mystic texts and processes, which is often extremely obscure, perhaps intentionally so.[3]

Like alchemy, the various forms of YOGA also strive for a liberation of the soul, for the state of 'detachment from objects' that the Hindus call *nirdvandva*, 'free from the opposites'. But whereas alchemy represented and experienced the transformation of the psyche symbolically in chemical substances, Yoga strives for transformation by physical and mental exercises which are thought to act directly on the psyche. The steps and stages are exactly prescribed and demand extraordinary psychic power and concentration. For Yoga 'the aim of spiritual existence [is] the begetting and perpetuation of a

---

[1] Ibid., par. 557.   [2] Ibid.

[3] Herbert Silberer pointed many years ago to the analogies between alchemy and modern depth psychology, particularly Jung's analytical psychology, in *Problems of Mysticism and Its Symbolism*.

psychic spirit-body ("subtle body") which ensures the continuity of the detached consciousness. It is the birth of the pneumatic man',[1] the Buddha, symbol of the spirit over against the transience of the body. Here again a 'vision' of inner 'reality', that is, an insight into the world of the pairs of opposites, is the prerequisite to the sought-for unity and wholeness. Even the sequence of images and stages recalls alchemy and the individuation process, once more bearing witness to the ever identical psychic foundations.

The *opus* which the alchemist brings forth and the *imaginatio*, which is the psychic instrument whereby the Eastern mystic 'produces' Buddha, are based on the *active imagination* that leads Jung's patients to the same experience of symbols and through them to the knowledge of their own 'centre', the self. This imagination has nothing to do with 'imagining' in the common sense of the word. 'The *imaginatio*,' says Jung, 'is to be understood here as the real and literal power to create images (*Einbildungskraft* = imagination)—the classical usage of the world in contrast to *phantasia*, which means a mere "conceit", "idea", or "hunch" (*Einfall*) in the sense of insubstantial thought.[2] . . . *Imaginatio* is the active evocation of (inner) images . . . an authentic feat of thought or ideation, which does not spin aimless and groundless fantasies "into the blue"— does not, that is to say, just play with its objects—but tries to grasp the inner facts and portray them in images true to their nature.' It is an activation of the profoundest depths of the soul, intended to promote the emergence of salutary symbols. The alchemists tried to attain it in chemical substance; the Yogis— and Loyola—through strictly prescribed and disciplined exercises; and Jungian psychology by helping the individual to descend consciously into the depths of his own soul, to know its contents, and to integrate them with consciousness. But, says Jung, these processes 'are steeped in mystery; they pose riddles with which the human mind will long wrestle for a solution, and perhaps in vain. For, in the last analysis, it is exceedingly doubtful whether human reason is a suitable instrument for this purpose. Not for nothing did alchemy style itself an "art",

---

[1] Cf. *Golden Flower*, par. 69.

[2] The active imagination must therefore be strictly distinguished from the passive imagination which is at work in daydreams, etc.

feeling—and rightly so—that it was concerned with creative processes that can be truly grasped only by experience, though intellect may give them a name.'[1]

With these brief remarks I have only wished to show that we possess, within our cultural horizon, many great intuitions and anticipations of important psychological insights, though more often than not they are disregarded or identified with superstition. And yet they are merely reflections of basic psychological facts which have changed so little that what was true two thousand years ago is still a living, effective truth.[2] A detailed account of all these strivings for the same goal would far exceed the scope of the present book. The reader is referred to Jung's exhaustive investigations[3] in this field; and at this point it might be well to repeat his well-founded warning that all attempts to imitate the alchemists or subject a Westerner to Yoga exercises are extremely dangerous. Such endeavours can never go beyond the conscious will and the neurosis is only increased. For a European starts from entirely different premises; he cannot simply forget his European knowledge and culture and accept the Eastern forms of life and thought. 'The widening of our own consciousness ought not to be practised at the expense of other kinds of consciousness, but ought to take place through the development of those elements of our psyche which are analogous to those of a foreign psyche, just as the East cannot do without our technique, science, and industry.... The East came to its knowledge of inner things with a childish ignorance of the world.' The European takes a different path. 'We, on the other hand,' says Jung, 'will investigate the psyche and its depths supported by a tremendously extensive historical and scientific knowledge. At this present moment, indeed, knowledge of the external world is the greatest obstacle to

---

[1] *Alchemy*, pars. 219, 564.

[2] See also C. A. Meier, *Ancient Incubation and Modern Psychotherapy*.

[3] Those of Jung's works which are most relevant in this connection are: 'Psychological Commentary on *The Tibetan Book of the Dead*'; *The Secret of the Golden Flower*; 'Yoga and the West'; 'The Visions of Zosimos'; Foreword to Suzuki's *Introduction to Zen Buddhism*; 'Psychology and Religion'; 'The Psychology of Eastern Meditation'; *Psychology and Alchemy*; 'The Psychology of the Transference'; 'A Study in the Process of Individuation'; 'Concerning Mandala Symbolism'; *Mysterium Coniunctionis*; *Flying Saucers: A Modern Myth*.

introspection, but the psychological need will overcome all obstructions.'[1]

Thus those who recognize the reality of the psyche experience it not with the instruments of the understanding but with other means that have been the same since time immemorial. Each epoch seeks and finds its own ways of illuminating the inner cosmos, but through them all runs a continuity and kinship. Sometimes it might seem as though mankind were weary of the arduous journey and would never again find its way in the darkness. But if we look more closely, we shall see that there has been no cessation and that everything that has happened up to now has been a meaningful chain of 'episodes in a drama that began in the grey mists of antiquity and stretches through all the centuries into a remote future. This drama is an *Aurora consurgens*—the dawning of consciousness in mankind.'[2]

ANALYTICAL PSYCHOLOGY AND RELIGION

Thus Jung's psychology and his attempt to open up the eternal processes of psychic transformation to Western man are only 'a step in the developmental process of a higher human consciousness that finds itself on the way toward unknown goals; it is not metaphysics in the ordinary sense. In the first place, and to that extent, it is only "psychology", but also to that extent it can be experienced, it is intelligible, and . . . it is real, a reality with which something can be done, a reality containing possibilities and therefore alive.' If in his teachings Jung contents himself with psychic experience and rejects metaphysical considerations, this does not imply scepticism toward religion or the higher powers. 'Every statement about the transcendental,' he writes, 'ought to be avoided because it is invariably a laughable presumption on the part of the human mind, unconscious of its limitations. Therefore, when God or Tao is named as a stirring of, or a condition of, the soul, something has been said about the knowable only, but nothing about the unknowable. Of the latter, nothing can be determined.'[3]

Accordingly, when Jung as a psychologist says that God is an archetype, he is referring to the ' "type" in the psyche. The word "type" is, as we know, derived from τύπος, "blow" or

[1] Cf. *Golden Flower*, par. 63.   [2] *Alchemy*, par. 556.
[3] Cf. *Golden Flower*, par. 82.

"imprint"; thus an archetype presupposes an imprinter. . . . The competence of psychology as an empirical science only goes so far as to establish, on the basis of comparative research, whether for instance the imprint found in the psyche can or cannot reasonably be termed a "God-image". Nothing positive or negative has thus been asserted about the possible existence of God, any more than the archetype of the "hero" proves the actual existence of a hero. . . . As the eye to the sun, so the soul corresponds to God. . . . At all events the soul must contain in itself the faculty of relationship to God, i.e. a correspondence, otherwise a connection could never come about. This correspondence is, in psychological terms, the archetype of the God-image.'[1]

From the standpoint of psychology no more can or should be said. 'The religious point of view understands the imprint as the working of an imprinter; the scientific point of view understands it as the symbol of an unknown and incomprehensible content.'[2] For in the mirror of the human psyche we can glimpse the absolute only as it is refracted by our limited human nature; we cannot know its true essence. This faculty is immanent in the psyche; but the psyche can never do more than clothe its intimation of the absolute in a perceptible image. Such an image can provide conclusive proof of the human aspect alone, but not of the transcendent, which the psyche can never fully express.

Religious faith is a gift of grace; no one, not even a psychotherapist, can force it on you. 'Religion,' says Jung, 'is a "revealed" way of salvation. Its ideas are products of a preconscious knowledge which, always and everywhere, expresses itself in symbols. Even if our intellect does not grasp them, they still work, because our unconscious acknowledges them as exponents of universal psychic facts. For this reason faith is enough—if it is there. Every extension and intensification of rational consciousness, however, leads us further away from the sources of the symbols and, by its ascendency, prevents us from understanding them. That is the situation today. One cannot turn the clock back and force oneself to believe "what one knows is not true". But one could give a little thought to what the symbols really mean. In this way not only would the in-

---

[1] *Alchemy*, pars. 15 and 11. [2] Ibid., par. 20.

comparable treasures of our civilization be conserved, but we should also gain new access to the old truths which have vanished from our "rational" purview because of the strangeness of their symbolism. . . . The man of today lacks the very understanding that would help him to believe.'[1]

Jung knows too much about the harmful consequences of 'force-fed' doctrines accepted without reflection; he knows too well that only what has grown organically, not what has been tacked on, can be truly alive and effective, to exempt those who trust themselves to his guidance from the need for making their own decisions and accepting their own responsibilities. He refuses to facilitate the task by telling them what attitude to take. For in experiencing the profound symbolic contents of his psyche, the believer will encounter the eternal principles which confirm the workings of God within him and reinforce his belief that God created man in his own image, while the unbeliever, the man who does not want to believe or who yearns for faith but whom no effort of the will or intellect can help to achieve it, will be led at least to a true *experience* of the eternal foundations of his being and in this way perhaps will attain, at the end of his struggle, to the charisma of faith.

Those who have travelled this path know that it leads through experiences which cannot be described in words and which can only be likened to the great inner upheavals experienced by the mystics and initiates of all times. The individuation process leads not to the intellectual knowledge that is alien to faith, but to an experienced knowledge, the force and reality of which are really lived, so that it becomes an unshakeable certainty. What is both fundamentally new and infinitely promising is that this should be possible within the framework of a scientific doctrine built on strictly empirical, phenomenological foundations.

TRANSFORMATION AND MATURATION

To go the 'middle way' is the task of the mature, for the psychological situation of the individual varies with his age. At the beginning of life, he must fight his way from infancy, which is still wholly immersed in the collective unconscious, to a

---

[1] 'A Psychological Approach to the Dogma of the Trinity', p. 199.

differentiation and definition of his ego. He must gain a foothold in real life and above all master the problems it raises: sexuality, profession, marriage, children, human relationships of all sorts. It is through the greatest possible differentiation of his constitutionally superior function that he acquires the tools needed for this work of adaptation. Only when this task, which belongs to the first half of life, is completed does an adaptation to the inner world become a concomitant necessity. Once the attitude of the personality toward the outside world has been built up and consolidated, the individual can turn his energies toward the intrapsychic realities that have been hitherto more or less disregarded, and so approach a true wholeness. For, says Jung, 'man has two aims: the first is the natural aim, the begetting of children and the business of protecting the brood; to this belongs the acquisition of money and social position. When this aim has been reached, a new phase begins: the cultural aim.[1] . . . A spiritual goal that points beyond the purely natural man and his worldly existence is an absolute necessity for the health of the soul; it is therefore the Archimedean point from which alone it is possible to lift the world off its hinges and to transform the natural state into a cultural one.'[2]

To build the wholeness of the personality is a task of the whole of life. It seems to be a preparation for death in the deepest sense of the word. Death is no less important than birth and like birth it is an inseparable part of life. Here nature herself, if we only understand her properly, takes us into her sheltering arms. The older we grow the more veiled becomes the outside world, steadily losing in colour, tone, and passion, and the more urgently the inner world calls us. In ageing the individual melts little by little into the collective psyche from which with a great effort he emerged as a child. The cycle of human life closes meaningfully and harmoniously; beginning and end coincide, an event that has been symbolized since time immemorial by the Uroboros, the snake biting its own tail.[3]

If the task has been performed in the right way, death must lose its terrors and become a meaningful part of the whole life process. Yet it must be admitted that many men—as numerous

---

[1] 'Unconscious', p. 73.   [2] 'Education', p. 86.
[3] Cf. Plates 9 and 15, in which the Uroboros encompasses the Face of Eternity.

infantile adults bear witness—prove unequal to the tasks even of the first half of life. Consequently only a few are privileged to round out their lives by self-realization. But these few have always been the creators of culture, in contradistinction to those who have only created and promoted civilization. For civilization is always a child of the *ratio*, the intellect; culture, however, grows from the spirit, and spirit is never wholly confined to consciousness like the intellect, but also encompasses, masters, and gives form to all the depths of the unconscious, of primordial nature.

It is the particular and individual destiny of Western man—because historical conditions, origins, and *Zeitgeist* always contribute to the psychological situation of man—that over the centuries his instinctual side has atrophied through the over-differentiation of his intellect. Particularly in recent years the headlong development of technology has so far exceeded his powers of psychic assimilation that he has almost wholly lost his natural bond with the unconscious. He has become so unsure of his instincts that he is tossed about like a cork amid the raging, swollen waters of his unconscious or—as recent events have brought home to us—he is actually engulfed by the waves. 'Inasmuch as collectivities are mere accumulations of individuals,' says Jung, 'their problems are accumulations of individual problems. One set of people identifies itself with the superior man and cannot descend, and the other set identifies itself with the inferior man and wants to go to the top. Such problems are never solved by legislation or tricks. They are solved only by a general change of attitude. And the change does not begin with propaganda and mass meetings, or with violence. It begins with a change in individuals. It will continue as a transformation of their personal likes and dislikes, of their outlook on life and of their values, and only the accumulation of these individual changes will produce a collective solution.'[1]

Thus self-realization is not a fashionable experiment but the highest task that an individual can undertake. For *himself*, it means the possibility of an anchor in what is indestructible and imperishable, in the primordial nature of the objective psyche. By self-realization he returns to the eternal stream in which

[1] 'Religion', p. 79.

birth and death are only stations of passage and the meaning of life no longer resides in the ego. Towards *others*, it raises up within him the tolerance and kindness which are only possible in those who have explored and consciously experienced their own darkest depths. Toward the *collectivity*, its special value is that it can offer society a fully responsible individual who knows the obligation of the particular to the general from his own most personal experience, the experience of his own psychic totality.

RESPONSIBILITY RESTS WITH THE INDIVIDUAL

Despite its close connection with the fundamental problems of existence, Jungian psychology sets itself up to be neither a religion nor a philosophy. It is a scientific system of psychic experience. Just as biology is the science of the living physical organism, so it aspires to be the science of the living organism of the psyche, of the implement with which man has shaped and experienced religions and philosophies since the beginning of time. And only such a science of the human psyche can provide a basis for a *Weltanschauung* which is not just taken over unreflectingly from tradition, but which every individual can work out and shape for himself. Small wonder that in this day and age, when the collective psyche is threatening to reduce the individual soul to nothing, this doctrine can offer comfort and inner security, and that the task it imposes on us, though one of the hardest of all time, represents so urgent a summons: to bridge the opposition between individual and collectivity through the *full personality* rooted in them both.

In the Western world man's reason, his onesidedly differentiated consciousness, has outdistanced his instinctive nature; the result is a highly developed civilization and triumphant technology which seem to have lost all contact with the soul. It will be possible to restore our lost equilibrium only if we call in the creative powers of our own psychic depths to help us, only if we reinstate them in their rights, and raise them to the level of our intellect. But, says Jung, 'such a change can begin only with individuals'.[1] For since every collectivity is the sum of its individual members, it bears the imprint of these

---

[1] *Alchemy*, par. 563.

individuals' psychic attitudes. If once the transformed individual has recognized himself as 'God's image and likeness' in the deepest sense, the sense of ethical obligation, he will, as Jung says, become 'on one side a being of superior wisdom, on the other a being of superior will'.[1]

The responsibility for our future culture lies more than ever with the individual.

[1] 'Relations', par. 396.

BIOGRAPHICAL SKETCH OF C. G. JUNG

CARL GUSTAV JUNG was born on July 26, 1875, in Kesswil (Thurgau Canton), Switzerland. When he was four years old, his parents settled in Basel, the home of his mother's family. His paternal ancestors were of German origin, his grandfather having moved to Switzerland in 1822 when Alexander von Humboldt obtained an appointment for him as professor of surgery at the University of Basel. Jung's father was a clergyman and his forebears on both sides included many members of the liberal professions. Jung spent his school years in Basel, where he also studied medicine, but it was in Zurich, in 1900, as assistant at the University Psychiatric Clinic, that he began his career as a psychiatrist. Here he remained for the next nine years, the last four as senior staff physician. In 1902, he took a leave of absence to study theoretical psychopathology for a term under Pierre Janet at the Salpétrière in Paris. On his return to Switzerland he did research under E. Bleuler, then director of the Burghölzli Clinic in Zurich. As a result of these investigations he published a number of important papers on galvanic phenomena and the word association tests, the first of which appeared in 1904 and won him a wide reputation, numerous invitations to lecture abroad, and, among other distinctions, an honorary degree from Clark University, in Massachusetts, U.S.A. In 1905 he became an instructor in psychiatry at Zurich University. In 1909 he gave up his position at the Psychiatric Clinic to devote himself to his work as a physician and a psychotherapist, to scientific research and literary activity. In 1903 he married Emma Rauschenbach, who remained his loyal and invaluable collaborator up to the time of her death in 1955. She bore him a son and four daughters, all of whom are married and have numerous children and grandchildren of their own.

Jung's first meeting with Sigmund Freud occurred in 1907. This was the beginning of his intensive interest in psychoanalysis, which confirmed his own independent findings in experimental psychopathology. There followed a period of lively human and scientific exchange, in the course of which Jung became editor of the *Jahrbuch für psychoanalytische und psychopathologische Forschungen*, sponsored by Bleuler and Freud. In 1911 he founded and became first president of the International Psychoanalytic Association.

In 1912 Jung published his *Wandlungen und Symbole der Libido*, in which he criticized Freud's theories. He was clearly moving away from Freud's ideas, and in 1913 he broke with Freud and the psychoanalytic school. In that year Jung gave up his teaching activity to concentrate on psychological research, particularly concerning the nature and phenomenology of the unconscious. The first basic results of his studies were set forth, after a fallow period, in 'The Psychology of the Unconscious Process' and 'The Concept of the Unconscious', in 1917, later expanded into *Two Essays on Analytical Psychology*. The fuller implications of these ideas were worked out in *Psychological Types* (1921). Other publications followed, dealing with the nature of the collective unconscious and its relation to consciousness and with what he called the 'individuation process', a course of analytically furthered psychic development aiming to realize the potential wholeness of the human psyche. Much of this work opened up entirely new areas of thought.

In line with his investigations of the unconscious and its phenomenology, Jung felt the need to study the psychology of primitive peoples at first hand. He spent several months in North Africa in 1921 and travelled among the Pueblo Indians of Arizona and New Mexico in 1924–25; in the following year he visited the inhabitants of the southern and western slopes of Mt. Elgon in Kenya. The striking analogies between the contents of a modern European's unconscious and certain manifestations of the primitive psyche encouraged Jung to delve still more deeply into ethnology and the psychology of religion.

Soon he turned to the philosophical and religious symbolism of the Far East which further broadened his views. An important step in this respect was his meeting with Richard Wilhelm (died 1930), then director of the China-Institut in Frankfurt, who had translated and commented on many of the great works of Chinese philosophy and literature. In 1930 Jung and Wilhelm collaborated in the publication of an ancient Taoist text, *The Secret of the Golden Flower*. In later years Jung collaborated with Heinrich Zimmer (died 1943), the German Indologist, whose last work Jung edited under the title *Der Weg zum Selbst* (1944). Still later he worked with Karl Kerényi, the Hungarian philologist and mythologist. The fruit of their labours was the *Einführung in das Wesen der Mythologie* (Amsterdam, 1942, translated into English as *Essays on a Science of Mythology*, London and New York, 1949).

In addition to his extensive practice as a psychotherapist, Jung delivered many lectures at the invitation of various congresses and universities such as Fordham, Clark, Yale, and Harvard. On the occasion of its tercentenary in 1936, Harvard University included him among the outstanding living scientists on whom it conferred honorary degrees. Other honorary degrees followed; invited to India by the committee for the celebration of the twentieth anniversary of the University of Calcutta, he received a Litt. D. from the Hindu University of Benares and from the Mohammedan University of Allahabad, and a Sc. D. from the University of Calcutta. In 1938 he received a Sc. D. at Oxford and was appointed a Fellow of the Royal Society of Medicine.

His scientific work, his worldwide interests, his extensive travels, and his openness to every exchange of ideas soon made Jung a leading figure in the field of psychological research. In 1930 he became honorary president of the Deutsche Ärztliche Gesellschaft für Psychotherapie (German Medical Society for Psychotherapy) and in 1933 president of the International General Medical Society for Psychotherapy. Until his resignation in 1939, he was editor of the *Zentralblatt für Psychotherapie und ihre Grenzgebiete*. In 1933 he resumed his academic lectures, now in the department of humane studies, Eidgenössische Technische Hochschule (Swiss Federal Polytechnic Institute) in Zurich. These lectures run to 11 privately circulated volumes. Between the years 1928 and 1939 he also delivered numerous seminars in English, [privately] issued in some 30 volumes, on dreams, visions, and the psychological interpretation of Nietzsche's *Thus Spake Zarathustra*.

For reasons of health he gave up his teaching at the Polytechnic Institute in 1942, but in 1944, though seriously overworked, he answered a call from the university of his home city of Basel to occupy a chair in medical psychology especially established for him. Unfortunately, illness forced him to resign in the following year. Since then he has given up his medical practice and devoted himself exclusively to his scientific and literary work. Among the distinctions with which his native land has honoured him may be mentioned the Literary Prize of the City of Zurich (1932), Honorary Membership in the Swiss Academy of Medical Sciences (1943), the honorary doctorates conferred on him in 1945, on the occasion of his seventieth birthday, by the University of Geneva and in 1955, on the occasion of his eightieth birthday, by the Federal Polytechnic Institute of Zurich.

During the last ten years he also devoted increasing interest to problems of the human collectivity. His widely-read essay 'The Undiscovered Self' (*Collected Works*, 10) bears eloquent witness to this interest. He even found time at the very end of his life, with the loyal assistance of Mrs. Aniela Jaffé, one of his pupils, to set down his penetrating autobiography *Memories, Dreams, Reflections*. After World War II Jung turned his attention more and more to the psychic centring processes and their symbolism. These studies gave rise to a number of important works, such as *Aion*, an investigation of the history of symbols, and the two massive volumes on the *Mysterium Coniunctionis*. He also showed renewed interest in the broad field of parapsychological manifestations, to which he had devoted his doctoral dissertation. His independent studies in this domain enabled him to develop new orientations and principles of explanation.

In his last twenty years Jung published a number of basic works, primarily dealing with the psychological connotations of alchemy and with the psychology of religion, on which subjects he has thrown an entirely new light. Jung's published works include some 30 books and 90 articles and essays of varying length. Not only has he opened up entirely new pathways in the psychology of the unconscious; he has also touched fruitfully on many other fields. Jung's works have been translated into almost all European and some non-European languages. They meet with steadily increasing interest even among specialists in disciplines apparently remote from psychology. A complete English edition has appeared simultaneously in the U.S.A. and England, and a German edition in Zurich; each comprises nearly 20 large volumes.

On June 6, 1961 Jung died after a short illness just before attaining his 86th year. In him we have lost one of the boldest and wisest of all who in our time have sought to heal and illuminate the mind of man. He has, however, left behind for us his great work and it is up to us loyally to carry it on.

THE C. G. JUNG INSTITUTE

In conclusion I should like to mention a particular milestone, the founding of the C. G. Jung Institute of Zurich, in 1948, on the initiative of various psychological societies and prominent scientists in Switzerland and abroad. Organized as a foundation, it is devoted to training and research in analytic psychology, having set itself the task of developing Jung's ideas in the spirit of their founder, of creating a centre for all endeavours in this direction, of extending their field of application, and producing a well-trained body of successors. The teaching staff is made up of highly experienced specialists trained by Jung himself; courses are given in English as well as German. Research scholars and students from all countries are admitted. An extensive library of the relevant literature is available to them.

To obtain an analyst's diploma, a student must attend the Institute for at least six semesters; he must pass a propaedeutic examination in the theoretical subjects and a final examination in the practical subjects, and he must submit a thesis. In addition, each student must undergo an analysis of roughly 300 sessions and conduct supervised analyses totalling at least 250 hours. In order that the lectures and research findings should at least in part be made available to a wider public, the Institute publishes a series of studies entitled *Studien aus dem C. G. Jung Institut, Zurich*, which are also being published in English.

SHORT TITLE LIST

The following abbreviations are used in the footnotes for the titles of certain of C. G. Jung's works to which reference is frequently made. For full bibliographical details see List of Works Cited: Works of C. G. Jung, below.

Alchemy	*Psychology and Alchemy*
'Dream Analysis'	'The Practical Use of Dream Analysis'
'Education'	'Analytical Psychology and Education'
'Energy'	'On Psychic Energy'
Golden Flower	Commentary on *The Secret of the Golden Flower*
'Nature'	'On the Nature of the Psyche'
'Relations'	'The Relations between the Ego and the Unconscious'
'Religion'	'Psychology and Religion'
Types	*Psychological Types*
'Unconscious'	'The Psychology of the Unconscious'

LIST OF WORKS CITED

I. WORKS BY C. G. JUNG

The edition of the Collected Works of C. G. Jung now in process is used for citations from his writings made in this volume. Particulars of this edition are given below. (C.W.=Collected Works.)

'The Aims of Psychotherapy.' in C.W. 16.
Aion: Researches into the Phenomenology of the Self. C.W. 9, ii.
'Analytical Psychology and Education.' In C.W. 17.
'Analytical Psychology and Weltanschauung.' In C.W. 8.
'Archaic Man.' In C.W. 10.
'Concerning Mandala Symbolism.' In C.W. 9, i.
'The Development of Personality.' In C.W. 17.
Essays on a Science of Mythology. (With C. Kerényi.) Translated by R. F. C. Hull. New York (Bollingen Series XXII), 1949; London (as *Introduction to a Science of Mythology*), 1950.
'Flying Saucers: A Modern Myth.' In C.W. 10.
Foreword to Suzuki's *Introduction to Zen Buddhism.* In C.W. 11.
'General Aspects of Dream Psychology.' In C.W. 8.

'The Gifted Child.' In C.W. 17.

'Instinct and the Unconscious.' In C.W. 8.

Introduction to M. Esther Harding, *Woman's Mysteries*, q.v. below under 'Works of Others'. (Also C.W. 18.)

Kindertraumseminare. Mimeographed for private circulation.

Mysterium Coniunctionis. C.W. 14.

'On the Nature of Dreams.' In C.W. 8.

'On the Nature of the Psyche.' In C.W. 8.

'On Psychic Energy.' In C.W. 8.

'On the Relation of Analytical Psychology to Poetry.' In C.W. 15.

'The Practical Use of Dream Analysis.' In C.W. 16.

Preface to *Collected Papers on Analytical Psychology*. Also in C.W. 4.

'Principles of Practical Psychotherapy.' In C.W. 16.

'Psychoanalysis and Neurosis.' In C.W. 4.

'A Psychological Approach to the Dogma of the Trinity.' In C.W. 11.

'Psychological Aspects of the Mother Archetype.' In C.W. 9, i.

'Psychological Commentary on the *Tibetan Book of the Dead*.' In C.W. 11.

'A Psychological Theory of Types.' In C.W. 6.

Psychological Types. C.W. 6.

Psychology and Alchemy. C.W. 12.

'The Psychology of the Child Archetype.' In C.W. 9, i.

'The Psychology of Eastern Meditation.' In C.W. 11.

'Psychology and Religion.' In C.W. 11.

'The Psychology of the Transference.' In C.W. 16.

'The Psychology of the Unconscious.' In C.W. 7.

'The Relations between the Ego and the Unconscious.' In C.W. 7.

'A Review of the Complex Theory.' In C.W. 8.

The Secret of the Golden Flower, Commentary on. In C.W. 13. (Original work in collaboration with Richard Wilhelm.)

'Some Crucial Points in Psychoanalysis.' In C.W. 4.

'The Soul and Death.' In C.W. 8.

'The Spiritual Problem of Modern Man.' In C.W. 10.

The Structure and Dynamics of the Psyche. C.W.8.

'The Structure of the Psyche.' In C.W. 8.

Studies in Word Association. (With others.) In C.W. 2.

'A Study in the Process of Individuation.' In C.W. 9, i.

Symbols of Transformation. C.W. 5.

'Synchronicity: An Acausal Connecting Principle.' In C.W. 8.

'The Transcendent Function.' In C.W. 8.

Two Essays on Analytical Psychology. C.W. 7.

'The Visions of Zosimos.' In C.W. 13.

Wandlungen und Symbole der Libido. Leipzig and Vienna, 1912. [Translated by B. M. Hinkle as *Psychology of the Unconscious,* 1916. Revised version, *Symbols of Transformation,* C.W. 5.]
'Yoga and the West.' In C.W. 11.

II. WORKS BY OTHER AUTHORS

Adler, Gerhard. *The Living Symbol.* New York and London, 1961.
Studies in Analytical Psychology. Second edition. New York and London, 1966.
Augustine, St. *Liber de diversis quaestionibus LXXXIII.* In J. P. Migne, *Patrologia Latina,* vol. 40, cols. 11–100.
Bash, K. W. 'Gestalt, Symbol und Archetypus.' *Schweizerische Zeitschrift für Psychologie* (Bern), V (1946), 2: 127–38.
Baynes, H. G. *Germany Possessed.* London, 1941.
Boehme, Jacob. *Theosophische Schrifften.* Amsterdam, 1682. (Consists of a number of parts variously bound up.)
Bohr, Niels. 'Das Quantenpostulat und die neuere Entwicklung der Atomistik.' *Die Naturwissenschaften* (Brunswick), XVI (1928), 245–57.
Bohr, Niels (*contd*). 'Wirkungsquantum und Naturbeschreibung.' *Die Naturwissenschaften* (Brunswick), XVII (1929), 483–86.
Chamisso de Boncourt, Louis Charles Adelaïde de. [*Peter Schlemihl's wundersame Geschichte.*] *The Shadowless Man, Peter Schlemihl.* Translated by Sir John Bowring. London, 1910.
Dionysius the pseudo-Areopagite. *On the Divine Names.* Translated by the Editors of the Shrine of Wisdom. Fintry (Surrey, England), 1957.
Freud, Sigmund. *The Psychopathology of Everyday Life.* Translated by Alan Tyson. Standard Edition of the Complete Psychological Works of Sigmund Freud, vol. 6. London and New York, 1960 [1961]. (Also in *The Basic Writings of Sigmund Freud,* New York (Modern Library), 1938.)
Die geheimen Figuren der Rosenkreuzer. Altona, 1785–88. 2 volumes.
Harding, M. Esther. *Woman's Mysteries.* Revised edition. New York, 1955.
Hesse, Hermann. *Steppenwolf.* Translated by Basil Creighton. London, 1929. (Original: *Der Steppenwolf.* Berlin, 1927.)
Huxley, Aldous. *Grey Eminence.* London, 1941.
I Ching. The German translation by Richard Wilhelm, rendered into English by Cary F. Baynes. 3rd edn., Princeton (Bollingen Series XIX) and London, 1967.

Jacobi, Jolande. *Complex/Archetype/Symbol in the Psychology of C. G. Jung*. Translated by Ralph Manheim. New York (Bollingen Series LVII) and London, 1959.

Two Essays on Freud and Jung. Zurich (privately printed for the Students' Association of the C. G. Jung-Institut, Zurich), 1958.

(with R. F. C. Hull) *C. G. Jung: Psychological Reflections: A New Anthology of His Writings 1905–1961*. Princeton (Bollingen Series XXXI) and London, 1970.

The Way of Individuation. New York and London, 1967.

Jaffé, Aniela. *The Myth of Meaning (in the Work of C. G. Jung)*. Translated by R. F. C. Hull. New York and London, 1971.

Jordan, Pascual. *Anschauliche Quantentheorie*. Berlin, 1936.

Die Physik des 20. Jahrhunderts. Brunswick, 1936.

Die Physik und das Geheimnis des organischen Lebens. Brunswick, 1941.

'Positivische Bemerkungen über die parapsychischen Erscheinungen.' *Zentralblatt für Psychotherapie* (Leipzig), 9 (1936), 3–17.

'Quantenphysikalische Bemerkungen zur Biologie und Psychologie.' *Erkenntnis* (Leipzig), 4 (1934), 215–52.

Jung, Emma. 'Ein Beitrag zum Problem des Animus', in Jung, C. G.: *Wirklichkeit der Seele* (Zurich, 1947). Translation: 'On the Nature of the Animus', by Cary F. Baynes, New York (Analytical Psychology Club), 1957.

Killian, Johann. *Der Kristall*. Berlin, 1937.

Knoll, Max. 'Transformations of Science in Our Age.' Translated by Ralph Manheim. In: *Man and Time*. Papers from the Eranos Yearbooks, 3. New York (Bollingen Series XXX, 3) and London, 1957.

'Quantenhafte Energiebegriffe in Physik und Psychologie', *Eranos-Jahrbuch* XXI (1952), Zurich, 1953.

Kranefeldt, Wolfgang W. *Secret Ways of the Mind*. Translated [from *Die Psychoanalyse, psychoanalytische Psychologie*] by Ralph M. Eaton. New York, 1932; London, 1934.

Meier, C. A. *Ancient Incubation and Modern Psychotherapy*. Translated by Monica Curtis. Evanston, 1967.

'Moderne Physik—moderne Psychotherapie.' In *Die kulturelle Bedeutung der komplexen Psychologie*. (Festschrift zum 60. Geburtstag von C. G. Jung), Berlin, 1935.

'Spontanmanifestationen des kollektiven Unbewussten.' *Zentralblatt für Psychotherapie* (Leipzig), XI (1939), 284–303.

Neitzsche, Friedrich. *Human, All-too-Human*. Translated by Helen Zimmern and Paul V. Cohn. (Complete Works, 6, 7.) London and New York, 1910, 1911. 2 vols.

Thus Spake Zarathustra. Translated by Walter Kaufmann. In: *The Portable Nietzsche*. New York, 1954.

Rosarium philosophorum. Secunda pars alchimiae de lapide philoso-phorum. Frankfort, 1550.

Schopenhauer, Arthur. *Aphorismen zur Lebensweisheit.* Translated in: *Essays from the Parerga and Paralipomena.* Translated by T. Bailey Saunders. London, 1951.

Scott, Walter (ed. and trans.) *Hermetica.* Oxford, 1924–36. 4 vols.

Shelley, Mary Wollstonecraft. *Frankenstein, or The Modern Prometheus.* London, 1818.

Silberer, Herbert. *Problems of Mysticism and its Symbolism.* Translated by Smith Ely Jelliffe. New York, 1917. (Original, Vienna, 1914.)

Stevenson, Robert Louis. *Strange Case of Dr. Jekyll and Mr. Hyde.* London, 1886.

Verworn, Max. *Kausale und konditionale Weltanschauung.* 3rd. edition. Jena, 1928.

Wilde, Oscar. 'The Fisherman and His Soul.' In: *A House of Pome-granates.* London, 1891.

Wolff, Toni. *Studien zu C. G. Jungs Psychologie.* Zurich, 1959.

Zimmer, Heinrich. *Der Weg zum Selbst.* Zurich, 1944.

BIBLIOGRAPHY OF WRITINGS BY
C. G. JUNG

GERMAN WRITINGS

Reprints are not generally recorded here. A few minor contributions to periodicals, forewords to books by other authors, and the like, have been omitted. (A full bibliography will be included in the final volume of the Collected Works.)

1. *Zur Psychologie und Pathologie sogenannter occulter Phänomene.* Leipzig: Mutze, 1902.

2. 'Ein Fall von hysterischem Stupor bei einer Untersuchungsgefangenen.' *Journal für Psychologie und Neurologie,* I (3), 1902

3. 'Über manische Verstimmung.' *Allgemeine Zeitschrift für Psychiatrie,* LXI (1), 1903.

4. 'Über Simulation von Geistesstörung.' *Journal für Psychologie und Neurologie,* II (5), 1903.

5. 'Ärztliches Gutachten über einen Fall von simulierter geistiger Störung.' *Schweizerische Zeitschrift für Strafrecht,* XVII, 1904.

6. 'Experimentelle Untersuchungen über Assoziationen Gesunder.' (With F. Riklin.) *Journal für Psychologie und Neurologie,* III (1-2, 4-6) and IV (1-2), 1904.

7. 'Über hysterisches Verlesen.' *Archiv für die gesamte Psychologie,* III (4), 1904.

8. 'Kryptomnesie.' *Die Zukunft,* 13th Year (50), 1905.

9. 'Experimentelle Beobachtungen über das Erinnerungsvermögen.' *Zentralblatt für Nervenheilkunde und Psychiatrie,* XXVIII (196), 1905.

10. 'Zur psychologischen Tatbestandsdiagnostik.' *Zentralblatt für Nervenheilkunde und Psychiatrie,* XXVIII, 1905.

11. 'Analyse der Assoziationen eines Epileptikers.' *Journal für Psychologie und Neurologie,* V (2), 1905.

12. 'Über das Verhalten der Reaktionszeit beim Assoziationsexperiment.' *Journal für Psychologie und Neurologie,* VI (1), 1905.

13. 'Psychoanalyse und Assoziationsexperiment.' *Journal für Psychologie und Neurologie,* VII (1-2), 1905.

14. 'Obergutachten über zwei sich widersprechende psychiatrische Gutachten.' *Monatsschrift für Kriminalpsychologie und Strafrechtsreform,* II (11-12), 1906.

15. 'Die psychologische Diagnose des Tatbestandes.' *Juristischpsychiatrische Grenzfragen,* IV (2), 1906.

16. 'Assoziation, Traum und hysterisches Symptom.' *Journal für Psychologie und Neurologie*, VIII (1–2), 1906.

17. 'Die psychopathologische Bedeutung des Assoziationsexperimentes.' *Archiv für Kriminalanthropologie und Kriminalistik*, XXII (2–3), 1906.

18. 'Die Hysterielehre Freuds, eine Erwiderung auf die Aschaffenburgsche Kritik.' *Münchener medizinische Wochenschrift*, LIII (47), 1906.

19. *Diagnostische Assoziationsstudien*. Vol. I. Leipzig: Barth, 1906.

    (1) Experimentelle Untersuchungen über die Assoziationen Gesunder. (With F. Riklin.) (See no. 6.)

    (2) Analyse der Assoziationen eines Epileptikers. (See 11.)

    (3) Über das Verhalten der Reaktionszeit beim Assoziationsexperiment. (See 12.)

    (4) Psychoanalyse und Assoziationsexperiment. (See 13.)

20. 'Statistisches von der Rekrutenaushebung.' *Correspondenz-Blatt für Schweizer Ärzte*, XXXVI (4), 1906.

21. *Über die Psychologie der Dementia praecox*. Halle: Marhold, 1907.

22. 'Über die Reproduktionsstörungen beim Assoziationsexperiment.' *Journal für Psychologie und Neurologie*, IX (4), 1907.

23. 'Die Freud'sche Hysterietheorie.' *Monatsschrift für Psychiatrie und Neurologie*, XXIII (4), 1908.

24. *Der Inhalt der Psychose*. Leipzig and Vienna: Deuticke, 1908.

25. 'Komplexe und Krankheitsursachen bei Dementia praecox.' (With E. Bleuler.) *Zentralblatt für Nervenheilkunde und Psychiatrie*, XXXI (N.S. XIX), (2), 1908.

26. 'Die Bedeutung des Vaters für das Schicksal des Einzelnen.' *Jahrbuch für Psychoanalytische und Psychopathologische Forschungen*, I, and as pamphlet, Leipzig and Vienna: Deuticke, 1909.

27. 'Vorbemerkung der Redaktion.' *Jahrbuch für psychoanalytische und psychopathologische Forschungen*, I, 1909.

28. *Diagnostische Assoziationsstudien*. Vol. II. Leipzig: Barth, 1909.

    (1) Assoziation, Traum und hysterisches Symptom. (See 16.)

    (2) Über die Reproduktionsstörungen beim Assoziationsexperiment. (See 22.)

29. 'Referate über psychologische Arbeiten schweizerischer Autoren' (bis Ende 1909). *Jahrbuch für psychoanalytische und psychopathologische Forschungen*, II, 1910.

30. 'Bericht über Amerika.' *Jahrbuch für psychoanalytische und psychopathologische Forschungen*, II, 1910.

31. 'Die an der psychiatrischen Klinik in Zürich gebräuchlichen psychologischen Untersuchungsmethoden.' *Zeitschrift für angewandte Psychologie*, III, 1910.

32. 'Ein Beitrag zur Psychologie des Gerüchtes.' *Zentralblatt für Psychoanalyse*, I (3), 1910.

33. 'Über Konflikte der kindlichen Seele.' *Jahrbuch für psychoanalytische und psychopathologische Forschungen*, II, 1910; and in pamphlet form, Leipzig and Vienna: Deuticke, 1910. 3rd edn., Zurich: Rascher, 1939.

34. 'Zur Kritik über Psychoanalyse.' *Jahrbuch für psychoanalytische und psychopathologische Forschungen*, II, 1910.

35. 'Randbemerkungen zu dem Buch von Fr. Wittels "Die Sexuelle Not".' *Jahrbuch für psychoanalytische und psychopathologische Forschungen*, II, 1910.

36. 'Ein Beitrag zur Kenntnis des Zahlentraumes.' *Zentralblatt für Psychoanalyse*, I (12), 1911.

37. 'Kritik über E. Bleulers "Zur Theorie des schizophrenen Negativismus".' *Jahrbuch für psychoanalytische und psychopathologische Forschungen*, III, 1911.

38. 'Morton Prince, M. D., "The Mechanism and Interpretation of Dreams". Eine kritische Besprechung.' *Jahrbuch für psychoanalytische und psychopathologische Forschungen*, III, 1911.

39. 'Wandlungen und Symbole der Libido.' *Jahrbuch für psychoanalytische und psychopathologische Forschungen*, III and IV, 1911–12. Also in volume form, Leipzig and Vienna: Deuticke, 1912; 3rd edn. 1938. (See 169.)

40. 'Neue Bahnen der Psychologie.' *Raschers Jahrbuch für Schweizer Art und Kunst* (Zurich), 1912. (See also 47.)

41. 'Zur Psychoanalyse.' *Wissen und Leben*, IX (10), 1912.

42. 'Über Psychoanalyse beim Kinde.' First International Congress of Pedagogy, Brussels, August 1911. Brussels: Misch et Thron, 1912.

43. 'Über die psychoanalytische Behandlung nervöser Leiden.' *Correspondenz-Blatt für Schweizer Ärzte*, XLII, 1912.

44. 'Versuch einer Darstellung der psychoanalytischen Theorie.' *Jahrbuch für psychoanalytische und psychopathologische Forschungen*, V, 1913; in volume form, Leipzig and Vienna: Deuticke, 1913; Zurich, Rascher, 1955.

45. 'Eine Bemerkung zur Tauskschen Kritik der Nelkenschen Arbeit.' *Internationale Zeitschrift für ärztliche Psychoanalyse*, I, 1913.

46. *Psychotherapeutische Zeitfragen*. Ein Briefwechsel mit C. G. Jung. Edited by R. Loÿ. Leipzig and Vienna: Deuticke, 1914.

47. *Die Psychologie der unbewussten Prozesse*. Zurich: Rascher, 1917. Revised and enlarged from 40. See also 54.

48. 'Über das Unbewusste.' *Schweizerland*, IV (9 and 11–12), 1918.

49. *Psychologische Typen*. Zurich: Rascher, 1921.

50. 'Über die Beziehungen der analytischen Psychologie zum dichterischen Kunstwerk.' *Wissen und Leben*, XV (19 and 20), 1922.
51. 'Psychologische Typen.' Lecture at Territet. *Zeitschrift für Menschenkunde*, I (1), 1925.
52. 'Die Ehe als psychologische Beziehung.' In *Das Ehebuch*, edited by Count Hermann Keyserling. Celle: Kampmann, 1925.
53. 'Geist und Leben.' *Form und Sinn*, II (2), 1926.
54. *Das Unbewusste im normalen und kranken Seelenleben*. Zurich: Rascher, 1926. (Revised and enlarged edition of 47.) (See 132.)
55. *Analytische Psychologie und Erziehung*. Heidelberg: Kampmann, 1926 (Later: Zurich: Rascher, 1936.) (See 145.)
56. 'Die Erdbedingtheit der Psyche.' In *Mensch und Erde*, edited by Count Hermann Keyserling. Darmstadt: Reichl, 1927.
57. 'Die Frau in Europa.' *Europäische Revue*, III (7), 1927.
58. *Die Beziehungen zwischen dem Ich und dem Unbewussten*. Darmstadt: Reichl, 1928. Later edition: Zurich: Rascher, 1935.
59. 'Heilbare Geisteskranke?' *Berliner Tageblatt*, 189 (April 21) Supplement, 1928.
60. 'Die Bedeutung der schweizerischen Linie im Spektrum Europas.' *Neue Schweizer Rundschau*, XXXIV (6), 1928.
61. 'Das Seelenproblem des modernen Menschen.' *Europäische Revue*, IV (2), 1928.
62. *Über die Energetik der Seele*. Zurich: Rascher, 1928. See also 153.

   (1) Über die Energetik der Seele.
   (2) Allgemeine Gesichtspunkte zur Psychologie des Traumes.
   (3) Instinkt und Unbewusstes.
   (4) Die psychologischen Grundlagen des Geisterglaubens.

63. 'Die Struktur der Seele.' *Europäische Revue*, IV (1 and 2), 1928.
64. 'Psychoanalyse und Seelsorge.' *Sexual- und Gesellschaftsethik*, V (1), 1928.
65. 'Der Gegensatz Freud und Jung.' *Kölnische Zeitung*, 2496 (Evening edition), May 7, 1929.
66. 'Tschung Scheng Schu. Die Kunst das menschliche Leben zu verlängern.' (With Richard Wilhelm.) *Europäische Revue*, V (2), 1929.
67. *Das Geheimnis der goldenen Blüte*. (With Richard Wilhelm.) Translated from the Chinese [into German] by Richard Wilhelm. European Commentary by C. G. Jung. Munich: Dorn, 1929. Second edition: Zurich: Rascher, 1938.
68. 'Die Probleme der modernen Psychotherapie.' *Schweizerisches medizinisches Jahrbuch*, 1929.
69. 'Die Bedeutung von Konstitution and Vererbung für die Psychologie.' *Die medizinische Welt*, III (47), 1929.

70. *Die Frau in Europa.* 57 republished as a pamphlet. Zurich: Neue Schweizer Rundschau, 1929. Later edition: Zurich, 1932.

71. 'Die seelischen Probleme der menschlichen Altersstufen.' *Neue Zürcher Zeitung*, March 14 and 16, 1930.

72. 'Nachruf für Richard Wilhelm.' *Neue Zürcher Zeitung*, March 6, 1930.

73. Introduction to W. M. Krancfeldt: *Die Psychoanalyse.* Berlin and Leipzig: De Gruyter, 1930.

74. 'Psychologie und Dichtung.' In *Philosophie der Literaturwissenschaft*, edited by E. Ermatinger. Berlin, 1930.

75. 'Der Aufgang einer neuen Welt.' Review of H. Keyserling: *America Set Free. Neue Zürcher Zeitung*, 2378, December 7, 1930.

76. Introduction to F. Wickes' *Analyse der Kinderseele.* Stuttgart: Hoffmann, 1931.

77. 'Der archaische Mensch.' *Europäische Revue*, VII (1/3), 1931.

78. Foreword to H. Schmid-Guisan: *Tag und Nacht.* Zurich: Rhein Verlag, 1931.

79. 'Die Entschleierung der Seele.' *Europäische Revue*, VII (2/7), 1931.

80. *Seelenprobleme der Gegenwart.* Zurich: Rascher, 1931.

    (1) Die Probleme der modernen Psychotherapie. (See 68.)
    (2) Über die Beziehungen der analytischen Psychologie zum dichterischen Kunstwerk. (See 50.)
    (3) Der Gegensatz Freud und Jung. (See 65.)
    (4) Ziele der Psychotherapie.
    (5) Psychologische Typologie.
    (6) Die Struktur der Seele. (See 63.)
    (7) Seele und Erde. (See 56.)
    (8) Der archaische Mensch. (See 77.)
    (9) Die Lebenswende. (See 71.)
    (10) Die Ehe als psychologische Beziehung. (See 52.)
    (11) Analytische Psychologie und Weltanschauung.
    (12) Geist und Leben. (See 53.)
    (13) Das Seelenproblem des modernen Menschen. (See 61.)

81. Foreword to O. A. Schmitz: *Märchen aus dem Unbewussten.* Munich: Hauser, 1932.

82. 'Die Hypothese des kollektiven Unbewussten.' *Vierteljahresschrift der Naturforschungen-Gesellschaft*, Zurich, Beer, 1932.

83. *Die Beziehungen der Psychotherapie zur Seelsorge.* Zurich: Rascher, 1932.

84. 'Nachruf für Dr. H. Schmid-Guisan.' *Basler Nachrichten*, April 1932.

85. 'Ulysses.' *Europäische Revue*, VIII (2/9), 1932.

86. 'Sigmund Freud als kulturhistorische Erscheinung.' *Charakter*, I (1), 1932.
87. 'Picasso.' *Neue Zürcher Zeitung*, CLIII (2), November 13, 1932.
88. 'Wirklichkeit und Überwirklichkeit.' *Querschnitt*, XII (12), 1933.
89. 'Über Psychologie.' *Neue Schweizer Rundschau*, I (1–2), 1933.
90. 'Bruder Klaus.' *Neue Schweizer Rundschau*, I (4), 1933.
91. Review of G. R. Heyer: *Organismus der Seele*. *Europäische Revue*, IX (10), 1933.
92. Preface to G. Adler: *Entdeckung der Seele*. Zurich: Rascher, 1934.
93. 'Zur gegenwärtigen Lage der Psychotherapie.' *Zentralblatt für Psychotherapie und ihre Grenzgebiete*, VII (1), 1934.
94. 'Zeitgenössisches.' Rejoinder to Dr. Bally's article 'Deutschstämmige Psychotherapie'. *Neue Zürcher Zeitung*, CLV (437–43), March 13–14, 1934.
95. 'Seele und Tod.' *Europäische Revue*, X (4), 1934.
96. *Wirklichkeit der Seele*. Zurich, Rascher, 1934.

    (1) Das Grundproblem der gegenwärtigen Psychologie. (See 79.)
    (2) Die Bedeutung der Psychologie für die Gegenwart. (See 89.)
    (3) Die praktische Verwendbarkeit der Traumanalyse.
    (4) Paracelsus.
    (5) Sigmund Freud als kulturhistorische Erscheinung. (See 86.)
    (6) Ulysses. (See 85.)
    (7) Picasso. (See 87.)
    (8) Vom Werden der Persönlichkeit.
    (9) Seele und Tod. (See 95.)
    (10)–(13) Papers by other authors.

97. 'Zur Empirie des Individuationsprozesses.' *Eranos-Jahrbuch 1933*, Zurich: Rhein-Verlag, 1934.
98. 'Ein neues Buch von Keyserling.' Review of H. Keyserling: *La Revolution mondiale*. *Sonntagsblatt der Basler Nachrichten*, XXVIII (19), May 13, 1934.
99. Preface to a popular edition of C. L. Schleich: *Die Wunder der Seele*. Berlin: Fischer, 1934.
100. 'Allgemeines zur Komplextheorie.' Aarau: Sauerländer, 1934.
101. 'Über die Archetypen des kollektiven Unbewussten.' *Eranos-Jahrbuch 1934*, Zurich: Rhein-Verlag, 1935.
102. 'Grundsätzliches zur praktischen Psychotherapie.' *Zentralblatt für Psychotherapie und ihre Grenzgebiete*, VIII (2), 1935.

103. 'Was ist Psychotherapie?' *Schweizerische Ärztezeitung für Standesfragen*, XVI (26), 1935.

104. Foreword to R. Mehlich: *J. H. Fichtes Seelenlehre und ihre Beziehung zur Gegenwart*. Zurich: Rascher, 1935.

105. Foreword to Esther Harding: *Der Weg der Frau*. Zurich: Rhein-Verlag, 1935.

106. Foreword to O. von Koenig-Fachsenfeld: *Wandlungen des Traumproblems von der Romantik bis zur Gegenwart*. Stuttgart: Enke, 1935.

107. Psychological Commentary to the 'Bardo Thödol'. In *Das Tibetanische Totenbuch*, ed. W. Y. Evans-Wentz. Zurich: Rascher, 1935.

108. 'Von der Psychologie des Sterbens.' *Münchener Neueste Nachrichten*, 269, October 2, 1935. See 96 (9).

109. 'Psychologische Typologie.' *Süddeutsche Monatshefte*, XXXIII (5), 1936.

110. 'Wotan.' *Neue Schweizer Rundschau*, III (11), 1936.

111. Review of G. R. Heyer: *Praktische Seelenheilkunde. Zentralblatt für Psychotherapie und ihre Grenzgebiete*, IX (3), 1936.

112. 'Traumsymbole des Individuationsprozesses.' *Eranos-Jahrbuch 1935*, Zurich: Rhein-Verlag, 1936.

113. 'Über den Archetypus, mit besonderer Berücksichtigung des Animabegriffes.' *Zentralblatt für Psychotherapie und ihre Grenzgebiete*, IX (5), 1936.

114. 'Die Erlösungsvorstellungen in der Alchemie.' *Eranos-Jahrbuch 1936*, Zurich: Rhein-Verlag, 1937.

115. 'Zur psychologischen Tatbestandsdiagnostik.' *Archiv für Kriminologie*, C (1–2), 1937.

116. 'Einige Bemerkungen zu den Visionen des Zosimos.' *Eranos-Jahrbuch 1937*, Zurich: Rhein-Verlag, 1938.

117. Introduction to D. T. Suzuki: *Die grosse Befreiung*. Leipzig: Weller, 1939.

118. 'Die psychologischen Aspekte des Mutterarchetypus.' *Eranos-Jahrbuch 1938*, Zurich: Rhein-Verlag, 1939.

119. 'Bewusstsein, Unbewusstes und Individuation.' *Zentralblatt für Psychotherapie und ihre Grenzgebiete*, XI (5), 1939.

120. 'Sigmund Freud. Ein Nachruf.' *Sonntagsblatt der Basler Nachrichten*, XXXIII (40), October 1, 1939.

121. 'Die verschiedenen Aspekte der Wiedergeburt.' *Eranos-Jahrbuch 1939*, Zurich: Rhein-Verlag, 1940.

122. *Psychologie und Religion*. Zurich: Rascher, 1940.

123. Preface to J. Jacobi: *Die Psychologie von C. G. Jung*. Zurich: Rascher, 1940.

124. *Das göttliche Kind.* (With K. Kerényi.) (Albae Vigiliae VI/VII.) Amsterdam and Leipzig: Pantheon Akademische Verlagsanstalt, 1941. (Contains 'Zur Psychologie des Kind-Archetypus'.)
125. *Das göttliche Mädchen.* (With K. Kerényi.) (Albae Vigiliae, VIII/IX.) Amsterdam and Leipzig; Pantheon Verlagsanstalt, 1941. (Contains 'Zum psychologischen Aspekt der Kore-Figur'.)
126. 'Rückkehr zum einfachen Leben.' *Du,* Schweizerische Monatsschrift, I (3), 1941.
127. 'Paracelsus als Arzt.' *Schweizerische medizinische Wochenschrift,* LXXI (40), 1941.
128. *Einführung in das Wesen der Mythologie.* (With K. Kerényi.) (Incorporates nos. 124 and 125.) Amsterdam: Pantheon Akademische Verlagsanstalt, 1941; later edn., Zurich: Rhein-Verlag, 1951.
129. *Paracelsica.* Zurich: Rascher, 1942.

    (1) Vorwort.
    (2) Paracelsus als Arzt. (See 127.)
    (3) Paracelsus als geistige Erscheinung.
    (4) Schlusswort.

130. 'Zur Psychologie der Trinitätsidee.' *Eranos-Jahrbuch 1940/41,* Zurich: Rhein-Verlag, 1942.
131. 'Das Wandlungssymbol in der Messe.' *Eranos-Jahrbuch 1940/41,* Zurich: Rhein-Verlag, 1942.
132. *Über die Psychologie des Unbewussten.* Zurich: Rascher, 1943. (Revised edition of 54.)

    (1) Die Psychoanalyse.
    (2) Die Erostheorie.
    (3) Der andere Gesichtspunkt: Der Wille zur Macht.
    (4) Das Problem des Einstellungstypus.
    (5) Das persönliche und das überpersönliche oder kollektive Unbewusste.
    (6) Die synthetische oder konstruktive Methode.
    (7) Die Archetypen des kollektiven Unbewussten.
    (8) Zur Auffassung des Unbewussten: Allgemeines zur Therapie.
    (9) Schlusswort.

133. 'Der Geist Mercurius.' *Eranos-Jahrbuch 1942,* Zurich: Rhein-Verlag, 1943.
134. 'Votum.' *Schweizer Erziehungs-Rundschau,* XVI (1), 1943.
135. 'Zur Psychologie östlicher Meditation.' *Mitteilungen der Schweizerischen Gesellschaft der Freunde ostasiatischer Kultur,* V, 1943.

136. 'Psychotherapie und Weltanschauung.' *Schweizerische Zeitschrift für Psychologie und ihre Anwendungen*, I (3), 1943.

137. *Psychologie und Alchemie.* Zurich: Rascher, 1944.

    (1) Einleitung in die religionspsychologische Problematik der Alchemie.
    (2) Traumsymbole des Individuationsprozesses. (See 112.)
    (3) Die Erlösungsvorstellungen in der Alchemie. (See 114.)
    (4) Epilog.

138. 'Über den indischen Heiligen.' Foreword to H. Zimmer: *Der Weg zum Selbst.* Rascher, Zurich, 1944.

139. 'Die Psychotherapie in der Gegenwart.' *Schweizerische Zeitschrift für Psychologie und ihre Grenzgebiete*, IV (1), 1945.

140. 'Medizin und Psychotherapie.' *Bulletin der Schweizerischen Akademie der medizinischen Wissenschaften*, I (5), 1945.

141. 'Nach der Katastrophe.' *Neue Schweizer Rundschau*, XIII (2), 1945.

142. 'Vom Wesen der Träume.' *Ciba-Zeitschrift*, IX (99), 1945.

143. 'Das Rätsel von Bologna.' Contribution to *Festschrift für Albert Oeri.* Published by Basler Nachrichten, Basel, 1945.

144. 'Der philosophische Baum.' *Verhandlungen der Naturforschenden Gesellschaft Basel*, LVI (2), 1945.

145. *Psychologie und Erziehung.* Zurich: Rascher, 1946.

    (1) Analytische Psychologie und Erziehung. (See 55.)
    (2) Über Konflikte der kindlichen Seele (See 33.)
    (3) Der Begabte. (See 134.)

146. *Aufsätze zur Zeitgeschichte.* Zurich: Rascher, 1946.

    (1) Wotan. (See 110.)
    (2) Die Psychotherapie in der Gegenwart (See 139.)
    (3) Psychotherapie und Weltanschauung. (See 136.)
    (4) Nach der Katastrophe. (See 141.)
    (5) Nachwort.

147. 'Zur Psychologie des Geistes.' *Eranos-Jahrbuch 1945*, Zurich: Rhein-Verlag, 1946.

148. *Die Psychologie der Übertragung.* Zurich: Rascher, 1946.

    (1) Vorrede.
    (2) Einleitende Überlegungen zum Problem der Übertragung.
    (3) Die Bilderserie des Rosarium Philosophorum als Grundlage für die Darstellung des Übertragungsphänomens.
    (4) Schlusswort.

149. 'Der Geist der Psychologie.' *Eranos-Jahrbuch 1946*, Zurich: Rhein-Verlag, 1947.

150. Foreword to Linda Fierz-David: *Der Liebestraum des Poliphilo*. Zurich: Rhein-Verlag. 1947.

151. 'Schatten, Animus und Anima.' *Wiener Zeitschrift für Nervenheilkunde und deren Grenzgebiete*, I (4), 1948.

152. *Symbolik des Geistes*. Zurich: Rascher, 1948.

    (1) Vorwort.
    (2) Zur Phänomenologie des Geistes im Märchen. (See 147.)
    (3) Der Geist Mercurius. (See 133.)
    (4) Die Gestalt des Satans im Alten Testament. (By Dr. R. Schärf.)
    (5) Versuch zu einer psychologischen Deutung des Trinitätsdogmas. (See 130.)
    (6) Zur Psychologie östlicher Meditation. (See 135.)

153. *Über psychische Energetik und das Wesen der Träume*. Zurich: Rascher, 1948.

    (1) Über die Energetik der Seele. (See 62.)
    (2) Allgemeines zur Komplextheorie. (See 100.)
    (3) Allgemeine Gesichtspunkte zur Psychologie des Traumes. (See 62.)
    (4) Vom Wesen der Träume. (See 142.)
    (5) Instinkt und Unbewusstes. (See 62.)
    (6) Die psychologischen Grundlagen des Geisterglaubens. (See 62.)

154. Foreword to Stewart Edward White: *Uneingeschränktes Weltall*. Zurich: Origo-Verlag, 1948.

155. Foreword to Esther Harding: *Das Geheimnis der Seele*. Zurich: Rhein-Verlag, 1948.

156. 'De Sulphure.' *Nova Acta Paracelsica*, V, 1948. (See 178.)

157. Introduction to Esther Harding: *Frauen-Mysterien*. Zurich: Rascher, 1949.

158. Introduction to C. A. Meier: *Antike Inkubation und moderne Psychotherapie*. Zurich: Rascher, 1949.

159. 'Über das Selbst.' *Eranos-Jahrbuch 1948*, Zurich: Rhein-Verlag, 1949.

160. Foreword to Erich Neumann: *Ursprungsgeschichte des Bewusstseins*. Zurich: Rascher, 1949.

161. Foreword to Gerhard Adler: *Zur analytischen Psychologie*. Zurich: Rascher, 1949.

162. *Gestaltungen des Unbewussten.* Zurich: Rascher, 1950.
    (1) Psychologie und Dichtung. (See 74.)
    (2) Über Wiedergeburt. (See 121.)
    (3) Zur Empirie des Individuationsprozesses. (See 97.)
    (4) Über Mandalasymbolik. (See 67.)
    (5) (Essay by another author.)
163. Foreword to F. Moser: *Spuk.* Baden bei Zurich: Gyr, 1950.
164. Foreword to Lily Abegg: *Ostasien denkt anders.* Zurich: Atlantis, 1950.
165. 'Grundfragen der Psychotherapie.' *Dialectica,* V (1), 1951.
166. Foreword to Carl Ludwig Schleich: *Die Wunder der Seele.* Frankfort a/M: Fischer, 1951.
167. *Aion. Untersuchungen zur Symbolgeschicte.* Zurich: Rascher, 1951.
168. 'Über Synchronizität. *Eranos-Jahrbuch 1951.* Zurich: Rhein-Verlag, 1952.
169. *Symbole der Wandlung.* (Revised version of no. 39.) Zurich: Rascher, 1952.
170. *Antwort auf Hiob.* Zurich: Rascher, 1952.
171. *Naturerklärung und Psyche.* (With W. Pauli.) Zurich: Rascher, 1952. (Includes 'Synchronizität als ein Prinzip akausaler Zusammenhänge'.)
172. 'Religion und Psychologie.' *Merkur,* IV (5), 1952.
173. *Von den Wurzeln des Bewusstseins.* Zurich: Rascher, 1954.
    (1) Über die Archetypen des kollektiven Unbewussten. (See 101.)
    (2) Über den Archetypus mit besonderer Berücksichtigung des Animabegriffes. (See 113.)
    (3) Die psychologischen Aspekte des Mutterarchetypus. (See 118.)
    (4) Die Visionen des Zosimos. (See 116.)
    (5) Das Wandlungssymbol in der Messe. (See 131.)
    (6) Der philosophische Baum. (See 144.)
    (7) Theoretische Überlegungen zum Wesen des Psychischen. (See 149.)
174. Foreword to G. Schmaltz: *Komplexe Psychologie und körperliches Symptom.* Stuttgart: Hippokrates Verlag, 1954.
175. *Welt der Psyche.* Zurich: Rascher, 1954.
    (1) Vom Wesen der Träume. (See 142.)
    (2) Psychologie und Dichtung. (See 162.)
    (3) Beiträge zur Symbolik des Selbst. (See 167.)
    (4) Theoretische Überlegungen zum Wesen des Psychischen. (See 173.)
    (5) Nachwort.

176. *Der göttliche Schelm.* (With Paul Radin and K. Kerényi.) Zurich: Rhein-Verlag, 1954.
177. 'Mandalas.' *Du* (Zurich), XXIII (4), 1955.
178. *Mysterium Coniunctionis, Part I.* Zurich: Rascher, 1955.
179. Psychological Commentary (Foreword) to *Das Tibetische Buch der grossen Befreiung.* Edited by W. Y. Evans-Wents. Munich: Barth, 1955.
180. 'Wotan und der Rattenfänger.' *Der Monat,* IX (97), 1956.
181. *Mysterium Coniunctionis, Part II.* Zurich: Rascher, 1956.
182. *Bewusstes und Unbewusstes.* Frankfort and Hamburg: Fischer-Bücherei, 1957.

    (1) (By E. Böhler.)
    (2) Über die Archetypen des kollektiven Unbewussten. (See 101.)
    (3) Einleitung in die religionspsychologische Problematik der Alchemie. (See 137.)
    (4) Zur Phänomenologie des Geistes im Märchen. (See 152.)
    (5) Zur Psychologie östlicher Meditation. (See 135.)
    (6) (By A. Jaffé.)

183. *Gegenwart und Zukunft.* Zurich: Rascher, 1957. (First appeared as Supplement to *Schweizer Monatshefte,* XXXVI (12), March 1957.)
184. Foreword to Victor White: *Gott und das Unbewusste.* Zurich: Rascher, 1957.
185. Foreword to Jolande Jacobi: *Komplex, Archetypus, Symbol in der Psychologie C. G. Jungs.* Zurich: Rascher, 1957.
186. Foreword to Eleanor Bertine: *Menschliche Beziehungen.* Zurich: Rhein-Verlag, 1957.
187. Foreword to Felicia Froboese-Thiele: *Träume, eine Quelle religiöser Erfahrung?* Göttingen: Vandenhoeck und Ruprecht, 1957.
188. 'Ein astrologisches Experiment.' *Zeitschrift für Parapsychologie und Grenzgebiete der Psychologie,* I (2–3), 1958.
189. 'Nationalcharakter und Verkehrsverhalten.' A Letter. *Zentralblatt für Verkehrsmedizin, Verkehrspsychologie und angrenzende Gebiete,* IV (3), 1958.
190. *Ein moderner Mythos. Von Dingen die am Himmel gesehen werden.* Zurich: Rascher, 1958.
191. 'Die transzendente Funktion.' (Written 1916.) In *Geist und Werk,* Festschrift for Dr. D. Brody. Zurich: Rhein-Verlag, 1958.
192. 'Das Gewissen in psychologischer Sicht.' In: *Das Gewissen.* Studien aus dem C. G. Jung-Institut, Zurich, VII. Zurich: Rascher, 1958.

193. 'Die Schizophrenie.' *Schweizer Archiv für Neurologie und Psychiatrie*, LXXXI (1–2), 1958.

194. *Praxis der Psychotherapie.* (Gesammelte Werke, vol. 16.) Zurich: Rascher, 1959.

195. Foreword to Aniela Jaffé: *Geistererscheinungen und Vorzeichen.* Zurich: Rascher, 1958.

196. Introduction and contribution to Otto Kankeleit: *Das Unbewusste als Keimstätte des Schöpferischen.* Munich and Basel: Reinhardt, 1959.

197. Foreword to Toni Wolff: *Studien zu C. G. Jungs Psychologie.* Zurich: Rhein-Verlag, 1959.

198. 'Neuere Betrachtungen von Schizophrenie.' *Universitas*, XIV (1), 1959.

199. 'Gut und Böse in der analytischen Psychologie.' In Wilhelm Bitter(ed.): *Gut und Böse in der Psychotherapie: Ein Tagungsbericht.* Stuttgart: Klett-Verlag, 1959.

200. Preface to Frieda Fordham: *Eine Einführung in die Psychologie C. G. Jungs.* Zurich: Rascher, 1959.

201. Commentary to W. Pöldinger: 'Zur Bedeutung bildnerischen Gestaltens in der psychiatrischen Diagnostik.' *Die Therapie des Monats* (Swiss edition), February 1959. Mannheim-Waldhof; C. F. Boehringer und Söhne.

202. *Psychologische Typen.* (Gesammelte Werke, vol. 6.) Zurich: Rascher, 1960.

203. Epilogue to Arthur Koestler: *Von Heiligen und Automaten.* Berlin: Scherz, 1961.

204. 'Ein Brief zur Frage der Synchronizität.' *Zeitschrift für Parapsychologie und Grenzgebiete der Psychologie*, V (1), 1961.

205. *Erinnerungen, Träume, Gedanken.* Recorded and edited by Aniela Jaffé. Zurich: Rascher, 1962.

206. *Zur Psychologie westlicher und östlicher Religion.* (Gesammelte Werke, vol. 11.) Zurich: Rascher, 1963.

207. Foreword to Cornelia Brunner: *Die Anima als Schicksalsproblem des Mannes.* Studien aus dem C. G. Jung-Institut, Zurich, XIV. Zurich: Rascher, 1963.

208. *Zwei Schriften über Analytische Psychologie.* (Gesammelte Werke, vol. 7.) Zurich: Rascher, 1964.

209. *Psychiatrische Studien.* (Gesammelte Werke, vol. 1.) Zurich: Rascher, 1966.

210. *Die Dynamik des Unbewussten.* (Gesammelte Werke, vol. 8.) Zurich: Rascher, 1967.

211. *Psychogenese der Geisteskrankheiten.* (Gesammelte Werke, vol. 3.) Zurich: Rascher, 1968.

212. *Der Mensch und seine Symbol.* (With M.-L. von Franz, Joseph L. Henderson, Jolande Jacobi, and Aniela Jaffé.) Olten and Freiburg im Breisgau: Walter, 1968.
213. *Mysterium Coniunctionis.* (Gesammelte Werke, vol. 14.) Zurich: Rascher, 1968. 2 vols.
214. *Freud und die Psychoanalyse.* (Gesammelte Werke, vol. 4.) Zurich: Rascher, 1969.
215. *Über Grundlagen der analytischen Psychologie. Die Tavistock Lectures 1935.* Olten: Walter, 1969.
216. *Mensch und Seele. Aus den psychologischen Schriften 1905 bis 1961.* Selected and edited by Jolande Jacobi. Olten: Walter, 1971.
217. *Über das Phänomen des Geistes in Kunst und Wissenschaft.* (Gesammelte Werke, vol. 15.) Olten: Walter, 1971.
218. *Briefe 1906–1961.* Selected and edited by Aniela Jaffé in collaboration with Gerhard Adler. Vol. 1: 1906–1945. Olten: Walter, 1971.

WRITINGS AND TRANSLATIONS IN ENGLISH

The following list does not generally record dates of reprints, except where later editions include important textual changes or additions. Cross-references are given to the German originals by their numbers in the preceding list; and to the volumes of the Collected Works of C. G. Jung in which the item in question has appeared or will appear. (G. = German bibliography, above; C.W. = Collected Works.) Prefaces, forewords, etc. written by Dr. Jung for books by other authors, and a few minor articles in periodicals, are omitted. (All these will be recorded in a complete bibliography of Dr. Jung's writings to appear in the final volume of the Collected Works.)

1. 'On Psychophysical Relations of the Associative Experiment.' *Journal of Abnormal Psychology* (Boston, Paris, London), I: 1907. (C.W. 2, ii.)
2. 'Psychophysical Investigations with the Galvanometer and Pneumograph in Normal and Insane Individuals.' (With F. Peterson.) *Brain* (London), XXX: 118, 1907. (C.W. 2, ii.)
3. 'Further Investigations on the Galvanic Phenomenon and Respiration in Normal and Insane Individuals.' (With C. Ricksher.) *Journal of Abnormal and Social Psychology* (Albany, N.Y.), II: 5, 1907–8. (C.W. 2, ii.)

4. *The Psychology of Dementia Praecox.* Trans. from G. 21 by F. W. Peterson and A. A. Brill. New York: Nervous and Mental Disease Publishing Co., 1909. (Retrans. by A. A. Brill alone, same publishers, 1936.) (C.W. 3.)

5. 'The Association Method.' *American Journal of Psychology* (Worcester, Mass.), XXI: 2, 1910. Later repub. in 11, below. (Cf. C.W. 2, ii and 17.)

6. 'On the Doctrine of Complexes.' *Transactions of Australasian Medical Congress* (1911), 9th Session, vol. 2, part 8, 1913.

7. 'Psychoanalysis.' Anonymous translation of 'Allgemeine Aspekte der Psychoanalyse'. *Transactions of the Psycho-Medical Society* (Cockermouth), IV: 2, Aug. 5, 1913. (C.W. 4.)

8. 'On the Importance of the Unconscious in Psychopathology'. *British Medical Journal* (London), II (Dec. 5), 1914. (C.W. 3.)

9. 'On Psychological Understanding.' *Journal of Abnormal Psychology* (Boston, Paris, London), IX, 1914. (C.W. 3.)

10. *The Theory of Psychoanalysis.* New York: Nervous and Mental Disease Publishing Co., 1915. Trans. from G. 44. First appeared in English in *Psychoanalytic Review* (New York), I: 1, 2, 3, 4; II: 1, 1913–15. (Cf. C.W. 4.)

11. *Collected Papers on Analytical Psychology.* Ed. by Constance Long. (Translations by M. D. Eder, A. A. Brill, Edith Eder, C. E. Long, and Dora Hecht.) London: Baillière, Tindall and Cox, 1916 (2nd edn., London; Baillière, Tindall and Cox, and New York: Moffat Yard, 1917).

Contents:

(1) 'On the Psychology and Pathology of So-called Occult Phenomena.' (G. 1; C.W. 1.)
(2) 'The Association Method.' (See 5 above; C.W. 2.) (Trans. from text written in German but unpublished.)
(3) 'The Significance of the Father in the Destiny of the Individual.' (G. 26; C.W. 4.)
(4) 'A Contribution to the Psychology of Rumour.' (G. 32; C.W. 4.)
(5) 'On the Significance of Number-Dreams.' (G. 36; C.W. 4.)
(6) 'A Criticism of Bleuler's "Theory of Schizophrenic Negativism".' (G. 37; C.W. 3.)
(7) 'Psychoanalysis.' (See 7 above.) (C.W. 4.)
(8) 'On Psychoanalysis.' (G. 41; C.W. 4.)
(9) 'On Some Crucial Points in Psychoanalysis.' (G. 46; C.W. 4.)

(10) 'On the Importance of the Unconscious in Psycho-pathology.' (See 8 above; C.W. 4.)

(11) 'A Contribution to the Study of Psychological Types.' (French 3; C.W. 6, ii.)

(12) 'The Psychology of Dreams.' (Later expanded as G. 62(2); C.W. 8.)

(13) 'The Content of the Psychoses.' (G. 24; C.W. 3.)

(14) 'New Paths in Psychology.' (G. 40; C.W. 7.)

In the second edition a revised version of (14) was substituted for it, under the title 'The Psychology of the Unconscious Processes'; and there was added:

(15) 'The Conception of the Unconscious.' (French 4; C.W. 7.)

12. *Psychology of the Unconscious.* Trans. from G. 39 by Beatrice M. Hinkle. New York: Moffat Yard; London: Kegan Paul, 1916. (Cf. C.W. 5.)

13. *Studies in Word Association.* Under the direction of C. G. Jung. Trans. by M. D. Eder from G. 19 and G. 28. London: Heinemann, 1918; New York: Moffat Yard, 1919. (Cf. C.W. 2, i and ii.)

14. 'Instinct and the Unconscious.' *British Journal of Psychology* (London), X: 1, 1919. Trans. by C. F. and H. G. Baynes from a German text, subsequently published in G. 62(3). (Cf. C.W. 8.)

15. 'On the Problem of Psychogenesis in Mental Disease.' *Proceedings of the Royal Society of Medicine* (London), XII: 3, Section of Psychiatry, 1919. (C.W. 3.)

16. 'The Psychological Foundations of Belief in Spirits.' *Proceedings of the Society for Psychical Research* (London), XXXI: 1. 1920. Trans. by (?) C. F. and H. G. Baynes from a German text subsequently published as G. 62(4). (Cf. C.W. 8.)

17. 'The Question of the Therapeutic Value of Abreaction.' *British Journal of Psychology* (London), II: 1, 1921. (Cf. C.W. 16.)

18. *Psychological Types.* Trans. from G. 49 by H. G. Baynes. New York: Harcourt Brace; London: Kegan Paul, 1923. (C.W. 6.)

19. 'On the Relation of Analytical Psychology to Poetic Art.' *British Journal of Medical Psychology* (London), III: 3, 1925. Trans. for G. 50 by C. F. and H. G. Baynes. (C.W. 15.)

20. 'Psychological Types.' In *Problems of Personality*: Studies presented to Dr. Morton Prince. New York: Harcourt Brace; London: Kegan Paul, 1925. Trans. from G. 51. Later retrans. as 22 (12) below. (C.W. 6.)

21. 'Marriage as a Psychological Relationship.' In *The Book of Marriage*, edited by Count Hermann Keyserling. New York: Harcourt Brace, 1926. Trans. from G. 52 by Therese Duerr. (C.W. 17.)

22. *Contributions to Analytical Psychology*. Translated by C. F. and H. G. Baynes. New York, Harcourt Brace: London, Kegan Paul, 1928.

    Contents:

    (1) 'On Psychical Energy.' (G. 62(1); C.W. 10.)
    (2) 'Spirit and Life.' (G. 53; C.W. 8.)
    (3) 'Mind and the Earth.' (Subsequently G. 80(7); C.W. 10.)
    (4) 'Analytical Psychology and Weltanschauung.' (Subsequently G. 80(11); C.W. 8.)
    (5) 'Woman in Europe.' (G. 57; C.W. 10.)
    (6) 'Marriage as a Psychological Relationship.' (G. 52; C.W. 17.)
    (7) 'The Love Problem of the Student.' (From an unpub. German MS.; C.W. 10.)
    (8) 'On the Relation of Analytical Psychology to Poetic Art.' (G. 50; C.W. 15.)
    (9) 'The Psychological Foundations of Belief in Spirits.' (C.W. 8.)
    (10) 'Instinct and the Unconscious.' (Subsequently G. 62(3); C.W. 8.)
    (11) 'The Question of the Therapeutic Value of Abreaction.' (Cf. C.W. 16.)
    (12) 'Psychological Types.' (G. 51; C.W. 6.)
    (13) 'Analytical Psychology and Education.' (Cf. G. 55; C.W. 17.)
    (14) 'The Significance of the Unconscious in Individual Education.' (From an unpub. German MS.; C.W. 17.)

23. *Two Essays on Analytical Psychology*. Trans. from G. 54 and G. 58 by C. F. and H. G. Baynes. New York: Dodd, Mead; London: Baillière, Tindall and Cox, 1928. (C.W. 7.)

24. 'Some Aspects of Modern Psychotherapy.' *Journal of State Medicine* (London), XXXVIII: 6, 1930. (C.W. 16.)

25. 'Your Negroid and Indian Behaviour.' *Forum* (New York), LXXXIII: 4, 1930. (CW. 10, as 'Complications of American Psychology'.)

26. 'Psychology and Poetry.' *transition* (Paris), 19–20, 1930. Translated from G. 74 by Eugene Jolas. (C.W. 15.)

27. 'The Spiritual Problem of Modern Man.' *Prabuddha Bharata* (Calcutta), Aug. and Sept. 1931. (G. 61; C.W. 10.)

28. 'Problems of Modern Psychotherapy.' *Schweizerische Medizinische Wochenschrift* (Basel), LXI: 35, 1931. Trans. from G. 68 by C. F. Baynes. (C.W. 16.)

29. *The Secret of the Golden Flower.* (With Richard Wilhelm.) Trans. by C. F. Baynes. New York: Harcourt Brace; London: Kegan Paul, 1931.

   Contents (by Jung):

   > (1) 'Commentary.' (G. 67; C.W. 13.)
   > (2) 'Examples of European Mandalas.' (C.W. 9, i.)
   > (3) 'In Memory of Richard Wilhelm.' (G. 72; C.W. 15.)

30. 'Sigmund Freud in his Historical Setting.' *Character and Personality* (Durham, N.C.), I: 1, 1932. Trans. from G. 86 by Cary F. Baynes. (C.W. 15.)

31. *Modern Man in Search of a Soul.* Trans. by W. S. Dell and C. F. Baynes. New York: Harcourt Brace; London: Kegan Paul, 1933.

   Contents:

   > (1) 'Dream Analysis in its Practical Application.' (Subsequently G. 96(3); C.W. 16.)
   > (2) 'Problems of Modern Psychotherapy.' (G. 68; C.W. 16.)
   > (3) 'The Aims of Psychotherapy.' (G. 80(4); C.W. 16.)
   > (4) 'A Psychological Theory of Types.' (G. 80(5); C.W.6.)
   > (5) 'The Stages of Life.' (G. 80(9); C.W. 8.)
   > (6) 'Freud and Jung: Contrasts.' (G. 80(3); C.W. 4.)
   > (7) 'Archaic Man' (G. 80(8); C.W. 10.)
   > (8) 'Psychology and Literature.' (G. 74; C.W. 15.)
   > (9) 'The Basic Postulates of Analytical Psychology.' (G. 79; C.W. 8.)
   > (10) 'The Spiritual Problem of Modern Man.' (G. 80 (13); C.W. 10.)
   > (11) 'Psychotherapists or the Clergy.' (G. 83; C.W. 11.)

32. 'Yoga and the West.' *Prabuddha Bharata* (Calcutta), Shri Ramakrishna Centenary Number, Feb. 1936. (C.W. 11.)

33. 'The Concept of the Collective Unconscious.' Parts I and II. *St. Bartholomew's Hospital Journal* (London), XLIV: 3 and 4, 1936–37. (C.W. 9, i.)

34. 'Psychological Factors Determining Human Behavior.' In: *Factors Determining Human Behavior*. Cambridge, Mass: Harvard University Press, 1937. (C.W. 8.)

35. 'Wotan.' *Saturday Review of Literature* (New York), XVI (Oct. 16), 1937. Translated and abridged from G. 110 by (Barbara Hannah?). (C.W. 10.)

36. *Psychology and Religion*. New Haven: Yale University Press; London: Oxford University Press, 1938. (Subsequently somewhat expanded as G. 122.) (Cf. C.W. 11.)

37. 'The Dreamlike World of India.' *Asia* (New York), XXXIX: 1, 1939. (C.W. 10.)

38. 'What India Can Teach Us.' *Asia* (New York), XXXIX: 2, 1939. (C.W. 10.)

39. 'On the Psychogenesis of Schizophrenia.' *Journal of Mental Science* (London), LXXXV: 358, 1939. (C.W. 3.)

40. *The Integration of the Personality*. Trans. by Stanley Dell. New York: Farrar and Rinehart, 1939; London: Kegan Paul, 1940.

    Contents:

    (1) 'The Meaning of Individuation.' (Subsequently, in shortened form, G. 119; Cf. C.W. 9, i: 'Conscious, Unconscious, and Individuation'.)

    (2) 'A Study in the Process of Individuation.' (G. 97; C.W. 9, i.)

    (3) 'Archetypes of the Collective Unconscious.' (G. 101; C.W. 9, i.)

    (4) 'Dream Symbols of the Process of Individuation.' (G. 112; C.W. 12.)

    (5) 'The Idea of Redemption in Alchemy.' (G. 114; C.W. 12.)

    (6) 'The Development of the Personality.' (G. 96(8); C.W. 17.)

41. 'Brother Klaus.' *Journal of Nervous and Mental Disease* (New York), CIII: 4, 1946. Translated from G. 90 by Horace Gray. (C.W. 11.)

42. 'The Fight with the Shadow.' The *Listener* (London), XXXVI: 930, 1946. (Cf. C.W. 10.)

43. 'The Bologna Enigma.' *Ambix* (London), II: 3–4, 1946. (G. 143; C.W. 14.)

44. *Essays on Contemporary Events*. London: Kegan Paul, 1947.

   Contents:

   (1) Preface. Trans. by Elizabeth Welsh.
   (2) Introduction: 'Individual and Mass Psychology.' (Repub., from 42 above, with new title.) (C.W. 10.)
   (3) 'Wotan.' Trans. from G. 146(1) by Barbara Hannah. (C.W. 10.)
   (4) 'Psychotherapy Today.' Trans. from G. 146(2) by Mary Briner. (C.W. 16.)
   (5) 'Psychotherapy and a Philosophy of Life.' Trans. from G. 146(3) by Mary Briner. (C.W. 16.)
   (6) 'After the Catastrophe.' Trans. from G. 146(4) by Elizabeth Welsh. (C.W. 10.)
   (7) 'Epilogue.' Trans. from G. 146(5) by Elizabeth Welsh. (C.W. 10.)

45. 'On the Psychology of Eastern Meditation.' *Art and Thought*. A Volume in honour of Ananda K. Coomaraswamy. London: Luzac, 1948. Translated from G. 135 by Carol Baumann.

46. *Essays on* (British edition, *Introduction to) a Science of Mythology*. (With C. Kerényi.) New York (Bollingen Series XXII): Pantheon Books, 1949; London: Routledge, 1950. Trans. from G. 128 by R. F. C. Hull.

   Contents by Jung:

   (1) 'The Psychology of the Child Archetype.' (C.W. 9, i.)
   (2) 'The Psychological Aspects of the Kore.' (C.W. 9, i.)

47. *Psychology and Alchemy*. (G. 179.) See Collected Works, 12. 1953.
48. *Two Essays on Analytical Psychology*. See Collected Works, 7. 1953.
49. 'Ulysses: A Monologue.' Translated from G. 131(6) by W. Stanley Dell. *Nimbus* (London), II: 1, 1953.
50. 'Picasso.' Translated from G. 131(7). *Nimbus* (London), II: 2, 1953.
51. 'The Spirit Mercury.' Translated from G. 133 by Gladys Phelan and Hildegard Nagel. New York: Analytical Psychology Club, 1953.
52. Psychological Commentary to *The Tibetan Book of the Great Liberation*. Edited by W. Y. Evans-Wentz. London and New York: Oxford University Press, 1954. (C.W. 11.)
53. *The Practice of Psychotherapy*. See Collected Works, 16. 1954.
54. *Spirit and Nature*. Papers from the Eranos Yearbooks, 1. New York (Bollingen Series XXX, 1): Pantheon Books, 1954; London: Routledge, 1955.

Contents by Jung:

    (1) 'The Phenomenology of the Spirit in Fairy Tales.'
        Translated from G. 152(2) by R. F. C. Hull. (C.W. 9, i.)

    (2) 'The Spirit of Psychology.' Translated from G. 149 by
        R. F. C. Hull. (C.W. 8, as 'On the Nature of the
        Psyche'.)

55. *The Development of Personality.* See Collected Works, 17. 1954.

56. *Answer to Job.* Translated from G. 213 by R. F. C. Hull. London:
Routledge, 1954; Great Neck (N.Y.): Pastoral Psychology
Book Club, 1956. (C.W. 11.)

57. *The Mysteries.* Papers from the Eranos Yearbooks, 2. New York
(Bollingen Series XXX, 2): Pantheon Books; London: Routledge, 1955. Contains, by Jung: 'Transformation Symbolism
in the Mass.' Translated from G. 131 by R. F. C. Hull.
(Cf. C.W. 11.)

58. *The Interpretation of Nature and the Psyche.* (With W. Pauli.) New
York (Bollingen Series LI): Pantheon Books; London: Routledge, 1955.

Contents, by Jung:

'Synchronicity: An Acausal Connecting Principle.' Translated from G. 214 (revised) by R. F. C. Hull. (C.W. 8.)

59. *Symbols of Transformation.* (G. 169.) See Collected Works, 5. 1956.

60. *Psychiatric Studies.* See Collected Works, 1. 1956.

61. 'Why and How I Wrote My "Answer to Job".' *Pastoral Psychology* (Great Neck, N.Y.), VI: 60, 1956. (Later repub. as Prefatory Note to 'Answer to Job' in C.W. 11.)

62. 'On the Psychology of the Trickster Figure.' Trans. from G. 176
by R. F. C. Hull. In *The Trickster: A Study in American Indian
Mythology.* By Paul Radin, with Commentaries by Karl
Kerényi and C. G. Jung. London: Routledge; New York:
Philosophical Library, 1956. (C.W. 9, i.)

63. 'Recent Thoughts on Schizophrenia.' A Broadcast for 'Voice of
America', 1956. *Bulletin of the Analytical Psychology Club* (New
York), XIX: 4, 1957. (Subsequently G. 198.) (C.W. 3.)

64. *Man and Time.* Papers from the Eranos Yearbooks, 3. New York
(Bollingen Series XXX, 3): Pantheon Books; 1957; London:
Routledge, 1958. Contains, by Jung: 'On Synchronicity'.
Trans. by R. F. C. Hull from a German original later ex-
panded into G. 214. (Cf. 58 above.)

65. 'The Transcendent Function.' Translated by A. R. Pope from a
German original written in 1916. Privately printed for the

Students' Association, C. G. Jung-Institut, Zurich, 1957. (C.W. 8.)

66. Psychological Commentary to *The Tibetan Book of the Dead*. Edited by W. Y. Evans-Wentz. London: Oxford University Press, 1957. Translated from G. 107 by R. F. C. Hull. (C.W. 11.)

67. *Psychology and Religion: West and East*. See Collected Works, 11. 1958.

68. *The Undiscovered Self*. Translated from G. 183 by R. F. C. Hull. Boston: Little Brown; London: Routledge, 1958. (C.W. 10.)

69. *Psyche and Symbol*. A Selection from the Writings of C. G. Jung. Edited by Violet S. de Laszlo, with a preface by C. G. Jung. Garden City, New York: Doubleday (Anchor Books), 1958.

70. *Flying Saucers: A Modern Myth of Things Seen in the Skies*. Translated by R. F. C. Hull from G. 190. New York: Harcourt Brace; London: Routledge, 1959. (C.W. 10.)

71. *The Archetypes and the Collective Unconscious*. See Collected Works, 9, i. 1959.

72. *Aion*. See Collected Works, 9, ii. 1959.

73. *The Basic Writings of C. G. Jung*. Edited by Violet S. de Laszlo. New York: Modern Library, 1959.

74. *The Psychogenesis of Mental Disease*. See Collected Works, 3. 1960.

75. *The Structure and Dynamics of the Psyche*. See Collected Works, 8. 1960.

76. *Spiritual Disciplines*. Papers from the Eranos Yearbooks, 4. New York (Bollingen Series, XXX, 4): Pantheon Books; London: Routledge, 1960. Contains, by Jung: 'Dream Symbols of the Individuation Process', trans. by R. F. C. Hull from G. 112. (Cf. C.W. 12.)

77. 'Good and Evil in Analytical Psychology.' Translated from G. 199. *Journal of Analytical Psychology* (London), V:2, 1960. (C.W. 10.)

78. *Freud and Psychoanalysis*. See Collected Works, 4. 1961.

79. 'The Symbolic Life.' *Darshana* (Moradabad, India), I:3, 1961. (A seminar talk originally given 1939 to the Guild of Pastoral Psychology, London. C.W. 18.)

80. *Memories, Dreams, Reflections*. Recorded and edited by Aniela Jaffé. Translated by Richard and Clara Winston. New York: Pantheon; London: Routledge & Kegan Paul and Collins, 1962.

81. *Mysterium Coniunctionis*. See Collected Works, 14. 1963.

82. *Civilization in Transition*. See Collected Works, 10. 1964.

83. *Man and His Symbols*. (With M.-L. von Franz, Joseph L. Henderson, Jolande Jacobi, Aniela Jaffé.) London: Aldus; New York:

Doubleday, 1964. (Jung, 'Approaching the Unconscious', in C.W. 18.)

84. *The Spirit in Man, Art, and Literature.* See Collected Works, 15. 1966.

85. 'The Realities of Practical Psychotherapy' (originally a lecture, 1937). In *The Practice of Psychotherapy*, 2nd edn. See Collected Works, 16. 1966.

86. *VII Sermones ad Mortuos.* Translated by H. G. Baynes. London: Stuart & Watkins, 1967. (Originally published privately, 1916. Also in *Memories, Dreams, Reflections* [No. 80], revised edn.)

87. 'Prefatory Note to the English Edition' (undated). In *Psychology and Alchemy*, 2nd edn. See Collected Works, 12. 1968.

88. *Alchemical Studies.* See Collected Works, 13. 1968.

89. *Analytical Psychology: Its Theory and Practice. The Tavistock Lectures.* New York: Pantheon; London: Routledge & Kegan Paul, 1968. (Originally given in London, 1935. In C.W. 18.)

90. *C. G. Jung: Psychological Reflections. A New Anthology of His Writings 1905–1961.* Princeton University Press (Bollingen Series XXXI); London: Routledge & Kegan Paul, 1970.

91. *Psychological Types.* See Collected Works, 6. 1971.

92. *The Portable Jung.* Edited by Joseph Campbell. New York: Viking, 1971.

93. *Experimental Researches.* See Collected Works, 2. 1972.

94. *C. G. Jung: Letters.* Selected and Edited by Gerhard Adler in collaboration with Aniela Jaffé. Vol. 1: 1906–1950. Princeton University Press (Bollingen Series XCIV); London: Routledge & Kegan Paul, 1972.

WRITINGS ORIGINALLY PUBLISHED IN FRENCH

1. 'Associations d'idées familiales.' *Archives de psychologie* (Geneva and Paris), VII: 26, 1907.

2. 'L'Analyse des rêves.' *Année psychologique* (Paris), XV, 1909.

3. 'Contribution à l'étude des types psychologiques.' *Archives de psychologie* (Geneva and Paris), XIII: 52, 1913. (C.W. 6, ii.)

4. 'La Structure de l'inconscient.' *Archives de psychologie* (Geneva and Paris), XVI: 62, 1916. (Written in German; trans. into French by M. Marsen.) (C.W.7.)

THE COLLECTED WORKS OF C. G. JUNG

The publication of the first complete edition, in English, of the works of C. G. Jung was undertaken by Routledge and Kegan Paul, Ltd., in England and by Bollingen Foundation in the United States. The American edition is number XX in Bollingen Series, which since 1967 has been published by Princeton University Press. Prior to his death, in 1961, the author supervised the textual revision, which in some cases is extensive. Sir Herbert Read (d. 1968), Dr. Michael Fordham, and Dr. Gerhard Adler compose the Editorial Committee; the translator is R. F. C. Hull (except for Volume 2) and William McGuire is executive editor.

In the following list, dates of original publication are given in parentheses (of original composition, in brackets). Multiple dates indicate revisions.

*1. PSYCHIATRIC STUDIES
   On the Psychology and Pathology of So-Called Occult Phenomena (1902); On Hysterical Misreading (1904); Cryptomnesia (1905); On Manic Mood Disorder (1903); A Case of Hysterical Stupor in a Prisoner in Detention (1902); On Simulated Insanity (1903); A Medical Opinion on a Case of Simulated Insanity (1904); A Third and Final Opinion on Two Contradictory Psychiatric Diagnoses (1906); On the Psychological Diagnosis of Facts (1905).

†2. EXPERIMENTAL RESEARCHES
   Translated by Leopold Stein in collaboration with Diana Riviere

   Studies in Word Association (1904–7, 1910):
      The Associations of Normal Subjects (by Jung and F. Riklin); An Analysis of the Associations of an Epileptic; The Reaction-Time Ratio in the Association Experiment; Experimental Observations on the Faculty of Memory; Psychoanalysis and Association Experiments; The Psychological Diagnosis of Evidence; Association, Dream, and Hysterical Symptom; The Psychopathological Significance of the Association Experiment; Disturbances in Reproduction in the Association Experiment; The Association Method; The Family Constellation.

* Published 1957; 2nd edn., 1970.   † Published 1972.

Psychophysical Researches (1907–8):
On the Psychophysical Relations of the Association Experiment; Psychophysical Investigations with the Galvanometer and Pneumograph in Normal and Insane Individuals (by F. Peterson and Jung); Further Investigations on the Galvanic Phenomenon and Respiration in Normal and Insane Individuals (by C. Ricksher and Jung); Appendix: Statistical Details of Enlistment (1906); New Aspects of Criminal Psychology (1908); The Psychological Methods of Investigation Used in the Psychiatric Clinic of the University of Zurich (1910); On the Doctrine of Complexes ([1911] 1913); On the Psychological Diagnosis of Evidence (1937).

*3. THE PSYCHOGENESIS OF MENTAL DISEASE
The Psychology of Dementia Praecox (1907); The Content of the Psychoses (1908/1914); On Psychological Understanding (1914); A Criticism of Bleuler's Theory of Schizophrenic Negativism (1911); On the Importance of the Unconscious in Psychopathology (1914); On the Problem of Psychogenesis in Mental Disease (1919); Mental Disease and the Psyche (1928); On the Psychogenesis of Schizophrenia (1939); Recent Thoughts on Schizophrenia (1957); Schizophrenia (1958).

†4. FREUD AND PSYCHOANALYSIS
Freud's Theory of Hysteria: A Reply to Aschaffenburg (1906); The Freudian Theory of Hysteria (1908); The Analysis of Dreams (1909); A Contribution to the Psychology of Rumour (1910–11); On the Significance of Number Dreams (1910–11); Morton Prince, "The Mechanism and Interpretation of Dreams": A Critical Review (1911); On the Criticism of Psychoanalysis (1910); Concerning Psychoanalysis (1912); The Theory of Psychoanalysis (1913); General Aspects of Psychoanalysis (1913); Psychoanalysis and Neurosis (1916); Some Crucial Points in Psychoanalysis: A Correspondence between Dr. Jung and Dr. Loÿ (1914); Prefaces to "Collected Papers on Analytical Psychology" (1916, 1917); The Significance of the Father in the Destiny of the Individual (1909/1949); Introduction to Kranefeldt's "Secret Ways of the Mind" (1930); Freud and Jung: Contrasts (1929).

‡5. SYMBOLS OF TRANSFORMATION (1911–12/1952)

* Published 1960. † Published 1961.
‡ Published 1956; 2nd edn., 1967.

*6. PSYCHOLOGICAL TYPES (1921)
   With Four Papers on Psychological Typology (1913, 1925, 1931, 1936).

†7. TWO ESSAYS ON ANALYTICAL PSYCHOLOGY
   On the Psychology of the Unconscious (1917/1926/1943); The Relations between the Ego and the Unconscious (1928); Appendix: New Paths in Psychology (1912); The Structure of the Unconscious (1916) (new versions, with variants, 1966).

‡8. THE STRUCTURE AND DYNAMICS OF THE PSYCHE
   On Psychic Energy (1928); The Transcendent Function ([1916]/1957); A Review of the Complex Theory (1934); The Significance of Constitution and Heredity in Psychology (1929). Psychological Factors Determining Human Behavior (1937); Instinct and the Unconscious (1919); The Structure of the Psyche (1927/1931); On the Nature of the Psyche (1947/1954); General Aspects of Dream Psychology (1916/1948); On the Nature of Dreams (1945/1948); The Psychological Foundations of Belief in Spirits (1920/1948); Spirit and Life (1926); Basic Postulates of Analytical Psychology (1931); Analytical Psychology and *Weltanschauung* (1928/1931); The Real and the Surreal (1933); The Stages of Life (1930–1931); The Soul and Death (1934); Synchronicity: An Acausal Connecting Principle (1952); Appendix: On Synchronicity (1951).

§9. Part I—THE ARCHETYPES AND THE COLLECTIVE UNCONSCIOUS
   Archetypes of the Collective Unconscious (1934/1954); The Concept of the Collective Unconscious (1936); Concerning the Archetypes, with Special Reference to the Anima Concept (1936/1954); Psychological Aspects of the Mother Archetype (1938/1954); Concerning Rebirth (1940/1950); The Psychology of the Child Archetype (1940); The Psychological Aspects of the Kore (1941); The Phenomenology of the Spirit in Fairytales (1945/1948); On the Psychology of the Trickster-Figure (1954); Conscious, Unconscious, and Individuation (1939); A Study in the Process of Individuation (1934/1950); Concerning Mandala Symbolism (1950); Appendix: Mandalas (1955).
   Part II—AION: RESEARCHES INTO THE PHENOMENOLOGY OF THE SELF (1951).

---

* Published 1971.   † Published 1953; 2nd edn., 1966.
‡ Published 1960; 2nd edn., 1969.   § Published 1959; 2nd edn., 1968.

*10. CIVILIZATION IN TRANSITION

The role of the Unconscious (1918); Mind and Earth (1927/1931); Archaic Man (1931); The Spiritual Problem of Modern Man (1928/1931); The Love Problem of a Student (1928); Woman in Europe (1927); The Meaning of Psychology for Modern Man (1933/1934); The State of Psychotherapy Today (1934); Preface and Epilogue to "Essays on Contemporary Events" (1946); Wotan (1936); After the Catastrophe (1945); The Fight with the Shadow (1946); The Undiscovered Self (Present and Future) (1957); Flying Saucers: A Modern Myth (1958); A Psychological View of Conscience (1958); Good and Evil in Analytical Psychology (1959); Introduction to Wolff's "Studies in Jungian Psychology" (1959); The Swiss Line in the European Spectrum (1928); Reviews of Keyserling's "America Set Free" (1930) and "La Révolution Mondiale" (1934); The Complications of American Psychology (1930); The Dreamlike World of India (1939); What India Can Teach Us (1939); Appendix: Documents (1933–1938).

†11. PSYCHOLOGY AND RELIGION: WEST AND EAST

Western Religion: Psychology and Religion (The Terry Lectures) (1938/1940); A Psychological Approach to the Dogma of the Trinity (1942/1948); Transformation Symbolism in the Mass (1942/1954); Forewords to White's "God and the Unconscious" and Werblowsky's "Lucifer and Prometheus" (1952); Brother Klaus (1933); Psychotherapists or the Clergy (1932); Psychoanalysis and the Cure of Souls (1928); Answer to Job (1952).

Eastern Religion: Psychological Commentaries on "The Tibetan Book of the Great Liberation" (1939/1954) and "The Tibetan Book of the Dead" (1935/1953); Yoga and the West (1936); Foreword to Suzuki's "Introduction to Zen Buddhism" (1939); The Psychology of Eastern Meditation (1943); The Holy Men of India: Introduction to Zimmer's "Der Weg zum Selbst" (1944); Foreword to the "I Ching" (1950).

‡12. PSYCHOLOGY AND ALCHEMY (1944)

Prefatory note to the English Edition ([1951?] added 1967); Introduction to the Religious and Psychological Problems of Alchemy; Individual Dream Symbolism in Relation to Alchemy (1936); Religious Ideas in Alchemy (1937); Epilogue.

* Published 1964; 2nd edn., 1970.
† Published 1958; 2nd edn., 1969.
‡ Published 1953; 2nd edn., completely revised, 1968.

*13. ALCHEMICAL STUDIES

Commentary on "The Secret of the Golden Flower" (1929); The Visions of Zosimos (1938/1954); Paracelsus as a Spiritual Phenomenon (1942); The Spirit Mercurius (1943/1948); The Philosophical Tree (1945/1954).

†14. MYSTERIUM CONIUNCTIONIS (1955–56)

‡15. THE SPIRIT IN MAN, ART, AND LITERATURE

Paracelsus (1929); Paracelsus the Physician (1941); Sigmund Freud in His Historical Setting (1932); In Memory of Sigmund Freud (1939); Richard Wilhelm: In Memoriam (1930); On the Relation of Analytical Psychology to Poetry (1922); Psychology and Literature (1930/1950); "Ulysses": A Monologue (1932); Picasso (1932).

§16. THE PRACTICE OF PSYCHOTHERAPY

General Problems of Psychotherapy:

Principles of Practical Psychotherapy (1935); What Is Psychotherapy? (1935); Some Aspects of Modern Psychotherapy (1930); The Aims of Psychotherapy (1931); Problems of Modern Psychotherapy (1929); Psychotherapy and a Philosophy of Life (1943); Medicine and Psychotherapy (1945); Psychotherapy Today (1945); Fundamental Questions of Psychotherapy (1951).

Specific Problems of Psychotherapy:

The Therapeutic Value of Abreaction (1921/1928); The Practical Use of Dream-Analysis (1934); The Psychology of the Transference (1946); Appendix: The Realities of Practical Psychotherapy ([1937] added, 1966).

¶17. THE DEVELOPMENT OF PERSONALITY

Psychic Conflicts in a Child (1910/1946); Introduction to Wickes's "Analyses der Kinderseele" (1927/1931); Child Development and Education (1928); Analytical Psychology and Education: Three Lectures (1926/1946); The Gifted Child (1943); The Significance of the Unconscious in Individual Education (1928); The Development of Personality (1934); Marriage as a Psychological Relationship (1925).

* Published 1968.
† Published 1963; 2nd edn., 1970.
‡ Published 1966.
§ Published 1954; 2nd edn., revised and augmented, 1966.
¶ Published 1954.

18. MISCELLANY
    Posthumous and Other Miscellaneous Works.

19. BIBLIOGRAPHY AND INDEX
    Complete Bibliography of C. G. Jung's Writings; General
    Index to the Collected Works.

INDEX

193